Forensic Comparative Science

Forensic Comparative Science

Qualitative Quantitative Source Determination of Unique Impressions, Images, and Objects

John R. Vanderkolk

ELSEVIER

AMSTERDAM • BOSTON • HEIDELBERG • LONDON
NEW YORK • OXFORD • PARIS • SAN DIEGO
SAN FRANCISCO • SINGAPORE • SYDNEY • TOKYO
Academic Press is an imprint of Elsevier

Elsevier Academic Press
30 Corporate Drive, Suite 400, Burlington, MA 01803, USA
525 B Street, Suite 1900, San Diego, California 92101-4495, USA
84 Theobald's Road, London WC1X 8RR, UK

This book is printed on acid-free paper. ♾

Library of Congress Cataloging-in-Publication Data
Application Submitted

British Library Cataloguing in Publication Data
A catalogue record for this book is available from the British Library

ISBN 13: 978-0-12-373582-9

For all information on all Elsevier Academic Press publications
visit our Web site at www.elsevierdirect.com

Printed in the United States of America

09 10 9 8 7 6 5 4 3 2 1

Contents

This book is dedicated to my wife, Pammy. Without your love, support, encouragement, advice, and trust, I would not have been able to experience and enjoy my endeavors in forensic comparative science. Thank you.

I also thank our children Robert, Lisa, Scott, Katie, Mark, Michael, and Stephen for their unique contributions to our family and my efforts. I will always remember Mark singing to me in 1999.

Acknowledgments

I could not have written this book without the help of others. Tremendous thanks goes to Billy Kreigh for providing invaluable support as my personal editor in this undertaking. Steve McKasson, Tom Busey, and my brother Father Pete Vanderkolk gave early critiques of these chapters and assisted me in clarifying my ideas. Without their help, I never would have accomplished this task.

The Indiana State Police Laboratory personnel have been extremely supportive of my efforts to learn and teach. I would like to thank those who helped me ask questions and seek answers. Bob Conley, Ed Littlejohn, Maurice Cooper, Bill Kuhn, Mike Oliver, Eric Lawrence, Troy Ballard, Jim Fazio, Todd Reynolds, Rick Oatess, Rick Hammer, Diane Tolliver, Dean Marks, John Kelly, Shannon Spreckelmeyer, and Steve Mayer all provided tremendous assistance and feedback to my endeavors. For the experience of working for the Indiana State Police Laboratory, the training you provided, the training you have encouraged me to give, and the research you have allowed me to pursue, thank you.

I am only going to mention a few influences in my learning outside the Indiana State Police Laboratory. There have been many more. Significant influences and inspirations were found in David Grieve, Alice Maceo, David Ashbaugh, Pat Wertheim, Alan McRoberts, Ron Smith, Kasey Wertheim, David Zauner, Roger Sherer, Ann Benson, and Father Dominique Carboneau. Special thanks again go to Tom Busey for letting me participate with him in novice and expert research at Indiana University, Department of Psychological and Brain Sciences, Bloomington. Learning through research has been a rewarding experience for me. All have shared tremendous writings, teachings, and visits with me throughout the years to help me develop experience, understandings, and judgments about seeing, thinking, knowing, and believing truth.

Thanks to Jacob Higgins, Hilary Wilson, Alexis Davidson, Linda McDonald, Serafina Salamo, and all the twins, especially Jami and Kami Hunt, for helping me study non-identical monozygotic twins.

To all who contributed to my development in understanding forensic comparative science throughout my career leading to this book, thank you. To all who worked with me in the Indiana State Police Laboratory at Fort Wayne, especially Sonja Sodano while I have been absent, and those many people not mentioned personally who challenged and contributed to my understanding and explanations and assisted me in my efforts, thank you.

Preface

Motivation to write this book has developed over my time and experience as a criminalist, or forensic scientist. Concurrently learning and practicing the disciplines of finger print, shoe print/tire print, firearm/tool mark examinations and the physical comparisons of broken and torn items challenged me to develop a philosophy that I could use within all of these disciplines by using common terminology and explanations for me, within my communities of peers, and with criminal justice system personnel. I did not look forward to explaining various terms, examination methods, thresholds for decisions, and standards for conclusions in one court during one trial with me as the one witness doing the explaining for many types of physical evidence. This effort to simply explain multiple forensic science disciplines under one generalized forensic comparative science domain evolved in my writings and teachings about determining the unique source of a unique image, no matter the source of the images under examination. Forensic comparative science is the process of measuring and judging two impressions, marks, objects, or images to determine whether they share common origin, no matter the origin.

I am writing this book for current examiners and those in training. This book is meant to be a supplement to the training programs provided in each domain or discipline. Using the approach presented in Chapters 1 through 6 as the foundation for the individual and associated disciplines presented in the remaining chapters, each image in forensic comparative science can be examined similarly. There is a significant lack of reference material associated with chapter 6 and beyond. Pick a specific discipline within forensic comparative science and there are libraries of available materials. Chapters 1-6 provide a foundation for knowing and believing pattern recognition of images. Thus, they provide some of the reference materials for doing what we do in comparative examination of evidence.

Science strives to validate and update its understandings and explanations. If science was stagnant, there would be no desire to improve our understandings, knowledge, and beliefs. As scientists move forward, my effort is to assemble a wide variety of forensic comparative sciences into a common and simply explained process of determining common or different origin of the two objects or images.

Many forensic comparative science disciplines within all of forensic science are under attack in the criminal justice system through Daubert, Frye, or Federal Rules of Evidence (FRE) type court challenges of expertise in science (Daubert, 1993; Frye, 1923; Moenssens, 2007, 3-110).

> In Daubert, the Court held that the *Frye* test is 'absent from and incompatible with the Federal Rules of Evidence.' It construed FRE 702 to require the trial court to make a two-fold inquiry: whether the expert testimony will assist the trier of fact and whether it amounts to scientific knowledge. Courts henceforth were expected to focus on how conclusions or opinions were reached. The Court identified a list of factors judges should consider in applying its definition of scientific knowledge. The Court stated the list was not a definitive checklist, but contained pertinent considerations. These considerations include: whether the proposition is testable and has been tested; whether the proposition has been subjected to peer review and publication; whether the methodology or technique had a known error rate; whether there are standards for using the methodology; and whether the methodology is generally accepted. The Court recognized that general acceptance of the methodology could be persuasive circumstantial evidence that the methodology is sound (Moenssens, 2007, 655).

The comparative science disciplines of finger prints, firearm/tool marks, shoe prints/tire prints, documents and hand-writing are just a few of the sciences being challenged. Forensic science has been involved in many other pattern recognition subject matters. Photographs of people and clothing have been examined to determine associations. Data bases in biometrics of faces, eyes, and people are being implemented. These comparative sciences can benefit from the use of one philosophy to determine the source of the image. These comparative sciences in conjunction with other related comparative sciences of foot or hand morphology, lip, elbow, or ear print examinations need a philosophy that is consistent among all of the forensic comparative science disciplines. There is no need to create a distinct strategy each time images from a variety of different sources are being examined. It does not matter what the source of the mark is and what the substrate is that bears the impression. As Daubert or other hearings take place to challenge the validity of the process of a comparative science, no matter the discipline, all should follow a similar explanation of the process.

With the current Daubert type hearings, we must remember that science has been attacked in the court room as long as experts have been presenting testimony. "Discontent with scientific expertise in the courts has existed as long as there have been scientific expert witnesses, and by the mid-nineteenth century, the debate over the meaning of these conflicts and the ways to resolve them had all the features that today are blithely assumed to be new…But it will, at least, reveal that these conflicts are less a product of human and institutional pathology than they are an illustration, should we need one, of the complexity of the ongoing social negotiations needed to harmonize laws of men and laws of nature and to cut truth and justice to human measure" (Golan, 2004, 4).

> The chronic inability of the courts to bridge the gap between experts and juries, the resultant fear of a credulous jury bewitched in the name of science by charlatans and opportunists, the difficulties of science in adjusting to adversarial procedures, the failure to create a better alliance between law and science adequate for litigation in the twentieth century—all these concerns played important roles in the Frye decision and even more so in turning it into a broad coherent rationale. No longer a passive umpire who watches over the rules of the game and counts the points gained by the parties, the twentieth-century trial judge became an active gatekeeper charged with the responsibility of screening unreliable scientific evidence (Golan, 2004, 263-264).

Understanding the explanations of the many comparative science disciplines as presented with generalizations as one domain will assist the gatekeepers of the laws of man in allowing the laws of nature to be presented by an expert scientist giving testimony in court.

My desire in this text is to start with a philosophy of knowing and believing in the truth and generality of science, followed by a description of the psychology of how we see, perceive, and carry through to the judgments and decisions we make about truth. Making judgments is part of science. Science would not exist without the scientist making judgments.

Science is about determining generalizations. The theme of this book will be "generalizing." Bringing forensic comparative science disciplines under one general philosophy of rules, terminology, examination process, and standards for conclusions forms the foundation of this book. Each specific discipline within forensic comparative science should not have its own specific set of rules and guidelines for examinations and making judgments with its indefinite variety of conditions of various types of evidence that could occur. By showing the relative similarities among these disciplines, explanations of each of the specific disciplines within forensic science will be simplified. The goal of any science is to simplify the explanations. The simpler explanation that correctly explains should be adopted. In whatever manner William of Ockham conveyed this centuries ago, the principle now known as Ockham's Razor is expressed similarly by a variety of scientists. "Although it is not included in his extant writings, the principle that 'entities should not to be multiplied beyond necessity' is traditionally attributed to the scholastic philosopher William of Ockham (c. 1285-1347)" (Curd and Cover, 1998, 672). "...the simplest theory which fits the data should be preferred" and "In the presence of noise, which is inevitable, there is bound to be some sort of trade-off between goodness-of-fit and simplicity. If there is a lot of noise then a simple model is better: there is no point in trying to reproduce every bump and wiggle in the data with a new parameter or physical law. On the other hand if there is very little noise, every feature in the data is real and your theory fails if it cannot explain it" (Coles, 2006, 62). "Put simply, this approach demands that we set aside complicated explanations for things when a simpler one will do" (Ball, 1999, 6). The 'intelligibility of science' (Dear, 2006) needs to be understandable and simple.

I might be accused of making the disciplines more complicated, or de-Ockhamizing (Curd and Cover, 1998, 593). The purpose of my efforts is to explain an overall philosophy of forensic comparative science in detail, to demonstrate the foundations of the comparative process, to relate the disciplines to each other, and then simplify it in the end. Understanding the foundations of the comparative process will assist the examiner in coordinating the explanation of the process. Experiencing, trusting, understanding, comparing, testing, judging, deciding, correcting, improving, knowing, and believing are parts of the process known as science.

To get there, we will consider physical objects that can break, tear, or deposit prints, impressions, markings, or images. Understanding the object or source and its surface will help us understand its images and our tolerance for variations in appearances of those deposited images. One of the great frustrations I had in my early years of applying the comparative science process was the lack of training in understanding the surface of the source of an image. Finger print training consisted of being told dogmatically that finger print skin is permanent and unique. Teachers within my community taught me it is "permanent and unique." Little explanation of why or how the skin is permanent and unique was given. Trust them, it is permanent and unique. I have to apologize here. As much as I emphasize understanding the source of an image, I am not going to document the development or construction of the source objects in these chapters. That would take many libraries to accomplish. The training programs within each discipline need to provide study of the development or construction of the source. Since this is a supplement to the available literature, additional efforts of studying the generation or construction of objects are necessary.

I am going to generalize the sources as "repeatable" and "unique" and change "permanent" to "persistent" throughout my writings. I will avoid use of the term "class characteristic," a label often attached to a group of something. Things that are unique can be grouped or things that are repeatable can be grouped. Friction skin arrangements and the prints from fingers have features that are generalized and classified for grouping, filing, and record keeping purposes according to specific rules. This results in a wonderful method to file record finger print cards of criminals. However, the general grouping utilizes unique features of the skin. The generality of the presence of grouped and labeled features recurs but the actual physical sequences and configurations of theses same structures are not repeated. In manufactured items, many shoes can be grouped based on the mold that generated the soles. Many guns are grouped based on make, model, and caliber. This classification relies on repeatable features of the structures of sequences and configurations of intentionally manufactured characteristics. Thus, to avoid confusion when discussing features of a class characteristic, I will be specific and use either the term repeatable or unique instead of class.

Before examining any type of evidence, the examiner must study that type of object and understand the repeatable and unique features and their persistency, or how long the surface of the source maintains its structure. No structure is really permanent. Persistency of source between the two events of depositing the impressions is needed and used in comparative science.

My firearms and tool mark trainers taught me about the manufacturing processes of tools, guns, and components of ammunition. Not only did we study the books and journal articles about the manufacturing processes, we traveled to the factories, asked questions of the design engineers and quality control personnel and learned about the guns and tools that would become sources of the images under examination. I watched the randomness of the finishing process on edges of tools. I developed first hand knowledge of the source from the communities that made the objects. This carried over to studying shoes and tires and as we read the articles and visited numerous factories and consulted with the designers and engineers. Also, we visited a factory and studied the manufacturing process of plastic bags to help us understand the repeatable and unique features of plastic film for a physical comparison examination to determine whether two pieces of plastic had shared common origin. Developing personal knowledge of science within the wider collaborating community of those who participate in the "instrumentality of science" (Dear, 2006) through manufacturing, expands our knowing and believing in forensic comparative science.

The foundation of forensic comparative science is "natural patterns are unique." Uniqueness is even present in those humanly made objects that have repeatable features, such as shoe soles from the same mold or tools from the same factory. Perceiving the uniqueness is a different challenge. A quick glance might not reveal unique features. The closer and clearer we observe the features of an object, the more we can realize actual uniqueness.

The frustration of different explanations of permanency or persistency of the source permeated through me and caused great anxiety in my early years of being a forensic comparative scientist. The features of the source of an image need to be sufficiently persistent between two depositions of its images for source of images to be determined. Is the ridged skin of the palms of the hands and soles of the feet really permanent, as was presented to me? Nothing else within forensic comparative science beyond the latent finger print training in my early experience spoke of permanency. None of the other disciplines relied upon permanency of the unique features of the source for determining the source of its images. Why do finger print examiners suggest the need for permanency of the source? How do the other disciplines function without permanency?

One of my great experiences in firearms training was shooting an older, dirtier gun and recovering the two consecutively fired bullets from a water tank. After conducting an examination utilizing the forensic comparison microscope, neither my trainer nor I was able to comparatively determine whether both bullets had been fired in the same gun, even though we had done the firing moments before. The bullets did not have sufficient patterns of corresponding striae for us to make the forensic comparative determination that both bullets had been fired from the same gun. The bias of us knowing the two bullets had been fired through the same gun did not overwhelm us to comparatively determine they had been fired from the same gun. The unique imperfections within the barrel had not been sufficiently persistent in this instance of firing two bullets through the same dirty bore. The condition of the bore changed between the two events of shooting the gun. This tool did not record similar markings of imperfections in both bullets. Something caused the recorded details to be different for determining both bullets had been fired through the same gun. Could it have been the lack of persistent features in the bore between the two events of shooting the gun? Firearms examiners do not require permanency of the source to conduct examinations. None of the other disciplines relied upon regeneration of the features of the source, like friction ridge skin. Once the feature was gone in objects of other disciplines, the feature was gone and the science carried on.

How do we relate the skin regeneration and permanency issues among the other disciplines? In my early years, I was taught to consciously avoid and not consider scars, creases, and cuts in volar skin. Why? Because, scars and imperfections were not permanent throughout the life of the person; they might not have existed in a previously obtained standard or print. All the other disciplines used unique imperfections, with sufficient persistency, to individualize the images back to the source. Why not volar print examinations? After all, volar skin has ridges, furrows, creases, and can have cuts, scars, warts, blisters, and other unique imperfections. All sort of guns, shoes, and other sources have unintended imperfections that are not permanent. The features of imperfections might be extremely persistent or they might be extremely fragile. The examiner needs to understand and use any feature of the source that is present, no matter the persistency. Persistency, and not permanency, of the features of the source as required for individualization will be emphasized within each of the discipline chapters.

After studying unique and persistent sources, the ranges of clarity of details in images from those sources will be discussed. No image of a source is completely homogeneous. Each natural image is heterogeneous: each varies from its source and among each other. The clarity throughout each image varies. These ranges of clarity of details are in images that exhibit the repeatable features and the unique features of the source. As each image is naturally deposited and created, each image will be unique. As an item breaks or separates, not all the connecting bonds separate the same on both sides of the break. Both sides of a bond in nature are parts of nature. As the bonds break, a perfect mirror image cannot be generated in the two opposing pieces. The corresponding part of a fracture examination is not a perfect negative image of the opposing piece. Elements within nature will not repeat, whether those parts are the natural depositions of impressions, marks, or images or the corresponding pieces in a fracture examination. These images are parts of nature. The genesis of each natural image is unique.

Detailed explanations of the examination process will occur. This examination process parallels descriptions of methods of human perceiving, knowing, and believing of phenomenon in the world. Acquiring knowledge and beliefs of phenomenon within a collaborating community is science. The examination process should be similar to naturally knowing and believing.

The threshold of sufficiency of details in images will be discussed in depth to help us understand the actual simplicity of using one general model for the threshold of sufficiency to determine the unique source of a unique image, no matter the source. The threshold for recognition by experts involves the training, experiences, understandings, and judgments of the community and the expert within the community. The type of threshold for sufficiency should not vary for each discipline. In each discipline, no matter the types of impressions or marks, the examiner will learn when two images share sufficiency to determine they came from the same or different sources. Also, the examiner will learn insufficiency. Then, ranges of conclusions based on sufficiency in this threshold will be addressed. This threshold works in all the forensic comparative science disciplines, even those disciplines that choose to use probable judgments when in the gray areas of doubt boundaries between sufficiency and insufficiency.

It must be remembered that all science and all models in science are open for refinement and improvement. Science is about learning, knowing, and believing and refining and improving knowledge and beliefs. Models help us understand. Models in science are imperfect. Science is imperfect, yet incredibly dependent on knowing and believing truth in nature. Science does not know everything there is to know within a particular discipline. I look forward to improvements of the models and philosophies presented in this effort. After all, I am a scientist who is combining a variety of knowledge and beliefs that help me understand and grasp the variety of disciplines and the applications of this knowing and believing into the goal of one forensic comparative science philosophy, this book.

REFERENCES

Ball, Philip. *The self-made tapestry: pattern formation in nature*, Oxford University Press, New York, 1999.

Coles, Peter. *From Cosmos to Chaos: The Science of Unpredictability*, Oxford University Press, Inc., New York, 2006.

Curd, Martin, and J. A. Cover. *Philosophy of Science: The Central Issues*, W. W. Norton & Company, Inc., New York, 1998.

Daubert v Merrell Dow Pharmaceuticals, Inc. 509 U.S. 579, 113 S.Ct. 2786 (1993).

Dear, Peter. *The Intelligibility of Nature: How Science Makes Sense of the World*, The University of Chicago Press, Chicago, 2006.

Frye v United States, 293 F. 1013 (D.C. Cir. 1923).

Golan, Tal. *Laws of Men and Laws of Nature: The History of Scientific Expert Testimony in England and America*, Harvard University Press, Cambridge, Massachusetts, 2004.

Moenssens, Andre A., Carol E. Henderson and Sharon G. Portwood. *Scientific Evidence in Civil and Criminal Cases – Fifth Edition*, Foundation Press, New York 2007.

CHAPTER 1

Recognizing Belief

CONTENTS

"Do you swear to tell the truth, the whole truth, and nothing but the truth?" These are the first words any expert witness in a trial expects to hear when testifying in court. How do experts examine evidence and prepare a report that may result in sworn testimony? How do forensic comparative scientists know and believe truth about the judgments and decisions rendered during an examination of evidence? How do examiners know and believe the threshold of sufficiency to enable the reporting and testifying to truth? How do forensic comparative scientists reach the level of comprehension needed in rendering expert opinions or judgment of examinations? How do scientists know and believe their judgment about the relationship between two objects or images is the truth? Experts seek the truth. If the experts are not seeking truth, what is the value in examining evidence, preparing reports, and testifying in court? The court expects the truth to be expressed because the witness has just sworn to speak the truth.

This chapter is an introductory journey into the processes that result in knowing and believing the truth of a judgment from an examination in a particular case. The way to know truth of judgment is to experience, understand, and judge what is known within the beliefs of the community that is continually challenged on its beliefs. There is no basis for truth if people do not know and believe truth within self and within the community. Forensic comparative scientists need to recognize the belief that accompanies the rendered conclusion made by self within the community. The study of philosophy and the workings of science is immense. The following is a limited effort on my part to describe how examiners make judgments and determinations to the origin of prints, impressions, images, or objects as evidence within the truths of science.

FORENSIC COMPARATIVE SCIENCE

Any science that is of interest to a court of law, a forum of organized debate, or a comparison of one object to another for the purposes of a potential inquiry in a forum of court is forensic science. Science is a systematic process of knowing and believing truths and operating under general laws about the reality of phenomenon within the universe by observing nature, forming questions about nature, answering those questions, and then challenging and testing those answers with more questions and answers. As the questions and answers accumulate into knowledge, that knowledge is shared among the communities of those interested in understanding the explanations of the phenomenon. This sharing of knowledge as belief is then tested with more questions and answers by those receiving the information. Because the development of knowledge and belief encompasses so much, science is broken down into many branches, with scientists within communities sharing and challenging the knowledge and beliefs in the advancement to better understanding. Science is not stagnant but rather a progression of inquiry leading the quest to know truth. Knowing and believing are justified as they lead to and then correspond to truth.

Preparation for forensic comparative examiners extends beyond the obvious need for adequate training and sufficient experience; it requires the development of a reasoned approach as a guiding philosophy before an examination begins. It includes an understanding of what constitutes science as well as the scientific principles involved. Forensic comparative scientists apply the studies, experiences, understandings, and judgments of physics, chemistry, biology, embryology, mathematics, psychology, philosophy, statistics, empirical observations, and experiments to the examination of an image, impression, object, or marking to determine its source. Science strives to reach intelligibility (Dear, 2006). The best explanations in science are the most general, simple, and intelligible, as expressed in Ockham's Razor, discussed in the preface.

According to McInerny and O'Callaghan (2005), "The first task of natural philosophy, accordingly, is to define and analyze physical objects." Forensic comparative science is the applying of intelligible general rules or laws of nature to the study of two physical objects, impressions, markings, or images of interest in an effort to determine whether they share a common origin. The scientist seeks and then understands the relevant and appropriate laws of nature, applies the laws to the images, compares the images to each other, and judges what the images depict. The details within the images are scrutinized to determine whether they correspond in shapes, sequences, and configurations by comparing their traits to each other. Judgments of the overall relationship of the totality of the sequential and configural comparative measurements of the details between two images are made by the forensic comparative scientist as a natural philosopher of physical objects.

Without the scientist, there would be no science, for science is the process of scientists seeking the knowledge and beliefs that result in truth. Richards (1994) states, "Recall that it is not forensic science that is called to testify, but the forensic scientist. The scientist, in collaboration with the community of forensic scientists, testifies as to what constitutes evidence, what shall be the truth of the case, and who shall say it."

Building upon experiences, understandings, and judgments of self and the communities to determine if the comparative science puzzles are being correctly solved, all relevant and appropriate questions must be asked about the science and the presented images to remove the irritation of doubt that may arise from those questions and puzzles. Examiners in forensic comparative science cannot prove infallibly that two images with variations in appearances came from the same source. They can only know it as critically inquiring observers, believe it within the collaborated community of scientists, and if needed, demonstrate it within the forensic community and to those outside the community.

TRAINING IN FORENSIC COMPARATIVE SCIENCE

Training is critical in forensic comparative science, as it provides the impetus to ask the initial questions and learn the answers. Through this training process, experience, understanding, and judgments form the initial knowing and believing of the science and the relationship of images to other images and to sources of images. As the application of that training carries over into practice, experience grows, building upon each other. According to Grieve (2007), "Experience provides efficiency that enables reinforcing the validity of the training or to reveal any deficiencies of the training."

Understanding comes from the practice of asking the relevant questions and correctly answering them. After the judgments of the understandings, knowledge is generated; science is generated. Just as knowledge and belief seek virtually unconditioned truth, so does the training in science.

SEEKING THE TRUTH IN SCIENCE

John Paul II (2003) once said, "All human beings desire to know [Aristotle] and truth is the proper object of this desire." Both laymen and scientists seek the objective reality of how things are. If people conclude that something is false, they refuse to accept it. If they find truth, they are satisfied. Not only is science pushed by this desire to know truth, it is its purpose and control. Koppl (2005, 255) states, "The proper function of forensic science is to extract the truth." And Carroll (2005, 14) adds that "the scientist's main constraint is the truth."

Humans who seek to know the truth must have the ability, aptitude, and desire to comprehend stimuli and data that inspire knowing truth. For the scientist, the desire to know needs to be pure, unrestricted, detached, and disinterested in what reality will bring to understanding and knowing (Lonergan, 1957). The nature of human understanding in science must be open, willing, and able to actually learn truth.

Truth is the correct determination of an object's relationship with another object. Investigating, seeking, explaining, or defining truth's relationship with reality is the mission of natural philosophers. Improving the intelligibility and simplicity of true explanations of nature is the method of science (Dear, 2006). Can an expert prove truth to the court? Can the expert only demonstrate why he or she knows and believes the truth of the judgment from an examination? If the jury and court are in different communities of knowing and believing relative to science, how do they accept as truth the judgments of an expert? When does trust come into the equation of knowing and believing truth?

Many explanations of truth exist. Examples are universal and absolute truth or virtually unconditioned and unconditioned truth (McKasson and Richards, 1998; Lonergan, 1957). *Universal*, the best known, refers to truth as determined and agreed upon by everyone who should know within the scientific community. *Absolute* denotes truth as perfect or infallible, complete and fixed where there are no further questions and answers *ever*. Truth can also be expressed as "truth" as known by scientists and people or "Truth." Truth with a capital T cannot be reached (Stewart, 2001).

Virtually unconditioned truth, similar to universal truth, exists when the community has essentially asked and answered all the known relevant questions and there are no known circumstances that would change the answers. It is virtually unconditioned because all human knowledge is open to adjustment and refinement as new and unforeseen conditions occur. This leads to the rule or law by which the community proceeds to investigate additional observations made in nature. Unconditioned truth, absolute truth, or Truth occurs when no more possible conditions that could better or change the understanding, knowing, or believing exist. Since humans cannot ever perfectly know absolute, unconditioned truth of reality, the best we can do is *know* virtually unconditioned or universal truth about any phenomenological topic (Lonergan, 1957; McKasson and Richards, 1998).

The goal of science is to have universal or virtually unconditioned truth as close as possible to absolute, unconditioned truth or reality. If scientists were capable of reaching and knowing absolute truth, infallibility would be a scientific human trait. The scientist seeks truth while conducting comparative measurements and making judgments, yet he or she must always keep in mind the potential of making mistakes. Scientists strive to reach truth.

If science disavowed the self-correcting process of knowledge and belief, of continual inquiry, of asking and answering questions, there would be no need or desire to conduct further scientific inquiry, study, and research. No science has all the answers to all the possible questions, past, present, and future. New relevant questions are generated and must be answered. Karl Popper (Thornton, 2006), a philosopher of science, describes science as being open to the potential to be falsified, or it can conceivably be determined as wrong if an opposing phenomenon of nature is discovered.

BIASES

Biases—whatever hinders asking and answering all relevant and appropriate questions about the evidence—get in the way of correct understanding and judgments. These include any abnormality of understanding that excludes insights and prevents the further questions and answers that would arise. A reason to do good for self-serving purposes, not asking the relevant and appropriate questions that are against the common interests of the group, a desire to confirm what has been determined before with the failure to ask and answer questions, a failure to ask and answer all the relevant and appropriate questions because a given answer is already expected, or a failure to ask and answer all the appropriate and relevant questions because of a given contextual situation are biases (Lonergan, 1957; Dror, 2005; Dror and Charlton, 2006; Koppl, 2005; Byrd, 2006).

Biases can result in a failure to ask and correctly answer all the relevant and appropriate questions about the topic. For instance, when asked to look through a telescope, some Aristotelian philosophers reported "either that they could see nothing new or that what they saw was mere optical illusion, tricks created by the telescope. Their mental bias is not hard to understand. They wanted to save at all costs the Aristotelian universe, which the telescope was shaking to its foundations" (Fermi and Bernardini, 2003, 59). Often, there are no further questions known by self or community that would cause a change in judgment, knowing, and believing; however, as further questions become known, they must be asked and answered.

KNOWING AND BELIEVING

Knowing and believing is the state of satisfaction that is reached when it appears all the currently known relevant and appropriate questions of the inquiry have been asked and answered about a topic. They are built upon the inspirations, insights, common sense, experiences, understandings, and judgments made by the inquirer and the trusted community in which the inquirer participates. These blend with the knowledge of trusted others because no one can have personally generated knowledge of everything and therefore must rely on the trusted knowledge of others within the community.

Belief is the receiving, grasping, and comprehending of trusted and shared knowledge of others upon whom the inquirer relies. One result of shared knowledge is that personally generated knowledge is questioned as new questions develop and new answers are generated and tested. Participation within the community leads to more insights; more experiences, understandings, and judgments; and more refined knowledge and beliefs (Hardwig, 1991; Fricker, 2002; Lonergan, 1957).

The state of satisfaction in inquiry is reached when the asking and answering of the relevant and appropriate questions lead to an awareness of no further questions. This can be described as the removal of the "irritation of doubt" (Peirce, 1877). Doubt drives the scientific inquiry, and the irritation of doubt indicates there are further questions and answers that need to be investigated before the removal of this irritation can lead to knowing and believing truth.

Good knowledge and beliefs exist; better knowledge and beliefs are possible. Likewise, mistaken beliefs may occur. Lonergan (1957, 735) states, "Mistaken beliefs exist, and the function of an analysis of belief is overlooked if it fails to explain how mistaken beliefs arise and how they are to be eliminated." Finding the cause of the mistaken belief in an inquiry fails its purpose if it fails to remove the reasons that developed into that mistaken belief. A biased interest that restricts the asking and answering of all the relevant and appropriate questions leads to errors in judging the truth. The relationship of an object to another object must be determined by the forensic comparative scientist who has no biased interest in the actual outcome of judgment. Truth must be the sole desired outcome.

THE ROLE OF DOUBT IN KNOWING AND BELIEVING TRUTH

Philosopher Rene Descartes believed in the human ability to reason and reach conclusions through long chains of reasoning and rejecting assumptions that could be doubted. Believing in human reasoning, he wrote of the doubting thinker. The only way to be sure of reaching conclusions was to first doubt and to keep doubting until doubt has been removed. The thinker avoids error in judgments by restricting beliefs to those of which he or she is obviously certain. American philosopher of science Charles Sanders Peirce (Peirce, 1877 and 1878; Bailey, 2002) wrote of pragmatism, or the meaning of a claim and its consequences, working through doubt by the method of inquiry and bringing beliefs into line with truth. The collaborative inquiry of science accepts that which currently has no doubt and inquiring into that which has doubt until it is replaced with accepted belief. Once the irritation of doubt is eliminated, belief occurs. When the irritation of doubt ceases to exist, or the "fixation of belief" occurs, there is no more need to inquire upon the subject (Peirce, 1877).

Knowing and believing are applied to puzzle solving within comparative science. Determining the answer to the puzzles of two images or pieces having common origin is comparative science. This scientific knowledge and belief must be open to confirmation, verification, refutation, or falsification. Once the questions have been answered, the irritation of doubt eliminated, and the answers judged, universal truth occurs. The scientist knows and believes that another scientist with similar trainings, experiences, understandings, and judgments would render the same conclusion.

SUBJECTIVITY AND OBJECTIVITY

Forensic science is the search for objective understanding of objects and their relationships to other objects within an aggregate of knowing and believing. Thus, science also has a subjective component in that the relationships are studied by scientists within experiences, understandings, and judgments of the community of scientists' experiences of objects' relationships to objects. Once the scientist does the observing and judging from a human perspective, subjectivity is involved. Dror (2005, 763) said, "At the one extreme, perceptions never have a full and total 'objective reality,' and at the other extreme end, hallucinations and delusions are not totally dissociated from reality." There is nothing wrong with subjectivity. If forensic science or any human endeavor was completely objective, there would be no need for the scientist, for all who viewed the images would know the same—objectively speaking. The trainings, experiences, understandings, and judgments of the expert within the community would not be needed. The court seeks the understandings and judgments of the object's relationship to another object as determined by the expert: a scientist. The court does not independently know the objective relationship between the two objects until it trusts the judgment of the expert.

The goal of the forensic comparative scientist is to determine whether comparative measurements agree with the objective dimensions of the objects. Eventually the examiner must make a conclusion, so when expert measurements and judgments are applied to the objective relationship between two things, they are not completely independent of each other. The scientist must comparatively measure object to object and judge the images within what is known within the community of scientists yet from his or her point of view in performing the observing and measuring. According to Saviano (2006, 880), "We must accept and recognize that our work is subjective as well as objective. In this way, we can be on our guard against any bias that may attempt to enter into the analysis."

There are objective and subjective components to the examinations of the images. The examiner conducts objective comparative measurements of the details in two images. The images are studied and comparatively measured as they relate to each other, object to object. The examined details must be present and visible to permit accurate comparative measurements. As the comparative measurements are made, judgments of similarity or dissimilarity occur, and then a judgment of actual agreement or disagreement and source of origin follow; hence, the subjective component of objective examination surfaces. Perfect matches cannot exist, for if they did, exact replication of a pattern would have occurred, and animate or inanimate patterns in nature cannot be replicated. Judgment of the expert then is part of each analysis, comparative measurement, and overall judgment of the examination.

Objective comparative measurements are not infallible. Fermi and Bernardini (2003, 108) state, "To Galileo experiments meant measurements, for in his maturity he considered proper subjects of science only those which are susceptible of measurement. He knew that if he repeated his experiments time after time, he should always expect small, accidental, irregular deviations of his measures from their average values, and that these deviations were unavoidable." Humans did the measuring in Galileo's days, and humans comparatively measure today.

JUDGMENT IN SCIENCE

Judging is part of science, part of knowing. Weed (2007, 139) had the following to say about this:

> Neither carefully crafted observations nor the accuracy of causal hypotheses are sufficient for this purpose. We need something else to help us decide what those causal relationships are. ... We need judgment. Expert judgment is inescapable and is as important as all that which surrounds science, feeds it, and feeds upon it: the funding and politics, the professional societies and journals, the universities, corporations, and the research institutions. It is as much a part of science as the theories, hypotheses, methodologies, and evidence. Judgment is an integral part of the history of science, its ethic, and its philosophy. In short, science would not be science without judgment.

Judgment, the evaluating or deciding based on previous experiences, understandings, and judgments by self and the trusted communities of participation, is part of the criteria of science, part of knowing and believing.

Judging is the consideration of propositions and then the answering of relevant questions. Premature judging is guessing. Once sufficient evidence for a judgment has been acquired on a question under deliberation, describing just what occurs during pondering and reflective insight is difficult.

INSIGHT

Insight, a sudden awareness of the answer to what had been a difficult question, often results from asking the question, "Why?" As inspirations accumulate, insights into the answers to relevant questions start to occur, and the answers seem obvious. Insights and knowledge are based in the senses of sight, touch, taste, smell, and hearing, and then by correctly answering the generated questions from experience.

In conjunction with the senses, people have the ability to think and critically reflect upon the phenomenon that is experienced, to ponder or reflect upon the significance of the answer that is grasped. The "eureka moment" of Archimedes resulted from his sudden insight into the problem of determining whether a gold crown had been mixed with other metal. As the story goes, when Archimedes got into a tub full of water and observed the water spilling over the rim, he realized that the volume of his body had displaced that amount of water. Thus, a weight of pure gold would have different volume than an equal weight of gold mixed with other metal. If the crown in question had been mixed with other metal, it would have displaced a different amount of water than the one of pure gold. Thus, Archimedes had an *insight*—a sudden comprehension that led to his better understanding of weight and volume. Carroll (2005, 14) said, "The greatest 'eurekas' in science combine both sensual aesthetics and conceptual insights."

INTELLIGIBILITY AND INSTRUMENTALITY OF SCIENCE

The explanations and understandings of an object's relationship to other objects in science must be intelligible in that they must make sense to the scientist and the community in the study of nature. The best explanations are those that are simplest and most intelligible, as William of Ockham, a fourteenth-century philosopher from England, taught us.

Science is about more than just knowing and believing. It is also about applying what is known and believed to other objects and using the knowledge as an instrument to do something. Intelligible natural philosophy supports instrumentality; instrumentality supports intelligible natural philosophy. Of this, Dear (2006, 6) said the following:

> Why are science's instrumental techniques effective? The usual answer is by virtue of science's (true) natural philosophy. How is science's natural philosophy shown to be true, or at least likely? The answer is by virtue of science's (effective) instrumental capabilities. Such is the belief, amounting to an ideology, by which science is understood in modern culture. It is circular, but invisibly so.

SOME PREVALENT PHILOSOPHIES OF EXPLAINING SCIENCE

Philosophers have been trying to explain science and its truths for centuries. Only a few of their explanations are included here. The concept that science must be open to refutation or "falsifiability" is attributed to the philosopher Karl Popper. Scientists determine rules or laws of nature and use the rules to know and believe in science. If something is observed and judged to falsify the rule or law, the observation, judgment, rule, and law must be revisited to determine what is wrong. Popper's concept of falsifiability is considered by many to be a hallmark of science, in that falsifiability must leave open the manner in which the rule or law can be identified as an error. He taught that scientists should seek more than just confirmation to support theories. Good scientific theory enlightens yet prohibits or forbids certain occurrences. A theory that cannot be refuted by any possible event is nonscientific. Testing a theory needs to be an attempt to falsify or refute it. Theories with greater risks of predictions are more testable and open to refutation. Valid but unsuccessful efforts to falsify a theory contribute to confirmation of the theory with corroborating evidence. Most unsuccessful theories are held up as valid for some time in an effort to avoid refutation. These theories, when found to be false, are often reinterpreted to try to avoid refutation. This is always possible, but it diminishes its claim as scientific (Popper in Curd and Cover, 1998; Bailey, 2002). According to Popper, "Logically speaking, a scientific law is conclusively falsifiable although it is not conclusively verifiable" (Thornton, 2006, 5). Scientists can never conclusively find and demonstrate all scenarios to prove or verify the law. Empirical studies support the law. Finding a conclusive error of the law would falsify it.

Philosopher Thomas Kuhn wrote of science as normal or extraordinary. Normal science solves puzzles by using accepted theories and models. Normal science would be the use of what is known and believed in the community and applying that knowledge and belief to the puzzles of forensic comparative examinations. The scientist applies what is known and continues the applications of the science to the puzzle placed before him. The inability of the scientist is the reason a specific puzzle is not answered correctly and not the fault of the science. According to Kuhn, Popper's falsifiability efforts do not occur in normal science in that scientists seek to answer the questions of the puzzle using normal theories. As a result, normal efforts to refute the theory do not take place.

Kuhn's explanation of extraordinary science includes specific challenges to the law or theory and concerted attempts to refute or falsify it. Once scientists find many puzzles that are not answered with the current theory, they seek answers to the questions addressing why the puzzles are not being solved.

A serious attempt to refute the theory will be considered and takes place. Extraordinary science is initiated and serious testing of the theory begins. If a theory is refuted with sufficient data, a better theory is required. In extraordinary science, a better theory becomes a revolution in science causing a new approach to studying the data. Kuhn introduced this as a paradigm shift, or a changing system of theoretical belief within science (Kuhn in Curd and Cover, 1998).

Imre Lakatos, another philosopher of science, offers the concept that mass belief does not make a theory or law a science. Lakatos also challenges Popper's views by stating that scientists rarely declare what would refute a theory before conducting the observations and experiments. Scientific change occurs when rivalry of community beliefs and research meet, when diverse communities have differing theories that come forward. Most scientists will follow a progressive theory that continues to predict novel facts and provide better solutions for problems. Better solutions for problems inspire more progressive research that will lead science (Lakatos in Curd and Cover, 1998).

LOGIC IN SCIENCE

Deduction, induction, and abduction are three types of logic in science that an examiner can use during inquiries in training and then in forensic comparative examinations (Peirce, 1877 and 1878; McKasson and Richards, 1998; Bailey, 2002; Peirce in Burch, 2006). Abduction adopts the rule generated from the logics of deduction and induction. The beginning of a specific inquiry in forensic comparative science needs to start with the rule in abduction, and if the rule is true, it leads the inquiry. In the study of logic, propositions lead to inference. A simple explanation of logic and inference could be found in the statements "A and B, therefore C," "B and C, therefore A," or "A and C, therefore B." Replacing A with "Case," B with "Rule," and C with "Result," the examiner can explain which logic is used (McKasson and Richards, 1998).

Deductive logic starts with the general and ends with the particular, inferring that the result is certain as long as the premises of the case and rule are true. For instance, the particular of the details between two images must agree if the examiner knows the two sufficient images did come from the same unique and persistent source. Likewise, deductive logic infers that the particular of the details between two images must disagree if the examiner knows the two sufficient images did not come from the same source and that the two sources are unique and persistent.

In forensic comparative science, deductive logic is used in training examiners. The trainer or trainee knows whether the two images of fingerprints, shoe or tire prints, fired bullets or cases, or broken pieces originated from the same source; he or she knows the rule of uniqueness and persistency of the source and knows whether the details in these two images agree or disagree. Deduction helps the examiner understand tolerance for variations in appearance or distortion of two independent images from the same source. Deductive logic is used during training exercises to learn agreement of details in sequences and configurations from the same source and to learn disagreement of details from different sources. For these images, "Case and Rule, therefore Result" becomes "The two images are known to have come from the same unique and persistent source, and individualization is possible because the features of the source are unique and persistent, so the details in the two sufficient images agree." Or "The two images are known to have come from different unique and persistent sources and exclusion is possible because the features of the sources are unique and persistent, therefore, the details in the two sufficient images disagree." Deductive logic in training, competency, and proficiency exercises and tests help develop the examiner's understanding of agreement of details from a common origin and disagreement of details from different origins. Learning sufficient agreement or disagreement of details is paramount in the training program. Understanding sufficiency and agreement or disagreement as explained by the Association of Firearm and Tool Mark Examiners (AFTE) (2007) through known sources of impressions is how an examiner learns.

Theory of Identification as It Relates to Toolmarks

1. The theory of identification as it pertains to the comparison of toolmarks enables opinions of common origin to be made when the unique surface contours of two toolmarks are in "sufficient agreement."

2. This sufficient agreement is related to the significant duplication of random toolmarks as evidenced by the correspondence of a pattern or combination of patterns of surface contours. Significance is determined by the comparative examination of two or more sets of surface contour patterns comprised of individual peaks, ridges and furrows. Specifically, the relative height or depth, width, curvature and spatial relationship of the individual peaks, and ridges and furrows within one set of surface contours are defined and compared to the corresponding features in the second set of surface contours. Agreement is significant when it exceeds the best agreement demonstrated between toolmarks known to have been produced by different tools and is consistent with agreement demonstrated by toolmarks known to have been produced by the same tool. The statement that sufficient agreement exists between two toolmarks means that the agreement is of a quantity and quality that the likelihood another tool could have made the mark is so remote as to be considered a practical impossibility.

3. Currently the interpretation of individualization/identification is subjective in nature, founded on scientific principles, and based on the examiner's training and experience.

Going from the particular to the general, or from results and case determination to the rule, is an example of inductive logic. Inductive logic is uncertain or probabilistic, even if the premises of case and result are true. The conclusion of the generalized rule cannot be ensured for the future based on past experience. All past experiences lead to the rule, but they do not guarantee the rule in the future. The determining that the details in two sufficient images agree and concluding they originated from the same source supports the rule of a source being unique and persistent. The determination that the details in two sufficient images disagree and that they originated from different unique and persistent sources also supports the rule of the sources being unique and persistent. Persistency of the source(s) must be sufficient between the depositions of the two images.

Studying all known sources is impossible. Examiners can never prove uniqueness and persistency of the source(s) through inductive logic; it can only be inferred probabilistically. Empirical observations and testing for more than a century support the law that natural patterns are unique. Inductive logic can never prove uniqueness of the past, nor definitely predict all of the future. It studies the past and present by making observations and establishes predictions about the future. Induction cannot prove the rule; it can only support the rule. Hume, Popper, and others write of this "problem of induction" (Curd and Cover, 1998; Bailey, 2002). In induction, "Case and Result, therefore Rule," becomes "The two images are known to have come from the same source, and the details in the two sufficient images agree, so individualization is probable because the features of the source are probably unique and persistent." Or "The two images are known to have come from different sources, and the details in the two sufficient images disagree, so exclusion is probable because the features of sources are probably unique and persistent."

In actual case work, abductive logic is used in examination of forensic comparative evidence. Examiners start with the fundamental principles—the laws or rules—of sources being unique and persistent, conduct an examination to determine similarities or differences, and then determine actual agreement or disagreement of details in two sufficient images, and make the determination whether the images came from the same source. Starting with a rule, determining a result of examination, and reaching a conclusion in a particular case is abductive logic. If the premises of rule and result are true, the conclusion in the case is true. No scientist has ever falsified the rule or the law "Natural patterns are unique." This law, which is open to falsification by the finding of natural patterns that have been replicated, is the foundation of forensic comparison science.

If repeated natural patterns from two known different sources would be determined, the rule or law would need to be revisited. This has not happened. "Rule and Result, therefore Case" becomes "Individualization is possible because the features of the source are unique and persistent and the details in the two sufficient images agree; therefore, the two images are now known to have come from the same source." Or "Exclusion is possible because the features of the sources are unique and persistent and the details in the two sufficient images disagree; therefore, the two images are now known to have come from different sources."

Deductive and inductive logic support abductive logic. Deductive logic, or "Case and Rule, therefore Result," works well in the training status to study images and learn tolerance for variations in appearances of images due to distortions. The trainer and trainee can impart distortions when depositing images and then study the images with various quality and quantity of visible details to develop experience, understanding, and judgments about two images from the same source or two other images from different sources. Inductive logic, or "Result and Case, therefore Rule," when used in the training status, supports the law of uniqueness that is utilized by the trainer and the trainee. The trainer creates examination exercises and knows the expected correct result and determination that is to be made in this particular case, and this will support understanding the rule of uniqueness and persistency. Normally the trainer will provide an abundant amount of known source images for searching and comparing. With this training and the resulting experience, understandings, and judgments within the collaboration of the community of scientists, the examiner develops knowledge and beliefs and becomes ready to conduct case work.

In actual case work, the examiner uses abductive logic, which is supported by the knowledge generated from the deductive and inductive inferential processing in training and starts with the rule, determines the result of the comparison, and makes a determination in the particular case examination. McKasson and Richards (1998, 80) said the following:

> Notice how both deduction and induction are involved in abduction: Induction helps to generate the formulation of the given, and deduction helps to show a logical relation of the premises of the given. Further, when abductive logic generates a Case, deductive logic explains the logical relation of Rule and Result, and inductive logic provides a relation of the Case to the Rule.

LAWS OF SCIENCE

Science is about generalizing nature with laws. Once universal truth is experienced repeatedly among a variety of situations, a generalized law can be established. Nature is organized by its rules or laws, and scientists strive to determine what those laws are (Saxe, et al. 2006; McRoberts, 1996; McKasson and Richards, 1998; Urry, 2007).

A law is the foundation on which the science stands. This universal belief allows the scientists to use the general law to know the specific in a particular case. An example of a universal truth, a virtually unconditioned truth, a generalization, or a law within the forensic comparative science community of collaborating scientists is the law "Every natural pattern is unique."

The law enables the scientist to give significance to the judgments of comparative measurements of details in images. Accepting the rule or law, judging the results of the comparisons, and determining the evaluation of the case are the responsibilities of the examiner within the community of scientists. The forensic comparative scientist must be cognizant of the images, the comparative measurements, and the community when making the judgments. The examiner must acknowledge the role, ethics, and responsibility of judging, an important component of the forensic comparative scientist. Without judging each comparative measurement and the overall relationship of the totality of the comparative measurements, there would be no forensic comparative science.

This has been a simple and limited discussion of defining science and its laws, rules, and methods of inquiry. As philosophers of science, Curd and Cover (1998, 79) offer this explanation:

> It is highly unlikely that any simple-minded, one- or two-sentence definition of science will yield a plausible demarcation criterion that we can use to label and condemn as pseudo-scientific those theories (and their advocates) that fail to meet the standards of good science. Ultimately, discriminating between science and its counterfeit depends on a detailed understanding of how science works.

My goals in this book are to describe one philosophy of how forensic comparative science works.

REFERENCES

Aristotle, (350 BC) *Metaphysics*, I, 1. From John Paul II 2003 *Fides et Ratio*.

Association of Firearm and Tool Mark Examiners Glossary, 2007, 5th Edition, Version 5.070207.

Bailey, Andrew. *First Philosophy: Fundamental Problems and Readings in Philosophy*. Broadview Press, Peterborough, Ontario, Canada, 2002.

Burch, Robert, "Charles Sanders Peirce", Edward N. Zalta (ed.), *The Stanford Encyclopedia of Philosophy* (Fall 2006 Edition). *<http://plato.stanford.edu/archives/fall2006/entries/peirce/>*.

Byrd, Jon. 'Confirmation Bias, Ethics, and Mistakes in Forensics,' *Journal of Forensic Identification*, 2006, 56 (4), 511–525.

Carroll, Sean B. *Endless Forms Most Beautiful: The New Science of Evo Devo and the Making of the Animal Kingdom*. W. W. Norton & Company, Inc., New York, 2005.

Curd, Martin, and J. A. Cover. *Philosophy of Science: The Central Issues*. W. W. Norton & Company, Inc., New York, 1998.

Dear, Peter. *The Intelligibility of Nature: How Science Makes Sense of the World*. The University of Chicago Press, Chicago, 2006.

Dror, Itiel E.. *Perception is far from perfection: The* role of the brain and mind in constructing realities, *Behavioral and Brain Sciences*, 2005, 28 (6), 763.

Dror, Itiel E. and D. Charlton. 'Why experts make errors,' *Journal of Forensic Identification*, 2006, 56 (4), 600–616.

Dror, Itiel E., D. Charlton and A. Peron. 'Contextual information renders experts vulnerable to erroneous identifications,' *Forensic Science International*, 2006, 156 (1), 74–78.

Fermi, Laura, and Gilberto Bernardini. *Galileo and the Scientific Revolution*. Dover Publications, Inc., Mineola, New York, 2003. (republication of the 1965 Fawcett paperback edition of the work first published by Basic Books, Inc., New York, 1961.)

Fricker, Elizabeth. 'Trusting others in the sciences: *a priori* or empirical warrant?' *Studies in History and Philosophy of Science*, 2002 (33), 373–383.

Grieve, David. Personal communication, 2007.

Hardwig, John. 'The Role of Trust in Knowledge,' *The Journal of Philosophy*, Vol. 88, No. 12. (December, 1991) 693–708.

John Paul II, [2003 05 09] *'Fides et Ratio,'* at: *http://www.vatican.va/edocs/ENG0216/_INDEX.HTM#fonte*.

Koppl, Roger. 'How to Improve Forensic Science,' *European Journal of Law and Economics*, 2005 (20), 255–286.

Lonergan, Bernard. *Insight: A Study of Human Understanding*. Longmans, Green & Co., London, 1957. Fifth edition, University of Toronto Press, Toronto, Canada, 2005.

McInerny, Ralph, John O'Callaghan. "Saint Thomas Aquinas," Edward N. Zalta (ed.), *The Stanford Encyclopedia of Philsophy* (Spring 2005 Edition), *<http://plato.stanford.edu/archives/spr2005/entries/aquinas/>*.

McKasson, Stephen C., Carol A. Richards. *Speaking as an Expert: A Guide for the Identification Sciences From the Laboratory to the Courtroom*. Charles C Thomas, Springfield, Illinois, 1998.

McRoberts, Alan. 'Nature Never Repeats Itself,' *The Print*, 1996, *12* (5), 1–3.

Nature editorial. 'Evolution and the brain,' *Nature*, Vol. 447, No. 7146, 14 June 2007, 753.

Peirce, Charles Sanders. 'The Fixation of Belief' *Popular Science Monthly*, 12 (November, 1877), 1–15.

Peirce, Charles Sanders. 'How to Make Our Ideas Clear' *Popular Science Monthly*, 12 (January, 1878), 286–302.

Richards, Carol. Letter to the editor, *Journal of Forensic Identification*, 1994, 44(1), 108–110.

Saviano, Jeffrey. 'The Pursuit of Objectivity in the Examination of Forensic Evidence' *Journal of Forensic Identification*, 2006, 56 (6), 877–884.

Saxe, Rebecca, Brett, Matthew, and Manwisher, Nancy. 'Divide and Conquer: A Defense of Functional Localizers,' *NeuroImage*, 2006, 30, 1088–1096.

Smith, Kurt 'Descartes' Life and Works,' The Stanford Encyclopedia of Philosophy 2007 (Summer Edition), Edward N. Zalta (ed.), forthcoming. <*http://plato.stanford.edu/archives/sum2007/entries/descartes-works/*>.

Stewart, Ian. *What Shape is a Snowflake?* W. H. Freeman and Company, New York, 2001.

Thornton, Stephen. 'Karl Popper', Edward N. Zalta (ed.), *The Stanford Encyclopedia of Philosophy* (Winter 2006 Edition). <*http://plato.stanford.edu/archives/win2006/entries/popper/*>.

Urry, Meg. 'The Secrets of Dark Energy,' *Parade*, May 27, 2007, 5, Parade Publications, New York.

Weed, Douglas. 'The Nature and Necessity of Scientific Judgment,' *Journal of Law and Policy*, 2007, 15 (1), 135–164.

CHAPTER 2

Believing Recognition

CONTENTS

Reed (2004, 2) said, "Cognitive psychology is the study of the mental operations that support people's acquisition and use of knowledge." Cognitive science is also the study of knowing again, or *re*cognition, when similar data is *re*presented to the viewer. Explaining how we recognize shapes is the mission of cognitive vision scientists. Palmer (2002, 377) explains:

> All of the theories we are about to consider are inadequate to capture the astonishing power, versatility, and subtlety of human shape perception. How people perceive shape is certainly among the most difficult problems in visual perception, so difficult that no satisfactory solution has yet been proposed.

The expert forensic comparative examiner sees and judges shapes. Explaining the process and thresholds is a challenge.

Much of life involves seeing, experiencing, understanding, judging, and then knowing or cognizing an object, storing it in memory, and then recognizing when it or a similar type of object is seen again at a later time. The question of level of recognition arises. Recognizing a constituent within a category is somewhat different from recognizing a specific entity within that group. Knowing an object is a chair is different from knowing that object is my favorite chair within a room of other chairs.

The degree or intensity of memory plays a role in recognition. The significance of relative mental measurements of sizes, shapes, sequences, and configurations of the features within an object results in a comparison of these features between the currently perceived object and that which has been previously perceived. These measurements of sizes, shapes, sequences, and configurations of features within each object and the resulting comparative measurements between the two items must be accompanied by judgments in knowing and believing. Through experiences, understandings, and judgments, the examiner must be able to determine correspondence or agreement of details that allows for the belief of recognition. The examiner must use judgments to believe in recognition if any conclusion of the same source of origin between two objects can take place in forensic comparative science.

THE VISUAL SYSTEM

The visual system of processing light from an object, to the eyes, through the nerves, and terminating in the brain is complex. The light from nature produces an image on the retina of the eye, which is transferred into generated energy that travels from the retina to the optic nerves and then to the brain for processing (Palmer, 2002). Because every visual perception of an object is by a viewer who has unique eyes, nerves, and brain that process the data, the viewing is unique. Dror (2005, 763) stated the following:

> We are different people, with different experiences, different views, and different brains and sensory mechanisms. This entails that we have different perceptions. Most people share sufficient perceptual commonalities that allow labeling and communication within everyday life activities. Nevertheless, the perceptions across people are far from identical. Furthermore, even if we did perceive the exact same thing, that percept is not necessarily a true and accurate reflection of the "objective reality." Perceptions fall along a multidimensional continuum and are subjective in nature. This individualization of perception derives from the active nature of cognition and the wide range of factors that affect what and how we perceive.

This visual process follows rules of perception that occur in nature and are now being determined by research scientists. Vision is adapted to complex natural images. Interestingly, vision scientists often study the unnatural to understand the natural. The activities of these research scientists bring forth the rules by which we perceive. As better rules of vision shed light on the process, improved understanding and explanations of the entire method of comparative measurements and recognition occur (Hoffman, 2000).

VISUAL INTELLIGENCE

Vision scientists might find it difficult to have their subjects study natural patterns during research. Many patterns found in nature have an abundance of composite parts with a variety of measurable features to judge the reasons for the subject's response. The researchers need to know what caused the response, so simple and controlled patterns of data are often presented. By studying the reactions to the variations of these patterns, scientists learn what features are important and the strategies used in the visual processing and ordering of details.

Vision scientist Donald Hoffman describes *visual intelligence* as an active construction of everything that is seen by people. People generalize simple parts that they construct into the whole complex object. By studying simple objects first, the rules of constructing parts into wholes and breaking down wholes into parts can be determined in complex objects (Hoffman, 2000). Visual intelligence construction of images in the brain is according to these rules, even though the scientists have not identified all of them.

The many aspects of the human visual system are being researched by many cognitive vision scientists, resulting in a conclusion that may seem obvious: "the realization that *vision is extremely difficult*" (Palmer, 2002, 60). Reed explains (Reed, 2004, 19), "Our superiority over computers as pattern recognizers has the practical advantage that pattern recognition can serve as a test.... However, the ease and accuracy with which people can recognize patterns make it difficult to study this ability."

Hoffman (2000, 1, 10) said the following:

> You are a creative genius. Your creative genius is so accomplished that it appears, to you and to others, as effortless. Yet it far outstrips the most valiant efforts of today's fastest supercomputers. To invoke it, you need only open your eyes. This might sound like the mantra of a new therapy or the babble of a fortune cookie. But it is, instead, the reasoned conclusion of researchers in the field of cognitive science. What happens when you see is not a mindless process of stimulus and response, as behaviorists thought for much of the twentieth century, but a sophisticated process of construction whose intricacies we are now beginning to understand.... So we share with all sighted animals a genius to construct and, in consequence, to err. This raises questions. When should we trust what we see?

The experiences, understandings, and judgments by self and within the community make possible this trust in perception. People do not see and remember like a camera and film.

Human perception is being studied to determine rules of vision and to improve the strategies and mathematical algorithms of computers. Efforts to simulate the human process with these computer efforts will never duplicate the natural process of human vision, but they do provide another source to aid in our understanding of this process. Multiple stages of visual construction occur based on the universal rules of vision. According to Hoffman (2000, 94–95), "You construct every line, curve, and 3D shape that you see. You then describe these constructions using, among other things, a language of parts. And you judge two of your constructions to be similar if you have given them similar descriptions."

The problem—that language and labeling of parts is generalized—frustrates the attempt of a complete description of uniqueness in natural patterns. Similarity of labeled parts is good for categorization. The beauty of forensic comparative science is not relying on generalized language to describe correspondence of unique parts but seeing the naturally unique patterns. When two or more people view unique structures with individualized perception, how can they see the objective reality of a thing as subjectively the same? The answer is they follow rules of vision.

Hoffman determined color, shading, texture, motion, shape, and the entire scene as some of the components of the rules of constructing images in perception. Stephen E. Palmer (2002), another research vision scientist, describes perceptual organization as the grouping and parsing of the elements of the details in the image based on proximity, color, shade, orientation, connectedness, common fate or movements, and past experience to determine that these components form into a unit.

Another component of shape perception is the determination of edges within an image. The four types of edges that Palmer describes are caused by variations in orientation, depth, illumination, and reflectance. Detecting edges as one element transitions to another element is paramount for the comparative scientist. The luminance that is generated to the eye is the basis for determining the edge location.

ATTENTION

Reed (2004, 2) said, "We can attend to only a small part of the physical stimulation that surrounds us, and only a small part of what we attend to can be remembered." To properly attend to physical evidence, the examiner needs to concentrate, focus, and select what needs attending to, requiring a mental effort. Attention must overcome contextual effects, or influences of surrounding or nearby data, in recognition of images (Dror, 2005). The context of one impression must not sway the processing of the data in the second image pattern. The context of the impression in relation to other evidence must not bias the examiner. Concentrating, focusing, selecting, and attending to two distinct images must occur during analyses, comparisons, and evaluations by the examiner in the process of forensic comparative science.

WORKING MEMORY

Intervening time between two independent situations of viewing, attention applied to both events, and influences on memory all contribute to what is remembered and considered when seeing the same or another object again.

The initial need and effort to actually remember what is seen the first time is another factor for consideration when encoding the details of that object into memory. Committing an item to long-term memory is different from knowing and then quickly forgetting irrelevant details in short-term memory. A variation of short-term memory is used in many functions of perception as working memory, which is utilized in forensic comparative science. In long-term memory, the mentally stored image cannot be brought back to its original condition for consideration against the current object. The mass quantities of data encoded into short-term memory for perception are quickly forgotten unless attended and rehearsed (Reed, 2004). There is no need, nor is it possible, to remember all data that are viewed while encoding into short-term memory.

Working memory is another kind of memory that is used specifically by the comparative scientist. Working memory uses short-term memory to briefly store elements of data to carry out a current activity using controlled and allocated attention as keys for succeeding in the task at hand (Palmer, 2002; Reed, 2004). The memory can be forgotten after the task is accomplished. Working memory in forensic science allows the comparative measurements and judgments to take place while viewing and quickly reconsidering both items during many observations of the process. The examiner can compare the two images with the exemplar as a template while considering the details and their configuration within themselves and to each other. The comparison helps the examiner to study and attend to the structures that are physically connected or grouped within a tolerable region.

The forensic comparative scientist does not rely on ordinary long- or short-term memory strategies to determine agreement or disagreement of details between two impressions or marks. Because long-term memory cannot recall all the details that had been perceived, and short-term memory quickly loses the insignificant influence of the current details, the comparative scientist uses two impressions or marks available for a recurring examination to determine whether corresponding details exist in both items. An unknown impression is compared as often as needed to an exemplar to determine agreement or disagreement of details. The images do not need to be stored in long-term memory, as each impression is available for reconsideration. Short-term memory quickly forgets the details. The processing of details with working memory continues until a decision is made. Many judgments are made in working memory throughout the process of reflectively contemplating the details in the available images. With these judgments building upon judgments, the knowing and believing of recognition occur. The data in the two images that the examiner uses to render a judgment can be retrieved and examined again, implementing working memory anew. The comparative scientist does not rely on long- or short-term memory.

Reed (2004, 181) had the following to say:

> Visual images preserve the spatial relations among the objects of a scene or the features of a pattern. The time it takes to mentally scan between two objects in an image is therefore a function of the distance between them. Visual images also make it possible to compare all the features of two patterns simultaneously when we try to match a visual pattern with an image of another pattern. In contrast, features described verbally must be compared one at a time because of the sequential nature of language.

The comparative scientist relies on the two images next to each other or in juxtaposition when presented for examination. The distance between them and time allotted can be controlled for the comparative measuring. A description of the comparison with language alone does not do justice to the visual processing that takes place under the attentive abstraction of details from the images. A forensic scientist realizes how much language is lacking when writing case notes. Notes of the examination and pictures allow for recollection of the examination later but are written in a linear mode. No matter how hard we try, notes, words, and pictures are still inadequate to completely replicate the recurring and complex perceptual processes that took place with the initial examination and when the sufficiency threshold for judgment was crossed.

Whether naturally perceiving, conducting examinations, or writing case notes, patterns can be compared and described using a variety of methods. The template theory considers an overlap of similarities. Feature theories, emphasizing distinct features, take the parts or components of an object and look for similarities. Structural theory follows the connection and relation of features to other features (Reed, 2004). Questioned impressions and known exemplars in comparative science can use all three strategies, applying working memory throughout the process. Test impressions or standards of a known shoe sole are often created on a transparent sheet. This becomes a template for the comparative measurements of sizes, shapes, sequences, and configurations with the unknown print. In feature theory, the features of a source and its marks can be compared by looking for details of its distinct unique components and determining whether they exist in relation to other features. In structural theory, the structures and relations of all features are considered, including the use of facets of a template strategy or similarities of distinct features. The actual structures and configurations of the details of the features within the whole are considered in forensic comparative science.

GROUPING

Elements within the same closed area will be grouped together. The transition from loose to simple proximity and then to actual connectedness indicates the difficulty of defining the thresholds of grouping. The grouping based on proximity, similarity, common region, element connectedness, good continuation, and common fate often result in an aggregate image as one perceived unit with the individual elements. A person's past experience with common elements provides a tendency to group similar elements similarly in present situations. The viewer's past familiarity with respect to the configuration of parts within an aggregate are considered the experience factor for this type of grouping (Palmer, 2002).

Texture analysis, or the defining of grouped regions, is not too different from the detection of luminance edges that would play a significant role in perception. Determining the variations in surfaces extracted from changes in luminance due to depth and shadowing in the image helps the viewer determine the components and the aggregate object of a group.

Some unnatural patterns are presented in Figures 2-1 through 2-6. Look at the patterns and, considering the rules of connectedness, proximity, shapes, color, and texture just presented, determine what general form or figure is embedded within each drawing. Using some of the rules of grouping, these figures are constructed by the viewer into shapes that represent known objects from the experience of the viewer.

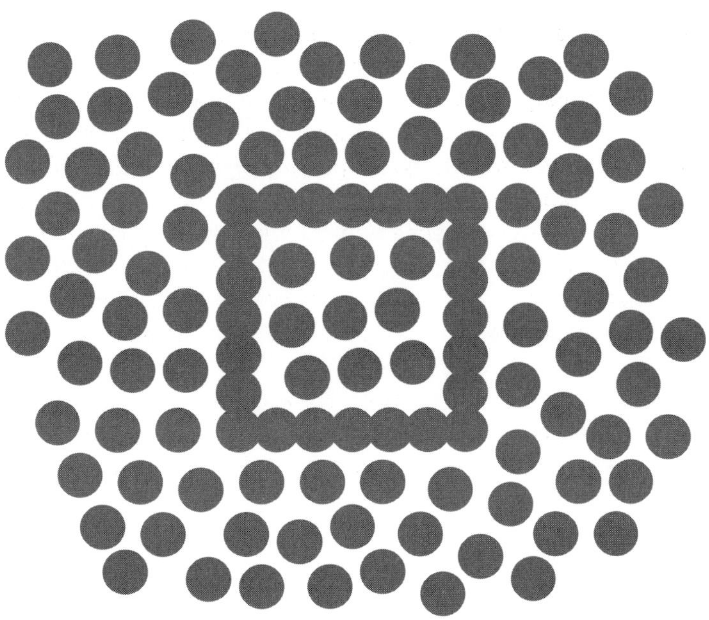

FIGURE 2-1
The principle of connectedness.

FIGURE 2-2
The principle of proximity.

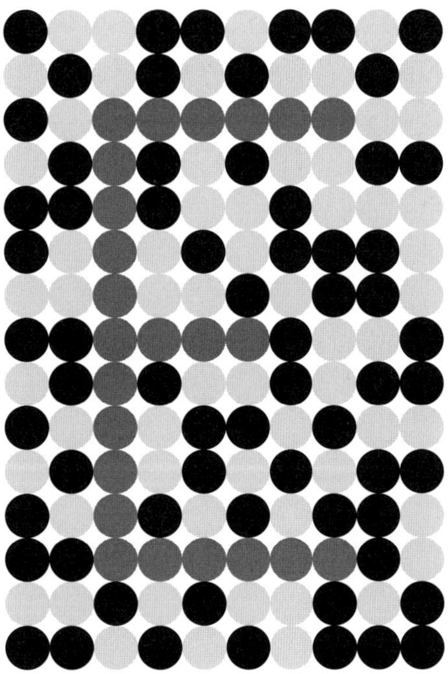

FIGURE 2-3
The principle of color.

FIGURE 2-4
The principle of shapes.

FIGURE 2-5
The principle of size.

PARSING

The visual system also organizes objects into parts. Parts are constructed by the visual system using a variety of interactions of the color, shape, and texture of the object, and the viewer's prior experience with them. Dividing whole objects into the sequences and configurations of their parts allows the viewer to search his or her memory of the vast categories of objects for correspondence. The parsing should not be influenced by a slight change of perspective or configuration if the parts remain in view. Distortions of objects within tolerance should generate the same construction of a part. The retinal image constructs the same parts in the brain even with slight variations of viewing, as the same object can never be viewed again exactly the same, but the viewer can construct similar parts from similar objects. Experience with a generalized wide variety of parts in wholes helps the construction process (Hoffman, 2000). Whether or not we know them, rules of nature and perception enable people to see and understand parts and whole entities.

Region segmentation is the process of parsing based on luminance, color, texture, motion, or variation. Edge detection is a likely process for segmenting the image into different parts. Parsing, depending on the shape of the object, determines what subdivisions of a perceptual unit are perceived as

FIGURE 2-6
The principle of texture.

being a component of the object. A solid circle and a straight line are individual objects without a contrasting place to naturally parse. The image is consistent throughout. Any measurable change of contrast would be a natural location for parsing. Parsing occurs where there is a change in the feature.

Parsing forms region segregation of an area within the object. This requires taking one perceptual object and dividing it into two or more parts, rather than grouping two or more parts and putting them together into a single unit. But there is no constraint on the order in which parsing and grouping must occur relative to each other; they could very well occur simultaneously.

Parsing can be based on texture through "normal" texture segregation or through "conscious scrutiny." *Scrutiny* is the focused attention on different parts of the image in an attempt to find shape differences between individual elements of the object (Palmer, 2002). Since objects are perceived by parsing and grouping, the issue is whether parts are perceived before the complete unit or the complete unit before the parts. Which occurs first in image processing may not be nearly as pertinent as determining how the processing is completed. Hoffman (2000, 104) says, "To construct objects, we must construct parts. But we must also… assemble these parts in coherent spatial relationships."

Perceived objects have an important aspect of being composed of distinct parts. A part is a restricted portion that could be considered an entity within the object. There are normal spatial and sequential relations among the parts that form the whole unit. The normal configuration of the parts of a table makes up the whole table. Construction using the same legs and top in a different configuration of attaching two legs to each side of the top results in something that might not be recognized as a piece of furniture. Examining the same parts in an unordinary arrangement might confuse the processor of the image details. The configuration of the parts is essential for the object. Examining parts in their normal configuration that emerges into the whole object is a strategy used in perception of objects because the viewer is familiar with the normal configuration of parts in that type of object. Fingerprint examiners usually view fingerprints in their upright position of tip at the top of the impression. The examiner learned the generalized parts that make up the print and their normal configuration. The ridges at the tip, core, and delta areas in a pattern usually indicate to an examiner the normal upright position. Having both prints in similar orientation is a benefit to the searching and comparison of prints. After orientating the generalized whole image, the parts that make up the image can be more closely scrutinized.

Some unnatural patterns are presented in Figures 2-7 through 2-12. Look at the patterns, and, considering the rules of parsing just presented, determine the number of comparative measurements that can be accomplished from the parsed sections. Consider lines, arcs, lengths, segments, insides, and outsides. Parsing is the segmenting of objects. Using arrangements of straight lines or circles in these figures, how many measured parts are depicted? How many parts do you choose to measure?

FIGURE 2-7
Eight straight lines.

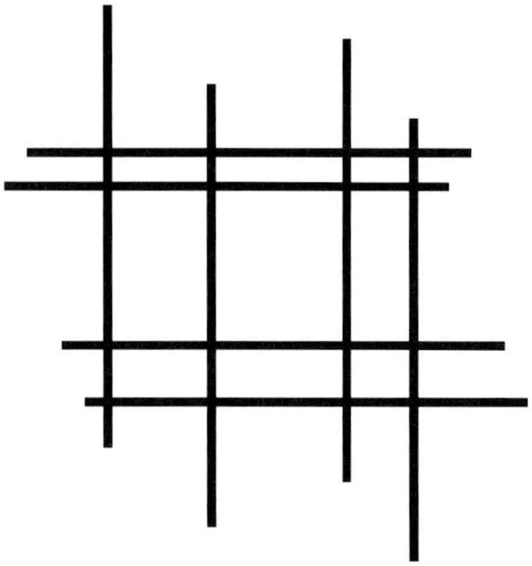

FIGURE 2-8
Many parts from eight straight lines.

FIGURE 2-9
Three circles.

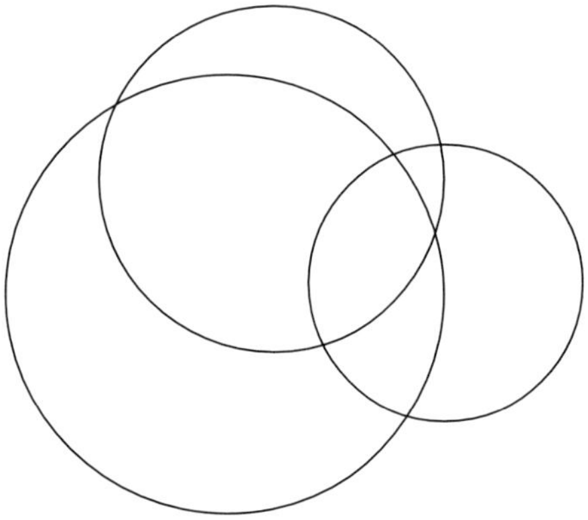

FIGURE 2-10
Many parts, or arcs, among three circles.

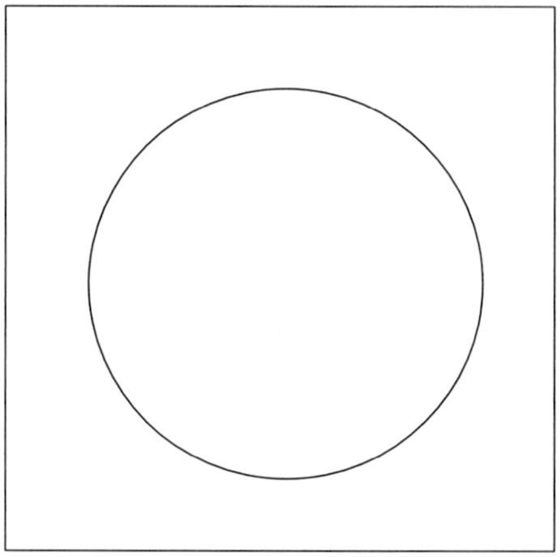

FIGURE 2-11
One circle and four lines making a box.

FIGURE AND GROUND

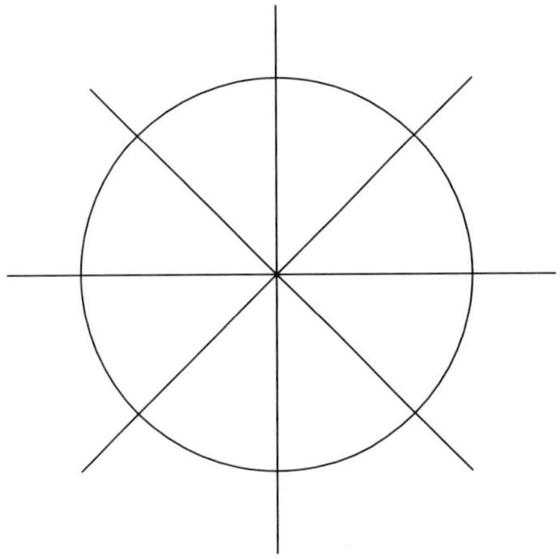

FIGURE 2-12
Many arcs from a circle and many parts from four straight lines.

The contrast between two parts of an image contributes to the judgment of what is the figure being viewed and what is the ground, background, or substrate in an image. The figure being perceived as being in front or on top of the ground region implies that figure/ground processing is related to depth perception. The figure becomes the focus of the perception based on the rules of the details associated with the image. The properties assigned to the figure are (1) it appears thinglike, (2) it is closer to the observer, (3) it is bound by contour, and (4) its shape is defined by its contour. The properties of the ground are (1) it does not appear thinglike, (2) it is further from the observer, (3) the dimensions extend beyond the contour in question, and (4) the ground does not possess shape at the contour.

The primary rules of figure/ground consideration are based on surroundedness, size, orientation, contrast, symmetry, convexity, and parallelism. If the other factors are equal, the object completely surrounded by another, the smaller region, the group that is vertical and horizontal versus oblique, the regions with greatest contrast to the surrounding area, the symmetrical regions, the convex regions, and the regions with parallel sides are usually perceived as figure and the other region as the ground. It is difficult to predict the judgment when a variety of factors are involved in the same image. Figure/ground organization must operate initially before either parsing or grouping can sensibly take place (Palmer, 2002).

Attention seems automatically drawn to the figure rather than attention determining the figure. It seems reasonable that people would attend to figures rather than grounds, because the figure is nearer and normally of more importance. It seems clear that there is a strong bias to attend to figures before the flexibility of attention studies either figure or ground, depending on the purposes of the examiner (Palmer, 2002).

A classic illustration of figure/ground consideration is a finger- or shoeprint (examples are presented in later chapters). Based only on experience, normally, the print is expected to be dark on a light background due to black ink or the development technique. There are occasions of color reversals in which the furrows appear dark and the ridges or tread elements appear light. The rules of textures, shapes, contrasts, and surrounding substrate must be considered. Knowing what to look for in an impression and being aware of possible color reversal is a component of examiner expertise. As rules of vision are understood, expert application of vision can be better accomplished.

CONFIGURAL PROCESSING

Perceptual processes seem to progress from the whole toward parts or simultaneously rather than sequentially (Palmer, 2002). The whole structure also influences the perception of parts by what cognition vision scientist Stephen Palmer calls "configural orientation effects." By seeing the whole, the viewer expects to see parts in their normal configurations. The whole is seen first, and then parts must be observed. The global or whole processing may be determined as primary because the awareness of parts improves when they are found within significant wholes. Significant wholes are those figures that are important to the viewer. Configural processing of wholes with their parts removes the likelihood that parts perception necessarily precedes that of the whole.

Gauthier and Tarr (2002, 432) explain this as follows:

> Holistic–configural effects arise when individual object parts are placed in the context of the other individual parts from the same object. Each individual part is better recognized in the original learned configuration than in the context of these same object parts in a new configuration. For instance, the nose of a familiar face, Bob, may be easier to pick out in a forced-choice test when the eyes of Bob are in the original configuration than when the eyes are moved apart.... This effect focuses on the unique contribution of configural processing to part identification.

Vision research scientist Thomas Busey found support for configural processing in visual observation of objects by experts. A fingerprint examiner who becomes familiar with the types and orientation of features as they relate to other features within prints expects to see those features in normal configurations. When prints are presented normally, the brain response is quicker than when they are presented in abnormal arrangements, such as inverted prints, because the brain response to those stimuli is delayed. Novices of this process did not demonstrate different brain responses when presented upright or inverted fingerprints, as configural orientation was not significant for their viewing (Busey and Vanderkolk, 2005). Expertise is developed in all disciplines of the comparative sciences. Configural processing would be expected within each as the experts learn what types of parts and their orientations are found in an impression.

Visual processing is about abstracting or withdrawing information out of the details in images. Cognitive scientist Stephen Reed (2004) describes this with three levels of abstraction that occur simultaneously when recognizing a written word: the features that make up each letter, the letter itself, and the grouping of letters into a word. Experience with parts of letters, letters, and words that make up the known language of the viewer enable recognition. Experience with comparative science evidence helps the examiner learn and recognize the salient features and configural orientation of things, enabling better judgments about those features that are most helpful for making conclusions. Knowing comparative science and the substantial exposure to images develops expertise.

People are not born with an innate expertise in forensic science; it must be developed. Simple aptitude is inadequate without experience taking place within the domain. Experience needs the process of learning, testing, correcting, understanding, judging, knowing, and believing within the community to develop expertise. Sabatini (2007) explains:

> Experiences shape our behaviour, memories, and perception. Mechanistically, they also influence the brain's circuitry, and cooperativity between neuronal contacts during learning may contribute to this process. Neuronal plasticity describes experience-related and development-associated structural and functional changes in the brain, which contribute to, among other processes, memory formation.… It is neuroscientists' goal to understand the plastic features of the brain that make storing memories and learning new behaviours possible. In trying to achieve this formidable goal, many neuroscientists hope that, by uncovering the mechanisms behind the regulation of individual synapses, they will reveal the rules that govern the wiring of the brain.

The brain is plastic in its functioning and needs stimuli to develop. As expertise develops, the brain develops.

Developing expertise is a process of knowing and believing truth in science. Making novice judgments without the needed experiences, understandings, and judgments about two images that vary in appearance is tantamount to guessing. The courts and juries do not want guessing. While the novice may guess correctly, how does that person and others know, believe, and trust that conclusion? Forensic comparative scientists must develop expertise so their knowing and believing can be trusted within and outside the community.

Reed (2004, 330, 349) said the following:

> One becomes an expert in the skills needed for success on ability tests in much the same ways that one becomes an expert in doing anything else—through a combination of genetic endowment and experience.… Our ability to reason and solve problems is influenced by the familiarity of the material.

Domain-specific expert knowledge develops through innate abilities and information processing; one without the other does not make an expert. Trainees who have the aptitude and physical ability to learn start the process of becoming an expert. Once sufficient trust, training, experience, understanding, and judgment occur within the community of the domain, expertise develops. Continuing the development of knowledge and beliefs within the community and exposure to the domain stimuli provide additional foundations for expertise. Experts learn the strategies of comparative measurements, tolerance for variations in appearances, and limits of rendering a conclusion. Experts must be aware of the beliefs within the community with all images that vary in appearance from the source.

Cognitive scientists study experts and novices to determine how people process information. Some people know and experience more about a domain than others. Many people know less about a domain. As people study a domain, become parts of communities that study the domain, participate within the community, and remain open to the community, accepting the notion of expertise is simple.

Nature follows natural laws. Cognitive scientists are striving to better explain natural laws of perception. As scientists better understand the natural laws, scientists will better understand experts. As the understanding of expertise improves, the explanations of the human activity of comparative measurements will improve. Experts who better understand comparative measurements will better understand their domain. There is no reason to abolish expertise simply because we do not have all the answers to how expertise is accomplished. Expertise is needed for science seeking the truth.

Determining letters and numbers from a poorly maintained scoreboard can be a challenge for a sports fan. Sports fans have been exposed to a wide variety of scoreboards and quality and quantity of data that are being presented. What are the names and numbers being depicted? The viewer attempts to determine what is represented and constructs numbers or letters based on experience and context of the presentation on this scoreboard. View the remaining figures in this chapter. What letter or number do you construct based on your knowledge of letters or numbers and scoreboards? Figures 2-13 through 2-20 represent a scoreboard and its lights. Determine all the acceptable letters or numbers that could be constructed from these dots. Consider the lightbulbs within the context of word, within the context of a score, or within either context of word or score. What letters do you construct? What numbers do you construct? What is the actual physical data that is presented when the context of the scoreboard is removed and only physical data of dots are available? No matter the presence or lack of context, the dots can be compared to other data.

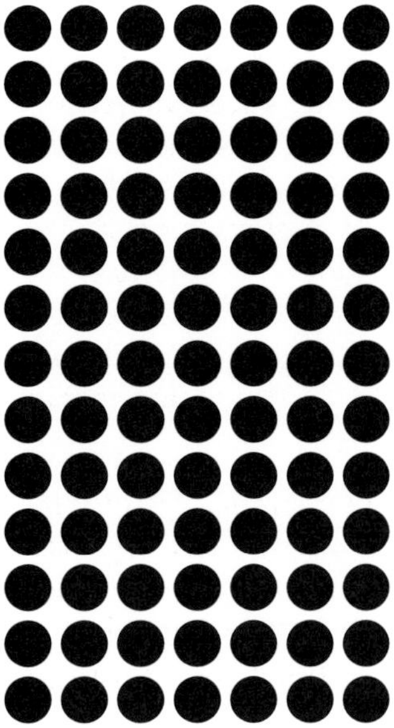

FIGURE 2-13
These black dots represent all the functioning lightbulbs in a panel of a scoreboard.

FIGURE 2-14
Lit lightbulbs in a scoreboard. Letters could be B, C, D, E, G, I, O, Q, S, and Z. Numbers could be 0, 2, 3, 5, 6, 8, and 9.

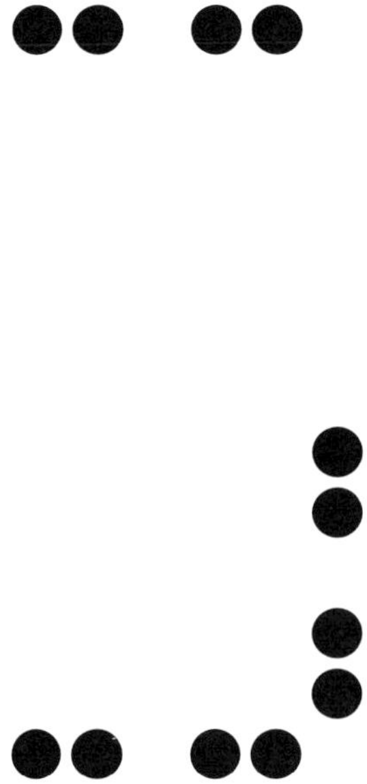

FIGURE 2-15
Lit lightbulbs in a scoreboard. Letters could be B, D, G, O, Q, and S. Numbers could be 0, 3, 5, 6, 8, and 9.

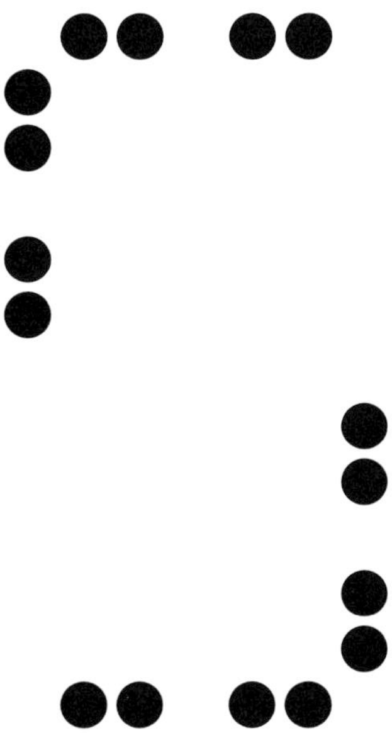

FIGURE 2-16
Lit lightbulbs in a scoreboard. Letters could be B, D, G, O, Q, and S. Numbers could be 0, 5, 6, 8, and 9.

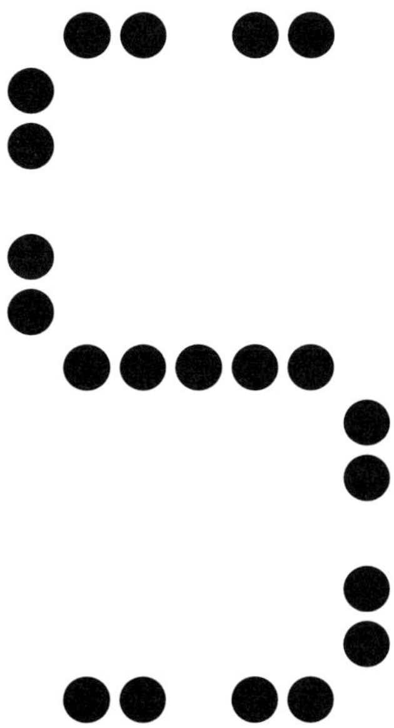

FIGURE 2-17
Lit lightbulbs in a scoreboard. Letters could be B and S. Numbers could be 5, 6, 8, and 9.

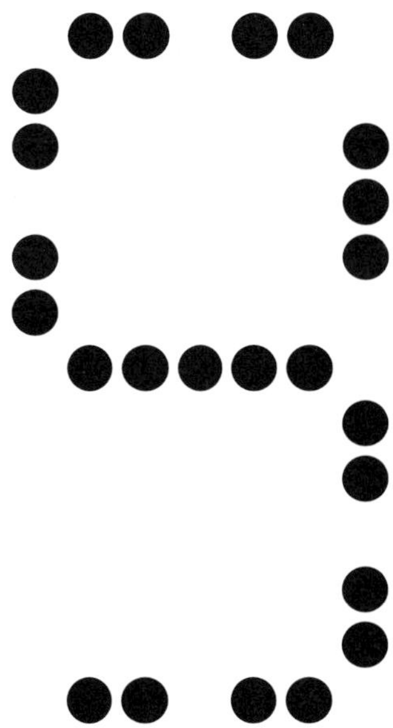

FIGURE 2-18
Lit lightbulbs in a scoreboard. Letter could be B. Numbers could be 8 and 9.

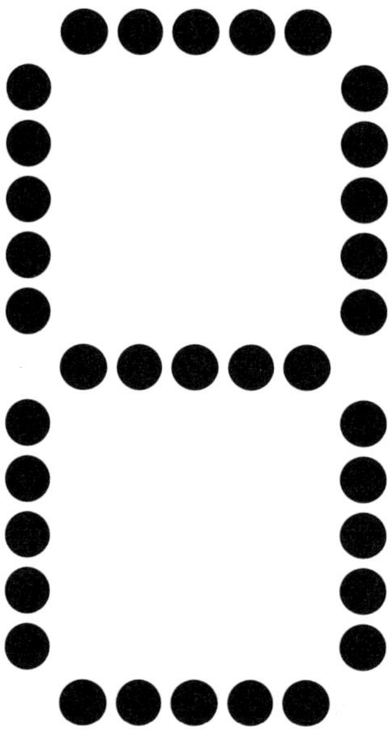

FIGURE 2-19
Lit lightbulbs in a scoreboard. Letter could be B. Number could be 8.

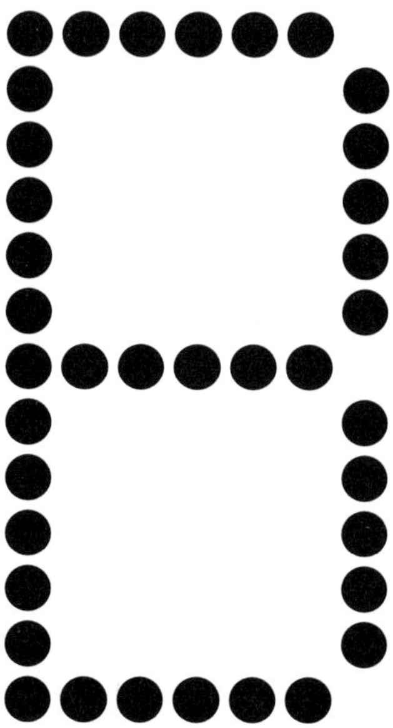

FIGURE 2-20
Lit lightbulbs in a scoreboard. Letter is B. Number is different than 8.

REFERENCES

Busey, Thomas A, and John R. Vanderkolk. 'Behavioral and electrophysiological evidence for configural processing in fingerprint experts,' *Vision Research*, 2005, 45, 431–448.

Dror, Itiel E. '*Perception* is far from *perfection*: The role of the brain and mind in constructing realities,' *Behavioral and Brain Sciences*, 2005, 28:6, 763.

Dror, Itiel E., Alisa E. Pèron, Sara-Lynn Hind, and David Charlton. 'When Emotions Get the Better of Us: The Effect of Contextual Top-down Processing on Matching Fingerprints,' *Applied Cognitive Psychology*, 2005, 19, 799–809.

Dror, Itiel E. 'Contextual information renders experts vulnerable to making erroneous identifications,' *Forensic Science International*, 2006, 156, 74–78.

Gauthier, Isabel, and Michael J. Tarr. 'Unraveling Mechanisms for Expert Object Recognition: Bridging Brain Activity and Behavior,' *Journal of Experimental Psychology: Human Perception and Performance*, 2002, Vol. 28, No. 2, 431–446.

Hoffman, Donald D. *Visual Intelligence—How We Create What We See*. W. W. Norton & Company: New York, 2000.

Palmer, Stephen E. *Vision Science – Photons to Phenomenology*. Massachusetts Institute of Technology, Cambridge, Massachusetts: 1999. Third printing 2002.

Reed, Stephen K. *Cognition—Theory and Application*. Wadsworth, a division of Thomson Learning, Belmont, California, 2004.

Sabatini, Bernardo L. 'Neighbourly synapses,' *Nature*, 27 December 2007, 450/20, 1173–1175.

CHAPTER 3

Unique and Persistent Surfaces of the Source

CONTENTS

THE LAW OF UNIQUENESS IN NATURE

Curd and Cover (1998, 805 and 806) said the following:

> Laws play a role in scientific reasoning. … Many also believe that we are justified in trusting scientific inferences because these predictions rest, in part, on well-confirmed laws. … Thus, according to Ayer's epistemic regulatory theory, a law is a true universal generalization about which we have certain beliefs and attitudes and that plays a characteristic role in science. … The regularity and necessitarian approaches share the conviction that laws of nature describe important facts about reality.

The first foundational rule for practicing forensic comparative science is the generalized law, "Every natural pattern is unique" or "Nature never repeats exactly" (Cummins and Midlo, 1943, 150). Determining and understanding the laws and rules of nature are the roles of the scientist. These laws or rules exist in reality, regardless if the scientist actually knows and can explain them. The declarations of laws or rules do not change nature but rather help us understand, explain, and study nature. If the declared law is determined to be flawed, it must be corrected.

Nature does not change its rules, or as Albert Einstein said in a letter about quantum mechanics to his colleague Max Born, "The theory says a lot, but does not really bring us any closer to the secret of the 'old one.' I, at any rate, am convinced that *He* is not playing at dice" (quoted in Born, 2005, 88). The "*He*" in Einstein's quote is assumed to be God. If Einstein was convinced that God does not change the laws of nature depending on a roll of dice, I can also be convinced. The key is not changing the rules of nature based on a roll of dice. Nature does not mislead, nor does it lie. Man might go astray on the paths of learning, but this is not nature's fault. Fermi and Bernardini (2003, 109) said, "In this way of proceeding, Galileo placed an absolute faith in the fact that nature cannot be deceitful; that between the mathematical, rational, and objective interpretation of phenomena and their actual happening and repetition, there can be no unpleasant surprise. Each experiment, if sensibly conceived, is a date with nature to which nature responds faithfully, at the exact time, without cheating or misleading."

Every natural pattern is unique. This is our foundation, our generalization, our rule, our law. According to Mairs (1995, 232), "Either Nature can produce duplicate patterns or she cannot." There is no indication, support for, or expectation that patterns in nature, animate or inanimate, have been, are, or ever will be replicated. There are no limitations of the law. The law prohibits replication of any size or type of natural pattern. If it is part of nature, its pattern is unique. And the patterns within its patterns are unique. This law bans repetition and is open to falsifiability. If actual replication of a natural pattern were to be found, the law would need to be qualified, improved, or changed. Every time you walk, look at the unique tapestries of nature's patterns and try to falsify the law. Try to find one natural pattern that is actually repeated. The search to find a repetitive pattern in nature is the gauntlet that is thrown down. The viewer must be aware when challenging the law that examining unclear and noisy patterns and being unable to determine difference is not the same as determining repetition.

FORM AND PATTERN

Form is the similar general shape that many objects have in common, which allows grouping or classification rules to be established. Patterns are the particular structures of shape within each object that has a form. Each specific pattern in nature does not need a specific explanation as to how that particular pattern developed uniquely but generalizations of how form naturally occurs are needed. Biologist D'Arcy Wentworth Thompson (1942) described the generalized explanations for development of forms in nature using mathematics as a tool throughout his work, *On Growth and Form*. He did not strive for an explanation and description of individuality of each object within a group. After all, most scientists are interested in the taxonomy or classification of objects to similar objects, not describing uniqueness with models and terminology. Specifically describing all individuality throughout nature would overwhelm the most ambitious of any scientist.

The judgment making of scientists in grouping, generalizing, and then "identifying similarities within difference" through the classification of common form is noted here as a challenge that is shared throughout science. Taxonomy has that challenge of applying mathematics and terminology to unique morphology that is to be generalized. It is good that humans have the capacity to determine specific patterns without the requirement to formally define each unique pattern within a category or classification of general form.

As an example, consider people. Lewontin (1982, 60) observed:

> People come in a continuous array of heights, weights, and colors, and they show extensive, subtle variation in their noses, ears, hairlines, and postures. Even those differences that are normally spoken of as qualitative—like "black" and "white"—show continuous variation when given a second glance. Eyes do not come in only two colors, blue and brown. Take any ten Europeans at random, and they will almost certainly be distinguishable one from another by their eye colors, just as ten randomly chosen "blacks" will vary in skin color enough to be told apart on that basis alone.

The ability to perceive these variations in form is affected by our conditioning of what we consciously, attentively, and comparatively measure from training, experiences, understandings, and judgments made by ourselves within the communities of people.

Other groupings occur besides just those on the outside of the human body. In cognitive neuroscience, the effort to classify regions of each brain is challenging, as each region of a brain is unique (Leslie, 2005; Muotri and Gage, 2006). As for the neuroscientists striving to pin down what areas manage specific brain functions, Saxe and colleagues (2006, 1089) said the following:

> Brain imaging relates function to locations in the brain. Because cognitive neuroscience is not about specific individuals but about people in general, we need some way to specify brain locations that will generalize across individuals. The problem is that the shape of each person's brain is unique, just like the challenge: What accounts as the same place in two different brains?... Once we can identify the "same place" in different brains, we are in a position to combine data across subjects, studies, and labs.

The good news for forensic comparative scientists is that on close inspection, the features of every object are unique.

THE ROLE OF TERMINOLOGY AND MATHEMATICS IN DESCRIBING GENERALITIES IN NATURE

Terminology and mathematics serve a purpose for both the taxonomist and the forensic scientist by providing tools that enable them to study and describe natural phenomenon. However, terminology and mathematics cannot completely describe the variations within each of nature's patterns. Terminology describes what remains after mathematics averages out the irregularities, imperfections, little bumps, edges, textures, or contours that will vary for each natural pattern within any general form (Ball, 1999). General terms tend to average the uniqueness and depict similarity among the unique parts. The perception of uniqueness has the potential to be lost because of the generalization caused by terminology.

In a discussion of perception within friction ridge examinations, David Grieve (1990, 110) states the following:

> The presence of such recognizable landmarks as dots, ridge endings, and bifurcations are necessary to the mechanism of identity, but have produced a detrimental consequence to the identification process. Unknown impressions tend to be viewed as mere summaries of their landmarks, expressed in shallow descriptions according to the number of named formations they contain. By reducing an impression to a collection of specific areas that lend themselves to nomenclature, the totality of the mark is shattered into a myopic concern over the quantity of the parts. An impression which exists as a unique entity is transformed during observation into a series of formations that must be rebuilt into something individual. This dismantling of ridge structure into a quantification of selected characteristics, or Galton points, may facilitate verbal descriptions or written standards, but does so at an enormous sacrifice to the remaining information in the impression.

In my earlier writings (Vanderkolk, 1993, 121–122), I state, "The more we, as examiners, attempt to describe something that is inherently unique, the more it will appear like something else, and, therefore, seem to lose its uniqueness. By confining our description of either latent or inked prints to labels such as whorls, loops, arches, bifurcations, ending ridges, and dots, we can easily lose track of the uniqueness of the ridge unit arrangements that comprise all the ridge structure. Uniqueness must not be compromised for the convenience of labels."

Terminology is needed for communication, and scientists must communicate. However, terminology diminishes the unique because it generalizes through the process of description. It is difficult, maybe impossible, for terminology to simply describe unique patterns and textures. It is also difficult for terminology to define when the patterns and textures of uniqueness blend into something else that is different yet equally unique. Saxe and colleagues (2006, 1095) said, "Imprecise boundaries are a feature of many scientifically respectable objects, including ocean currents like the Gulf Stream, geographical features like Mt. Fuji and human body parts like knees and elbows.... So it is important that researchers recognize that a name is a tool, not a conclusion." When does the knee become the shin within each leg? When does the elbow become the arm in each person? When does a structure in three-dimensional volar skin with the label "ending ridge" actually transition into a structure that bears the name "bifurcation"? There is no predefined boundary for this transition of topography of volar skin.

Terminology is imprecise when describing the blending of features of uniqueness into other features of uniqueness. A generalized name of a uniquely patterned feature is a tool to verbally describe the perception of details in images. The generalized names of the details must not diminish the perception and understanding of the actual nature of the textures, contours, sequences, or configurations within an object. Terminology must not impart commonality upon the features of the object or the details in the images being examined.

Mathematics, like terminology, is a tool to study forms and enables the building of models to explain and represent the generalities of form. Models are humanly made imperfect representations of whatever natural or unnatural objects they represent. As science seeks general laws of nature, mathematics is used to build general models within those laws. The generality of models is studied to understand the specific. However, models are inadequate when studying uniqueness because they cannot be just like the objects they represent.

van den Bergh (2007) once said, "Albert Einstein and many others have commented on the effectiveness of mathematics for formulation of the laws of nature. As a result, science sometimes evolves in those directions in which mathematics can be applied. However, several areas, including friction, turbulence, and morphological classification, remain largely in the mathematical wilderness. Progress in galaxy morphology has mainly resulted from the remarkable human capacity to recognize patterns." It is good that the forensic comparative scientists have a remarkable ability to recognize patterns within the "mathematical wilderness" applied to the study of morphological classification of forms.

ADEQUACY OF MODELS IN SCIENCE

A recent effort to deal with the generalized models of unique variations within the human body is exposed in the works of Gunther von Hagens (2005). He uses processes of plastination to preserve various structures, tissues, and systems within a deceased human body. The tissues of interest are preserved, and unneeded tissues are removed. He presents these objects and systems of the bodies for study and research. Building general models of bodies was limiting the understanding of the individuality of each human. von Hagens strives to learn structures and their relationships from the vast tapestries of systems found within each body. Studying the unique patterns within many bodies helps in understanding the vast variations among all people. He found that models were insufficient and chose to preserve, present, and study many varieties of unique patterns within many unique human bodies. According to von Hagens (2005, 20), "Artificial anatomical models can also make only limited contributions to understanding anatomy as they … are not capable of showing fine details and cannot convey the individuality of the human body. One model is the same as the next one. Anatomical variations, however, are significant from one individual to another."

A challenge of creating models for the understanding of natural unique patterns is the problem of reducing symmetry from the averaging found in the mathematical models of forms to the generation of lower broken symmetry that results in natural unique pattern formation. As nature produces its components that result in patterns, the natural symmetry breaks into the unique shapes, textures, and alignments and forms something exactly like nothing else, cloned or modeled. Mathematical models of structures and form are based on average tendencies within nature. Once many components of different yet similar natural objects are measured and averaged for a model, the model will be different from each of the originals. Since each natural object is unique, there is no practical need in trying to make a perfectly dimensioned model. Symmetry in nature is found only by averaging the actual unique patterns that had been generated. Studying the breaking of form's symmetry is needed for the forensic comparative scientist's understanding of the uniqueness found in all of nature's tapestries.

UNIQUE NATURAL PATTERNS

The law that patterns in nature will never be replicated is supported by the empirical studies of natural pattern formations (Ball, 1999). There are no restrictions or specifics on the size or qualities of the natural patterns in these studies. No levels of uniqueness exist. Uniqueness does not cease as it gets larger or smaller. A corollary to the law of uniqueness is, as McKasson (2007) states, "Complexity does not derive from simplicity. There is just finer-grained complexity."

The universe is unique (Coles, 2006, 2). Each photon of light is unique (Ball, 2002). From the entire universe to each photon of light and everything in between, nature is unique. The galaxies within the universe are unique. van den Bergh (2007) said, "Galaxies are like people: The better you get to know them, the more peculiar they often seem." There is only one Earth within the universe. Mountain ranges on Earth are not repeated. Individual mountains within the ranges are without a match. The same canyons and rivers within these mountains will not be created again. Every pebble near each river is unique. Ball (2006) said it this way:

> What shape is a pebble? The answer, of course, is "pebble-shaped"; but now, thanks to research by a team in France and the United States, it's possible to define what that means. Technically speaking, says material physicist Doug Durian of the University of Pennsylvania in Philadelphia and his colleagues, a pebble is a rounded body with a near-gaussian distribution of curvatures. While no two pebbles are exactly alike, all seem to end up with this mathematical form.

Stone pebbles are unique even though they can be described with a general mathematical form. Even the inside of each pebble is not replicated. In a discussion of stones, laser beams, and holographic memory, Liesbeth Venema (2007) writes, "As each stone is unique and irreproducible, only the stone that is used to store the information can retrieve it again.... Because each piece of mineral has a unique composition, the random pattern of reference beams produced cannot be replicated by any other stone." Figure 3-1 is a picture of many unique rocks or pebbles.

FIGURE 3-1
Many stones or pebbles displaying some of the variety of textures and patterns in nature.

Snowflakes are like the aforementioned pebbles. Stewart (2001, 6, 9, 214) stated the following:

> Snowflakes have a puzzling combination of features. On the one hand, they reveal sixfold symmetry, like the mathematician's hexagon but much fancier. They have treelike branches, and—so the saying goes—every snowflake is different. If the regularity is the result of mathematical laws, where does the variety come from? If the variety is the result of the complexities of stormclouds, or the rest of the universe, where does the regularity come from? What shape is a snowflake? ... It has almost perfect sixfold symmetry, six copies of the same shape—but that shape is like nothing ever seen in Euclid's geometry. It isn't exactly random, but you won't find its name in any dictionary. What shape is a snowflake? Any shape it wants to be—but snowflakes have no wants. ... They come into being in huge, towering clouds of water vapor—atoms of hydrogen and oxygen, bound together in threes, scarcely noticing their neighbors until they crash into them. The dance of the water molecules is pure physics, complex but disorganized, mass movement of infinitesimal molecules.... What shape is a snowflake? Snowflake-shaped.

The "almost perfect symmetry" comment emphasizes how close nature can produce, but not quite reach, any perfect replications of patterns.

The outline of a forest of trees on a mountain is unique. All of the structures of a leaf on any one of those trees or any other tree will never occur again. Individual structures of cells, molecules, and atoms within each leaf are not repeated. And the water molecules that bond and form into a six-sided, symmetrically imperfect, uniquely formed snowflake are like no other. Each hydrogen atom differs from every other hydrogen atom (Lonergan, 2005). Nothing in nature is truly featureless when scrutinized closely enough.

All objects in the universe are unique in their patterned structure. Scientific photographer Lucia Covi (2006) presents images at the nanometric level, or below the wavelength of visible light, in her book *Blow-up: Images from the Nanoworld*. Images of nanometric, or billionths of a meter, proportions are being studied for the benefit of all sorts of technological advances, or applying instrumentality to intelligibility within science. Nanotechnology uses top-down and bottom-up technology efforts to manufacture tools and instruments to image and control the making of objects below the visible wavelength of light threshold. Top-down nanotechnology uses already formed objects that are sculpted into the final product, often using focused ion beam technology. Bottom-up nanotechnology tries to control natural formation of the developing object using artificial influences to shape and align the components into the desired product.

In a discussion of shaping nanometric tools and instruments using top-down nanometric technology for the purposes of studying surfaces at nanometric levels, Covi (2006, 29, 73) writes, "Each time it is a game with ingredients that are offered by nature and therefore are never the same. Full of inhomogeneities, surprises: This is what always makes the landscapes unexpected and research always an original challenge." Later, as she writes of "bottom-up" nanofabrication, "Here we find structures where matter self-assembled spontaneously, as in the nanowires of the 'sea urchin' or in those made of tin oxide. … The resulting structures are not perfectly ordered, nor are they exactly of the same shape, which might be a problem. … Many images in this section emphasize shapes, irregularities or symmetries of a surface: They emerged during the growth of the crystal, or when it was modified by some external agent, or decorated by the deposition of molecules and atoms during one of the processes that we use in our research. Understanding and guiding these phenomena is an important part of our work." The patterned beauty in the images exists in the vast array of unique tapestries of interrelationship of the nanometric features. In all the images presented in her book, there were nanometric textures on the surfaces and edges of every object. Nature is noisy in its breaking of symmetry. Nothing was smooth. There were no straight lines. There were no round circles. Symmetries of specific patterns broke.

Symmetry breaks in all natural patterns, as the observer can determine by looking closely enough at each natural object. Symmetry breaking is the result of developmental "noise" in all natural patterns.

DEVELOPMENTAL NOISE

All patterns in nature are "noisy." They all have elements of noisy randomness that influence the variations in the surface contours, textures, or features. Noise is caused by expected variations and interactions within all the influences of forces such as but not necessarily limited to chemistry, physics, biology, temperature, and timing interactions within the developmental environment of the natural pattern formation. Pattern formation in nature is much too complicated, much too noisy, for one simple explanation of how all the unique patterns are created. Natural tapestries of incomprehensible variations of patterns can be similar in form yet will be unique in a specific noisy pattern. Ball (1999, 253) said, "Pattern appears when competing forces banish uniformity but cannot quite induce chaos. It sounds like a dangerous place to be, but it is where we have always lived."

Noise in natural patterns also exists in the vision perceptual system. From each unique photon of light, the noise in nature influences the unique structures of all eyes, nerves, and brains that process the data that influences how people see and think. With the unique perceptions of objects, the scientists must remember the generalizations that have become the laws and methods of the particular domain and remain within tolerance of the community for judgments rendered.

IDENTICAL TWINS ARE NOT IDENTICAL

Identical (monozygotic) twins are not identical because of developmental noise. Biological clones or monozygotic twins are different than exact copies of the other (Ball, 2002). Lewontin (1982, 1) said, "When we think about human beings, we are struck with an apparent contradiction in the nature of our own species: Human beings are alike, yet they are all different.... Even identical twins who act and dress alike can be readily told apart by their parents, their siblings, and others who know them well."

If natural patterns could be replicated anyplace, they would replicate between monozygotic or "identical" twins. They would have indistinguishable DNA as tested in most current forensic science laboratories. However, DNA might be genetically indistinguishable, but the results of DNA's instructions to create form produce a unique phenotypic expression of patterns. Raser and O'Shea (2005) said the following:

> Genetically identical cells and organisms exhibit remarkable diversity even when they have identical histories of environmental exposure. Noise, or variation, in the process of gene expression may contribute to this phenotypic variability. ... Any individual in a population of living

> organisms or cells is unique. Much of population variability is due to genetic differences, but environment and history also contribute to variability in cellular phenotype. Indeed, identical twin humans or cloned cats differ in appearance and behavior.

Using the levels of discrimination available in many forensic science laboratories of the alleles that are detected in DNA, monozygotic twins are usually indistinguishable. Indistinguishable DNA is part of the generation of human form of the twins, not the generation of the phenotypic specificity of those noisy patterns within each of those human forms. The form might be considered symmetrical, but the actual noisy patterns within the form are not.

As technology improves, DNA and the human genome are found to be more variable than previously thought. Indistinguishable DNA of today might be distinguishable tomorrow. Pearson (2006) said the following about Redon and colleagues:

> These differences make each person genetically unique—influencing everything from appearance and personality to susceptibility to disease. ... They [Redon et al.] have identified surprisingly large chunks of the genome that can differ dramatically from one person to the next. 'Everyone has a unique pattern,' says one of the lead authors, Matthew Hurles at the Wellcome Trust Sanger Institute in Cambridge, UK. ... The precise degree to which each person's DNA differs from another may not become clear until geneticists devise a way to read through the entire genome of many different people and compare them all in detail, something that is far too expensive and time consuming today but may become possible with the advent of faster, cheaper sequencing techniques.

SYMMETRY AND ASYMMETRY

Chris McManus, professor of psychology and medicine at the University College London, writes and presents discussions and pictures about asymmetry of patterns within general forms in his book *Right Hand, Left Hand: The Origins of Asymmetry in Brains, Bodies, Atoms and Cultures*. Bilateral symmetry of specific patterns does not exist in nature. The organism's general form supports all the subtle and unavoidable textured, bumpy, noisy, unique variations and anomalies among the individuals of that organism (Ball, 1999).

Symmetry of general form may exist but not symmetry of natural pattern. The appearance of symmetry in natural patterns occurs because of the averaging of the activities of the atoms, molecules, and cells within the system, within regions or among regions within the system of the generalized common form.

FIGURE 3-2
The right side of a cow with measurable pattern. (Figures 3-2 through 3-6 courtesy of Terry Neuenschwander.)

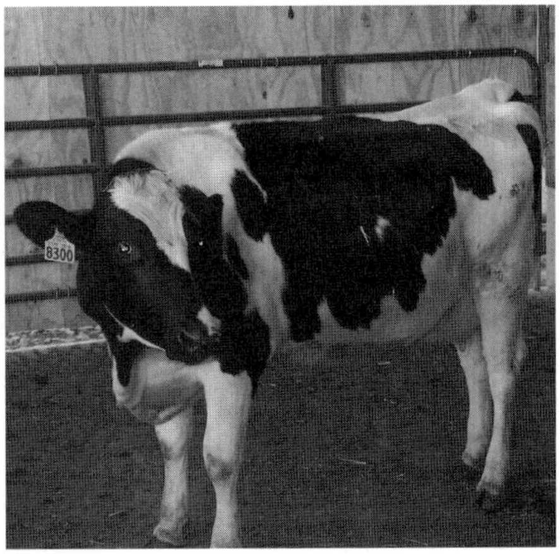

FIGURE 3-3
The left side of the cow in Figure 3-2.

FIGURE 3-4
The right side of the cow in Figure 3-2 with the image reversed depicting bilateral asymmetry as Figure 3-3.

However, at the atomic scale there is random disorder and atomic vibrations. Symmetry of form breaks when the actual specific patterns of the object develop. Asymmetry of patterns is found in left and right hands, left and right sides of brains, left and right sides of atoms, left and right sides of faces, and left and right sides of nature (McManus, 2002). Nature is also noisy within each side of each object, within each part of each side. If replication of a specific pattern could be expected, it should be found in bilaterally symmetrical forms within one body. But this replication or mirror image of symmetrical pattern does not occur in any body in nature. Nature is not going to silence its noise. Figures 3-2 through 3-6 show cows that have asymmetrically unique black-and-white patterns. No matter the natural pattern that is perceived, that pattern is asymmetrically unique.

Bilateral symmetry of pattern does not occur in leaves on a tree. Figures 3-7 through 3-12 illustrate the variation in patterns of the structures of leaves. The left side of a leaf is patterned differently from the right. The patterns within the patterns are also different. There are no mirrored images of patterns within any leaf.

The series of images in Figures 3-13 and 3-14 represent the natural patterns not being replicated between monozygotic twins and the breaking of symmetry of patterns between the left and right side of each body. Using DNA polymerase chain reaction technology in 2005, the determination was made that the twins Jami and Kami are currently genetically

FIGURE 3-5
Three cows with different patterns on their heads and near their muzzles.

FIGURE 3-6
The three cows from Figure 3-5 with the image reversed depicting bilateral asymmetry.

indistinguishable. Figure 3-13 is a picture of Jami's and Kami's faces in correct orientation. Figures 3-14 is a reversed position or mirror image of Figure 3-13. Notice the variations of patterns between Jami and Kami in both figures and the bilateral variations of patterns between the normal and mirrored image of each of the twins. Note all variations of patterns

FIGURE 3-7
The natural patterns in a leaf.

FIGURE 3-8
The natural patterns in another leaf from the same tree.

FIGURE 3-9
A closer view of the leaf in Figure 3-7.

FIGURE 3-10
A closer view of the leaf in Figure 3-8. Note the variations in patterns between this leaf and the leaf in Figure 3-9.

FIGURE 3-11
An extremely close view of the patterns within a small section of the leaf in Figure 3-9.

FIGURE 3-12
An extremely close view of the patterns within a small section of the leaf in Figure 3-10.

within Jami, within Kami and between Jami and Kami, in the normal and reversed positions. Stephen's face is shown in Figure 3-15 and a reversed image is shown in Figure 3-16. The large amount of freckles can be easily examined for the lack of patterned bilateral symmetry in nature.

Patterned symmetry is broken in the left and right thumbs of Jami and Kami, as shown in prints of their thumbs in Figures 3-17 and 3-18. Figures 3-19 and 3-20 are reversed or mirrored images of Figures 3-17 and 3-18.

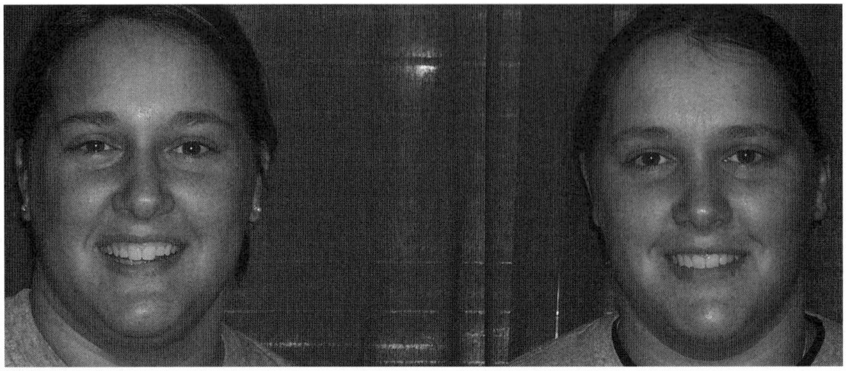

FIGURE 3-13
Monozygotic twins Jami and Kami. Note the variations of phenotypic expressions with the same genotype between the twins. These "identical twins are not identical." (Figures 3-13, 3-14, and 3-17 through 3-24 courtesy of Jami and Kami Hunt.)

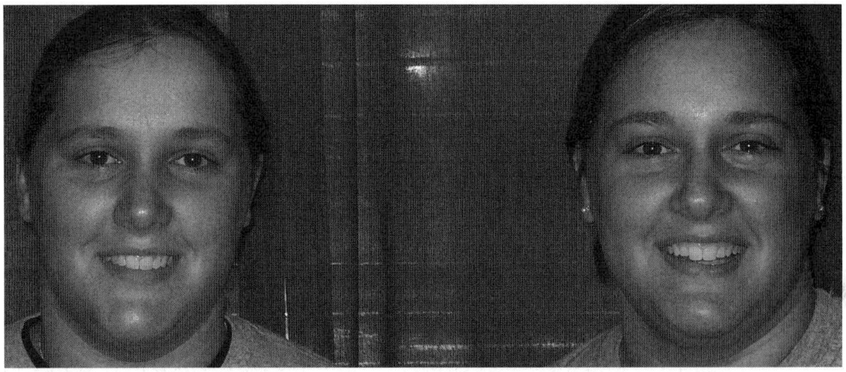

FIGURE 3-14
Images of twins Jami and Kami in reversed positions. Note the bilateral variations within each twin and the bilateral variations between each twin as compared to Figure 3-13.

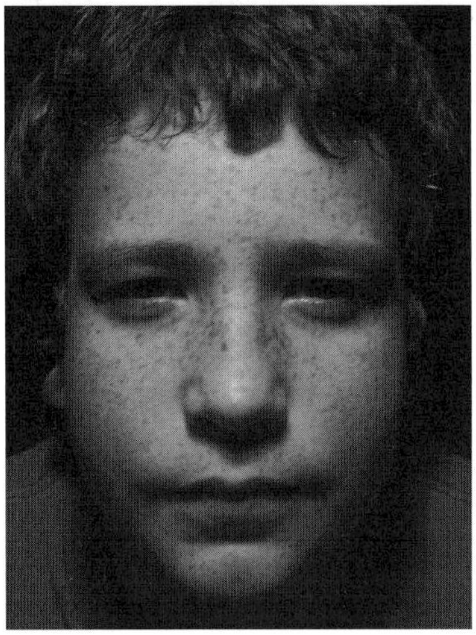

FIGURE 3-15
Stephen's face. Note the many measurements that can be accomplished with freckles. (Figures 3-15 and 3-16 courtesy of Stephen Vanderkolk.)

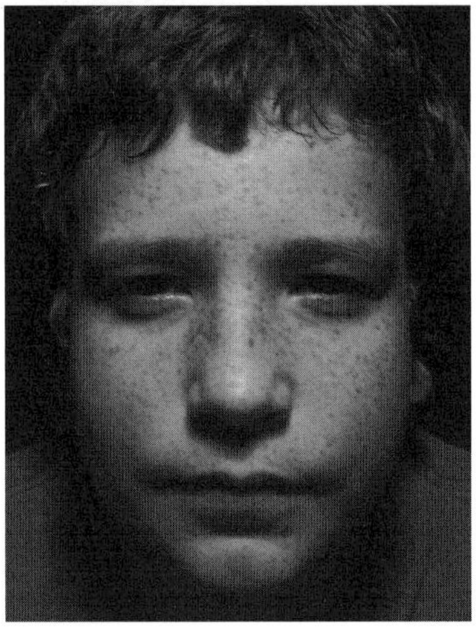

FIGURE 3-16
Stephen's face, reversed image, for comparison to Figure 3-15.

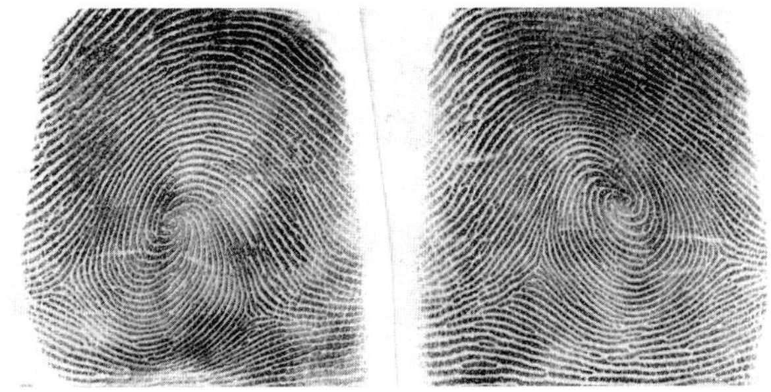

FIGURE 3-17
Jami's left and right thumbprints.

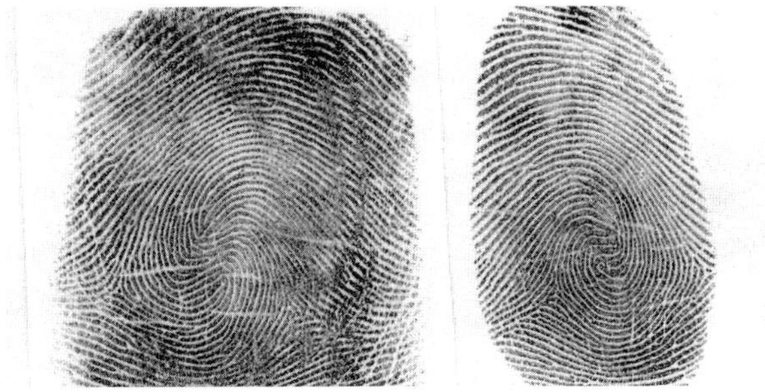

FIGURE 3-18
Kami's left and right thumbprints.

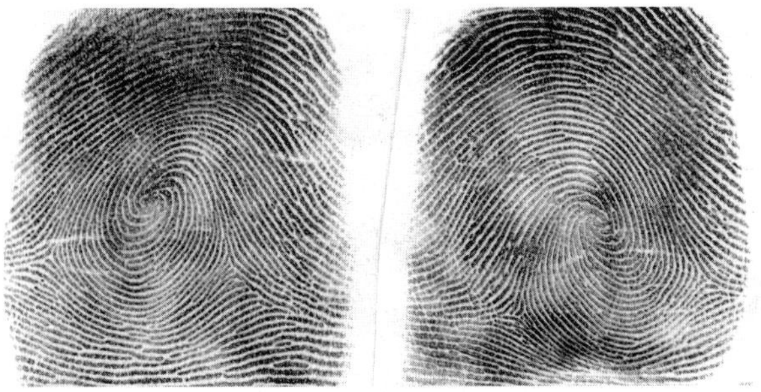

FIGURE 3-19
Jami's left and right thumbprints, reversed image.

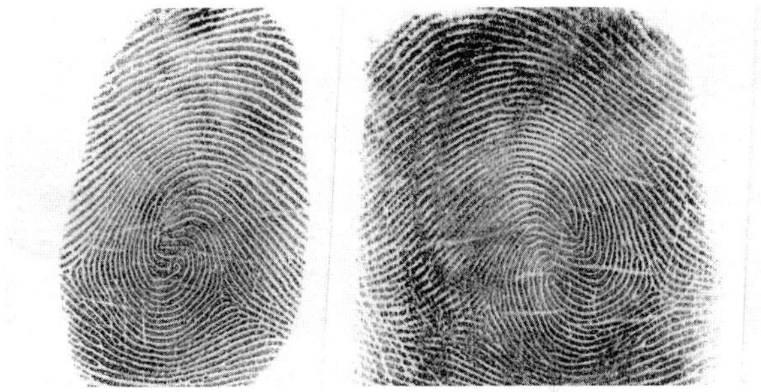

FIGURE 3-20
Kami's left and right thumbprints, reversed image.

Each thumb is patterned differently from a mirrored image of the opposing thumb within each twin. Each thumb is patterned differently from the corresponding thumb of the twin. Bilateral symmetry of pattern is broken.

Patterned symmetry is broken in the lips of Jami and Kami, as shown in prints of their lips in Figures 3-21 and 3-22. Within each lip, the left side of each lip is patterned differently from the right side, as depicted in reversed position Figures 3-23 and 3-24. The patterns vary bilaterally within and between each set of individual lips.

Each part of each pattern in Figures 3-1 through 3-24 depicts a minuscule amount of patterns of unique features that result from noisy broken symmetry. Indistinguishable DNA was a limited part of the noisy processes that produced monozygotic twins that resulted in the universal truth that "identical twins are not identical." So if monozygotic twins are neither bilaterally identical within self nor between the other twin in their natural patterns, can any object be identical with any other object? The answer is no; perfectly cloned patterns in nature cannot exist.

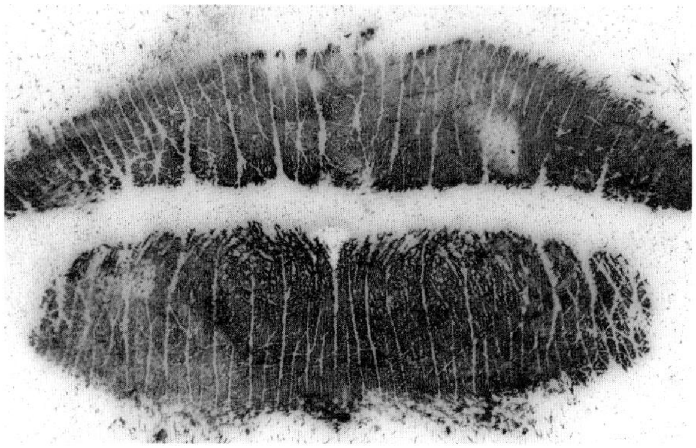

FIGURE 3-21
Jami's lipprint.

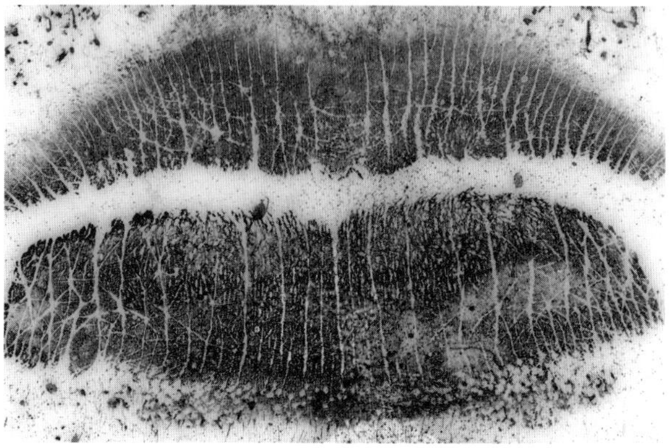

FIGURE 3-22
Kami's lipprint.

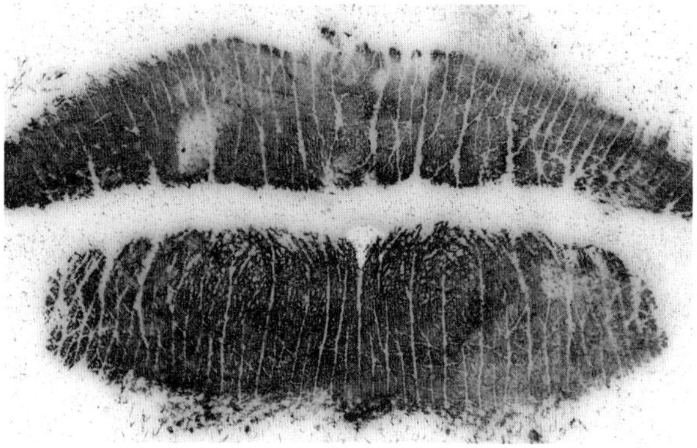

FIGURE 3-23
Jami's lipprint, image reversed.

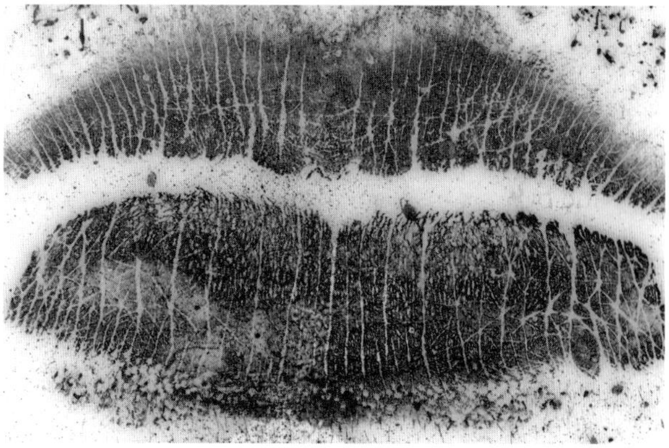

FIGURE 3-24
Kami's lipprint, image reversed.

UNNATURAL REPEATABLE FEATURES

The term *class characteristic* is often used in science. *Class* refers to a grouping of objects that share something in common. Restrictions of which objects belong within a given class are decided upon by the scientists doing the grouping and the measurements made of the objects. Even though natural objects are unique, they can be grouped together under specified parameters. For record-keeping purposes, unique fingerprints are classified into groups of whorls, loops, and arches. Unnatural objects can also be grouped. Shoes from the same mold share the same class characteristics of features with repeatable dimensions. I am intentionally avoiding the use of the term *class characteristics* because I want to emphasize the unique features in natural items and repeatable and unique features in unnatural items. I do not want to confuse unique with repeatable when the term *class characteristics* could blend these two types of features.

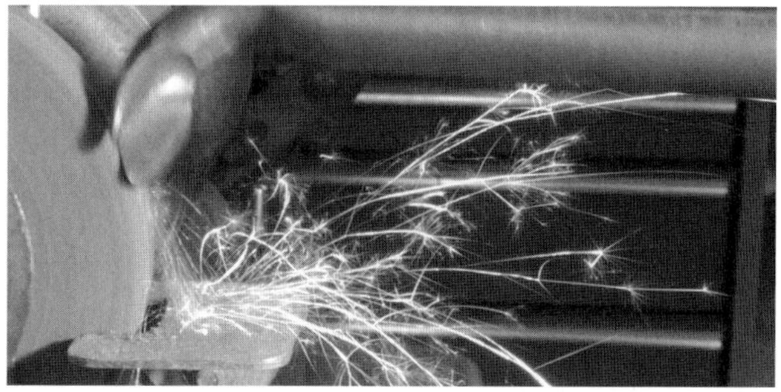

FIGURE 3-25
The grinding of metal sends patterns of sparks flying in many directions. These patterns cannot be replicated or symmetrical. The grinding of the metal surface results in a unique texture on the tool from the unique separations of particles from the surface of the tool.

All objects are unique even if they have unnatural repeatable features made by humans using a wide variety of manufacturing processes. Humans can construct visibly and measurably repeatable features in the production of many items. Mass production of unnatural objects such as shoes, tires, and tools through the use of forms, molds, or design specifications can generate features with the same visible repeatable patterns. The measurable surface components that can be repeated on the mass-produced objects are, or can be, indistinguishable. Thus, these elements of the object are repeatable as far as the visible comparative measurements of the manufacturer and the examiner are concerned. One of the goals of manufacturing unnatural items is to make them interchangeable or indistinguishable among themselves. However, upon close scrutiny, unique patterns will be detected.

At and beneath the surface of the visible repeatable features are the uniquely shaped and bonded molecules. As the surfaces of repeatable features continue through the manufacturing finishing process, then wear down, get cut, or break, different unique molecules become the surface. As the shapes of the molecules are unique and the bonds among these molecules have different strengths, the molecules do not separate or break apart from one another with the same patterns of separation, breaking, or tearing. A unique texture is generated at the surface of these objects. A demonstrable image of molecules being separated from an object is represented in Figures 3-25 and 3-26. The grinding of a metal surface distributes sparks whizzing away from the object. The bonds of metal molecules are forcibly broken. The force of application of the tool to the grinder varies. A new texture of molecules is generated on the surface of the blade. The macroscopic and microscopic edges of the blade of the surface of the tool have changed its patterns as have the many bonded submicroscopic structures.

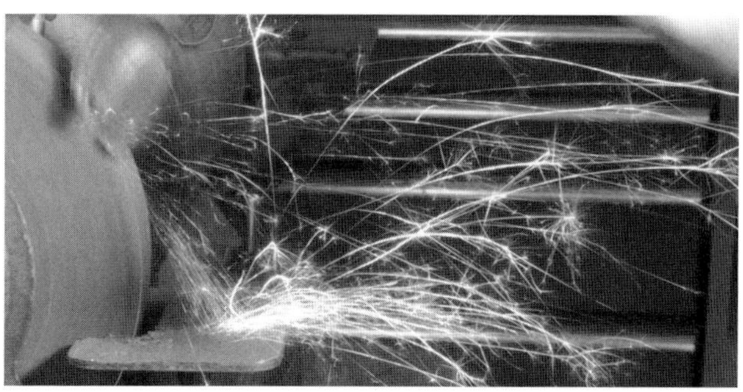

FIGURE 3-26
More grinding of the same tool results in different patterns of sparks and a different surface on the tool.

Unnatural objects, or humanly manufactured items, can have measurable features of repeatable patterns within tolerance of the person and tool used in measuring. In humanly manufactured items, such as guns, tools, shoes, and tires, repeatable features are designed into the dimensions of these items. Many guns have nominally the same dimensions of bore caliber, number, widths, and measurements of lands and grooves. Many shoe soles are manufactured with the measurably same features generated from the same mold. As the surfaces of these items become worn, cut, abraded or damaged, the bonded molecules underlying the surface structure become the surface. The uniqueness of the sole presents itself on the surface as the manufactured texture wears away or is damaged. The generalization, or law, is that natural patterns and structures of the underlying molecules in nature are unique, even when manmade form is replicated on the surface. Even the surfaces of these unnatural repeatable objects are unique if perceived closely enough. After all, stacked and bonded molecules and atoms make up every surface.

PERSISTENCY OF FEATURES

No natural pattern is permanent. No unnatural pattern is permanent. The pattern can be persistent or durable, but it cannot be permanent. The patterned structure can age, be damaged, or destroyed. It can fade. The change of pattern may be fast or slow. While patterns change before our eyes as the clouds blow across the sky, the peaks of mountains change much more slowly. What is needed by the forensic comparative scientist is the persistency of patterns in objects between the times and events of making the questioned image and the standard image. Persistency, not permanency, is required by the forensic comparative scientist. Fingerprint examiners have long said the ridges of the skin are permanent. It must be remembered; skin heals from trauma and ages. Skin regenerates itself with new cells that are not perfect replicates of the preceding cells. Therefore, the cellular surface structure is not permanent. The visible patterns that result in skin are remarkably persistent but not permanent.

Some objects do not regenerate their features. Once the feature wears away or is damaged, the original features of that object have changed. Some objects, such as skin, can regenerate features. However, regeneration does not result in a same permanent structure. Regeneration cannot result in perfect duplication because of the uniqueness of atoms, molecules, and cells. The source regenerates with similar but different cells. It ages. Homeostatic regeneration and aging of skin will be discussed in more detail in Chapter 10. However, believing in the uniqueness of cells, the regeneration of the aging skin is an example of the subtle change in structure of the cellular surface of the skin. Skin is not perfectly permanent in its structures, but structures of skin are remarkably persistent. In forensic comparative science, persistency of the source is needed, whether the consideration of persistency is for repeatable or unique features.

UNDERSTANDING THE SOURCE

"Surface of the source" is used differently from "source" or "object" throughout this book because of issues of the persistency and locations of the features on a surface of an object. The actual surface of the part of an object that had made contact with a substrate to deposit an image is the source of the image from the greater aggregate of the object. The left side of a finger is a different source from the right side of the same finger. The left index finger is a different source from the right index finger. The left hand is a different source from the right hand. But these different sources all represent one human body as the object. The surface of the source can change. The aging and healing of skin vary the features of the source.

As another example of the surface of a source, consider a shoe that made an unknown shoeprint. Over time, it significantly wears, and the unique features on the surface of the source change. This shoe is obtained and known standard impressions are made. In reality, this shoe is the source of both the unknown and known impressions. However, the surface of the source of the impressions changed. Details of unique features in the first impression are different from those found in the second impression. Excluding the shoe as the source of the first print is not acceptable in answering the question "Did the shoe make the print?" Wear on the bottom of the shoe causes changes to the surface that generated the later image. The same shoe or object can produce two images that had been produced between significant wear on the surface of the object, or the source. In reality, the shoe is the same source of both images; however, the surface of the source changed significantly, preventing this determination. An object can be determined as the source of two images if the object's surface is sufficiently persistent and details of the same unique features are found in both.

Likewise, the two sides of a flat-bladed screwdriver are different surfaces of the sources of images from the same screwdriver. Each side of the blade of the screwdriver will make different striae patterns from the same screwdriver. Significantly changing the angle of the application of the blade to substrate will make differing striae patterns from the same side of the same blade of the same screwdriver. Different edges of the same side of one blade are different surfaces of the sources of images. As parts of the blade of a screwdriver wear away, persistency of the source influences the variations in the images generated. The heel of a shoe sole is a different source of images than the toe area of the same sole. As a sole of a shoe wears away, persistency of the surface of the source influences the images generated. As chewing gum that is stuck to the bottom of a shoe wears away, the persistency of the shape of the gum influences the images that are deposited from the same gum on the same sole. Persistency of source influences the images generated.

Persistency of the surface of the source in forensic science is related to the ancient philosophical concept credited to Heraclitus that once a person steps into a river and removes some of the water, it is no longer the same river (Graham, 2007). If the Wabash River near my home floods, and the dimensions of the river bank change, is it still the Wabash River? Once some of the dirt on the banks of the river is washed away, are they the same banks after the flood recedes? But I know I can still identify, or individualize, many parts of the banks of the Wabash River. I know it is still the Wabash River. The change in the persistent nature of the banks of the river before and after a flood is often insignificant. Persistency is the degree of maintaining structure of the condition of the source or surface of the item. If the change of persistency is insignificant, persistency of the surface is acceptable for individualizing or excluding the source as having made the questioned image.

As the surface of the source wears away, or changes, persistency is affected. The object or source remains, but the surface changed between two depositions of images. With significant wear, even though the object generated both images, the surface changed significantly, and the source of the first impression cannot be determined. Excluding the object as making the first impression would be a mistake. In addition to the repeatable and unique features of a source, persistency of the source that made an image, impression, or mark is another relevant question that must be answered when examining images. The second fundamental rule of determining the source of images is "The source must be persistent between the times and events the two images were made." Without sufficient persistency, the surface of the source would change too much so that another image with corresponding details could not be recorded.

Variability between different features on a natural object is not very different from variability of change of one feature. As change occurs, the original feature is lost and a new feature surfaces. McInerny and Callaghan (2005) said the following:

> The analysis of change and the product of change begins with surface changes. Some enduring thing changes place or quality or quantity. But enduring things like men and trees and horses and the like have also come into being and are destined some day to cease to be. Such things are called substances. It is a given that there are substances and that they come to be and pass away. The question is: Can the analysis of surface change be adjusted and applied to substantial change? What would its subject be?

Parts of substances, or surfaces of objects, change. These changes must be insignificant or insubstantial for the results of the analyses, comparisons, and evaluations of efforts to determine the source of images to be meaningful.

The contour or edge of the object's surface, or source of an image, may change, sometimes insignificantly and sometimes significantly. The surface that significantly changes actually changes the source and the resulting images from the object. If enough parts of its features remain sufficiently persistent, the surface of the source is suitable for examinations. The source is the conditioned surface structure of the object that had made a particular image. The examiner must understand persistency of the features of the source.

Examples of variations of persistency would be found among the various physical realities of features on Earth. If shown a photograph of a mountain, you would not rely on the images of the clouds above the mountain to locate the mountain, unless the image had just been captured moments earlier. You might rely on the patterns of snow on the peak, depending on the durability of the patterns within the variety of influences of weather, time, and environmental noise. Most likely, you would rely on the most persistent features of the textures, contours, and configural silhouette of the mountain. You may rely on the textures and configural contours of the crevices of the mountain from its base to its peak. Persistency of the surfaces that made an image is needed for determining whether a source made an image. There are various levels of persistency throughout the many surfaces of objects that become the source of images under consideration in the examination.

Understanding the repeatability, uniqueness, persistency, and surface features of sources that produce images is the foundation of forensic comparative science. Forensic scientists need to study sources before studying images of a source.

Each discipline within forensic comparative science needs to consider the persistency of the surfaces before studying images. When examining source items and their images, the examiner must know and believe which features on the source are unnaturally repeatable and which features are unique. The two types of features are separate and distinct. They can and do coexist. Patterns in nature are only unique. Unnatural objects can have repeatable and unique patterns.

IMAGES OF THE SOURCE

No two separate and distinct items in nature, animate or inanimate, have exactly the same appearance or patterns of features, including the independently deposited impressions, markings, or images of a source. If they actually did perfectly possess the same appearance, the same patterns, and the same qualities and quantities of details of the features of the source, they would be replications of each other in conflict with the law. The law would have to be adjusted. If an examiner says two naturally deposited images are exact or perfect matches of each other, the examiner must revisit the law, revisit the images, and revisit the comparative measurements and judgments and determine what aspect of determining the final judgment is wrong. No two separately deposited images of volar skin possess the same appearance. No two fired bullets from the same gun possess the same appearance. No two prints from the same shoe sole possess the same appearance. No two broken cross-sectional edges of corresponding plastic possess a perfectly mirrored appearance of each other. There are always variations in the appearances of two separate and distinct prints of the same finger, bullets fired from the same gun, prints from the same sole, and edges from broken plastic. There is no such thing as a perfect match between two separately and distinctly deposited images of a source. Every independently deposited impression, mark, or image of an object will be unique.

The stacking of atoms, molecules, or cells that become the features of the source; the processes of applying the source to the substrate; the molecules in the matrices or residues that are transferred to or from the receiving substrate; the molecules in the components of the technique used to develop the image; and even the light that strikes the objects and then reaches the eyes and is processed through the vision system are all unique. These interactions of these variations are parts of the noise that cause each independently deposited image of the source to be unique.

TOLERANCE

With variations of appearances of each independent image, tolerance for the variations must be learned by the examiner (Ashbaugh, 1999). Without accepting the variations of appearances, the examiner would never be able to reach a definitive conclusion of recognition of anything because, objectively speaking, all matches are less than perfect, and judgment is involved in every comparative measurement.

The examiner must learn tolerance of comparative measurements and judgments through training exercises by applying known sources to substrates to create a variety of images. Additional variations in the types of residues on the source or substrate; the amounts of those residues; the nature of the environment before, during, and after applying the source to the substrate; and methods of lighting, visualizing, and capturing the image need to be studied. Learning the effects of distorted sources, distorted substrates, and variations in residues or matrices, substrates, environments, pressures, directions, and motions of applying the source to the substrate to create an image will help enable the examiner to understand variations of appearances and the judgments of comparative measurements.

Believing in uniqueness, the sources, matrices, receiving substrates, development processes, and viewings, are all parts of the overall noisy influences that result in unique images from unique sources. This limited listing of factors that cause the developmental noises that generate the variations of appearances of each deposited pattern needs to be studied for understanding each natural image as a unique variation of a recording of the source. Acceptance of the comparative measurements of these variations must be learned through a variety of training exercises provided by a trainer in which the images are known to have come from a specific source.

REFERENCES

Ashbaugh, David R. *Quantitative-Qualitative Friction Ridge Analysis: An Introduction to Basic and Advanced Ridgeology*. CRC Press LLC, Boca Raton, 1999.

Ball, Philip. *The self-made tapestry: pattern formation in nature.* Oxford University Press, New York, 1999.

Ball, Philip. *'Physics bans cloning', news@nature.com, http://www.nature.com/news/2002/020520/full/020520-1.html.* Retrieved on May 21, 2002.

Ball, Philip. *'What shape is a pebble? Scientists head to the beach to find out.', news@nature.com, http://nature.com/news/2006/060710/full/060710-15.html.* Retrieved on July 14, 2006.

Born, Max. *The Born—Einstein Letters 1916–1955: Friendship, Politics and Physics in Uncertain Times.* Macmillan, New York, 2005.

Carroll, Sean B. *Endless Forms Most Beautiful: The New Science of Evo Devo and the Making of the Animal Kingdom*. W. W. Norton & Company, New York, 2005.

Coles, Peter. *From Cosmos to Chaos: The Science of Unpredictability*. Oxford University Press, Inc., New York, 2006.

Covi, Lucia. *Blow-up. Images from the nanoworld.* Damiani editore, Bologna, Italy, 2006.

Cummins, Harold, and Charles Midlo. *Finger Prints, Palms and Soles – An Introduction to Dermatoglyphics*. Dover Publications, Inc., New York, 1961, an unabridged and corrected republication of the work first published by The Blakiston Company, 1943.

Curd, Martin, and J. A. Cover. *Philosophy of Science: The Central Issues*. W. W. Norton & Company, Inc., New York, 1998.

Fermi, Laura, and Bernardini, Gilberto. *Galileo and the Scientific Revolution*. Dover Publications, Inc., Mineola, New York, 2003, republication of the 1965 Fawcett paperback edition of the work first published by Basic Books, Inc., New York, 1961.

Graham, Daniel W., "Heraclitus", In Edward N. Zalta, ed., *The Stanford Encyclopedia of Philosophy* (Spring 2007 Edition). *<http://plato.stanford.edu/archives/spr2007/entries/heraclitus/>*.

Grieve, David. 'Reflections on Quality Standards—An American Viewpoint,' *Fingerprint Whorld*, April 1990.

Leslie, Mitch. 'Cerebral Surveying,' *Science*, Vol. 310, 27, 7 October 2005.

Lewontin, Richard. *Human Diversity.* Scientific American Books, An imprint of W. H. Freeman and Company, San Francisco, 1982.

Lonergan, Bernard. *Insight: A Study of Human Understanding.* Longmans, Green & Co., London, 1957. Fifth Edition, University of Toronto Press, Toronto, Canada, 2005.

Mairs, G. Tyler. 'Can Two Identical Ridge Patterns Actually Occur—Either on Different Persons or on the Same Person?' *Finger Print and Identification Magazine,* November 1945, 27 (5), reprinted in *Journal of Forensic Identification,* 45 (2), 1995, 231–241.

McInerny, Ralph and O'Callaghan, John. "Saint Thomas Aquinas," In Edward N. Zalta, ed., *The Stanford Encyclopedia of Philosophy* (Spring 2005 Edition). <*http://plato.stanford.edu/archives/spr2005/entries/aquinas/*>.

McKasson, Stephen C. personal communication, 2007.

McManus, Chris. *Right Hand, Left Hand: The Origins of Asymmetry in Brains, Bodies, Atoms and Cultures.* Harvard University Press, Cambridge, Massachusetts, 2002.

Meyer, Jannik, A. K. Geim, M. I. Katsnelson, K. S. Novoselov, T. J. Booth and S. Roth. 'The structure of suspended graphene sheets, *Nature,* Vol. 446, 1 March 2007; 60–63.

Muotri, Alysson R. and Fred H. Gage. 'Generation of neuronal variability and complexity,' *Nature,* Vol 441, 29 June 2006; 1087–1093.

Pearson, Helen. 'Human genome more variable than previously thought—Surprisingly large segments of DNA found to differ from person to person,' news@nature.com, *http://www.nature.com/news/2006/061120/pf/061120-9_pf.html.*

Raser, Jonathan M. and Erin K. O'Shea. 'Noise in Gene Expression: Origins, Consequences, and Control,' *Science,* Vol. 309, 23 September 2005, 2010–2013.

Saxe, Rebecca, Matthew Brett, and Nancy Manwisher. 'Divide and conquer: A defense of functional localizers,' *NeuroImage,* Vol. 30, 2006; 1088–1096.

Stewart, Ian. *What Shape is a Snowflake?* W. H. Freeman and Company, New York, 2001.

Thompson, D'Arcy Wentworth. *On Growth and Form.* Dover Publications, Inc. New York, 1992, first published as On Growth and Form: A New Edition Cambridge University Press, Cambridge, England, 1942.

van den Bergh, Sidney. 'Out of Order', *Nature,* Vol 445, 18 January 2007; 265.

Vanderkolk, John R. 'Class Characteristics and "Could Be" Results,' *Journal of Forensic Identification,* 43 (3), 1993; 119–125.

Venema, Liesbeth. 'The Secret of the Stone,' *Nature,* Vol. 447, 14 June 2007; 787.

von Hagens, Gunther and Angelina Whalley. *Body Worlds—The Anatomical Exhibition of Real Human Bodies,* Institut for Plastination, Heidelberg, Germany, 6th printing 2005, English translation of the 14th German printing.

CHAPTER 4

Ranges of Levels of Details in Images

CONTENTS

So with no such thing as a perfect match and with variations of appearances between images, how does an examiner describe details in images? David Ashbaugh (1999) introduced the fingerprint examiner community to three levels of details that describe the clarity in images recorded from features of the volar skin. Three levels of details in images are also described by Vanderkolk (1999) and the Scientific Working Group on Friction Ridge Analysis, Study and Technology (SWGFAST). Steve McKasson and Carol Richards (1998) express a variation of this concept with a descriptive approach of sets, subsets, and sub-subsets even with a continuation to newer and deeper levels. There is no requirement for using only three levels. This amount can be divided into more levels if desired. When patterns exist in nature, patterns exist within patterns which exist within patterns. The structures of subpatterns do not cease to exist until the object that bears the patterns ceases to exist. The three levels of clarity is a simple amount to use for form and pattern description.

The object possesses the features of the surface of the source that makes the image. The source has persistency that affects the image produced. The image then possesses details of the features of the source. There will always be lesser qualities and quantities of details in each of the images than there are features in the source. There will always be variations in appearances of the details in each image of the source, as each image is a unique recording of the source.

The clarities of recorded features as first-level details in an image are the recordings of the forms of features in an object. The image depicts a general flow of directions of paths and general sizes and shapes, or dimensions, of features of the source. As discussed earlier, form in an image cannot be determined as specific to an object. Only limited and general comparative measurements of details can occur if clarity in the image is restricted to first-level details of form. Specific measurements of first-level details cannot occur.

However, first-level details can be sufficient to exclude some objects as possessing corresponding features to the details in the image. Details of round features are depicted differently than details of straight parallel features at first-level clarity and should be sufficient to determine any difference between the objects that deposited the images. First-level clarity is not sufficient to differentiate somewhat similar but different specific patterns of features compared to other features. The features on the actual objects can be measured as different but the quality of the details are too poor to make accurate measurements in images recorded with only first-level clarity. If shown pictures of houses that are poor (but not too poor) quality, I can determine that the pictures represent houses. I should be able to exclude many pictures of one-, three-, and some two-story houses as my house based on first-level form but would be unable to determine when my house is depicted among the many other two-story houses. First-level details allow me to know what I should consider for determining difference, but first-level details by themselves cannot tell me when I have found sameness.

The clarities of recorded features as second-level details are the specific dimensions, paths, lengths, widths, and positions of details of the major measurable features within the source. The clarity of second-level details allows the examiner to conduct some critical comparative measurements of patterns of the features of the source. Specific paths, dimensions, or patterns of second-level details cannot exist without the presence of the first-level details of form. Many patterns can be excluded based on first-level form. More patterns can be excluded with second-level measurements of sequences and configurations of patterns along the form. Specific pattern can be determined if sufficient second-level measurements of sequences and configurations of details of features can be made from the images. The general must exist for the specific to exist. Form does not cease because pattern is present. Second-level details depict specific patterns within the form of first level. First- and second-level details allow me to know what I should look for, what I can disregard, and when I have found it. When shown better-quality pictures of houses, I can now see details of specific sequences and configurations of patterns of features. These same patterns within the form allow me to determine that a particular picture represents my house.

The clarities of recorded features as third-level details depict the edges, textures, contours, and anomalies along the paths, or within the boundaries or dimensions, of the second-level details of patterns. Think of third-level details as the patterns within second-level patterns, which are all within first-level form. First-level form and second-level details of pattern support third-level details of patterns within patterns. First-, second-, and third-level details allow me to know what I should look for, what I can disregard, and when I have found it, not needing as large an area as when presented just first and second-level details. When shown very good-quality pictures of houses, I can now see details of specific sequences and configurations of patterns of features within different objects of the house. The form, patterns, and patterns within patterns allow me to determine the specific components of the alignments of the cement steps on the front porch, the chipped paint on the front door, the scratch on the garage door, and other features that make up the smaller components of my house. These individual components are clear enough to determine they are parts of my house.

When only a restricted area of first-level form with limited second-level pattern is available with sufficiently clear third-level details in an unknown image, the challenge is to find a suitable location in a standard to compare to the third-level patterns of the unknown image. Knowing where to look on the standard images based on previous training and experience enables the examiner to be more efficient in finding the locations to compare to small area of unknown images containing first, second, and third-level details. In a visible image, the quality and quantity (QQ) of first-level form can range from extremely partial to almost complete as compared to the originating object. From very limited first-level to very clear form, second-level paths of details within the area of form can vary from indeterminable to nearly complete. Once the second level becomes determinable, both first and second-level details are available for consideration in the examination. Within those second-level paths and first-level form, third-level textures can range from indeterminable to almost complete. Once third-level details can be determined, first-, second-, and third-level details are available for the examination.

Limited quality and quantity of form do not banish the possibilities of sufficient second- and third-level details. Limited form and second-level does not prohibit third-level details. Limited form might hinder, but does not prevent, the searching process for locating comparable details in another image. Details of a few friction ridges of simple form might possess sufficient ridge paths that bear extremely clear third-level textures that permit source determination if the correct location can be found on sufficient standards. Details of the form of one element of shoe tread that bears some second-level path of wear marks with sufficiently clear third-level texture can result in source determination if the correct location can be found on sufficient standards. The totality of first, second, and third levels of details in the marks determine the value of each and their relation to the other.

There are ranges of quality and quantity of details within each unique image. Think of a source as being 100% of the available quality and quantity of measurable features of an object that can be recorded, with images resulting in varying and lesser quality and quantity of details than what is present in the features of the source. The quantity of available measurable features in a persistent source is fixed with that particular source, realizing each source is different. The quantity depends on how clear and how closely the features are measured.

The value of the image depends on the quality of the details recorded in that image. The quality throughout the image is the level of clarity of the parameters of those details as they depict the parameters of the features of the source. Quality is less than 100% clarity of the source, for it cannot be a perfect match with the source and greater than 0% clarity of the source, for if there was no quality of detail in an image, there would be no image of that feature; therefore, quality of detail ranges between 0 and 100% clarity throughout the image of the source. Quality is not homogeneous throughout any natural image. Think of quality as a scale of potential accuracy of the measurability of the details in the images. Clearer details can be measured more accurately than less clear details. Critics of comparative science will want a number representing clarity. Clarity throughout the images is complex. The scale of 0 through 100% is the range from no clarity to complete clarity; neither will occur in any natural image; all images are somewhere between. The inhomogeneous nature of the image will make an average percentage even more difficult to calculate.

So what is a quantity in identification? There is no basic unit of quantity in identification because uniqueness has no lower limit. A unique unit is complex, which causes the quantity value to be complex. A unit of uniqueness in one image must be different from that of its source, as the image is a lesser-quality recording of the source. As a unit of uniqueness becomes clearer, more units become visible and can be measured. The former single unit is now composed of many smaller units with the improved quality. Quantity is the amount that can be comparatively measured in an image. This depends on the clarity of details that can be measured, what the examiner chooses to measure, and how the examiner chooses to do the measuring. Many varieties of comparative measurements take place. Quantity starts with the area of the image, or how big the image is. Measuring and comparing components within the area of first-level details to other first-level details contribute to quantity. Measuring and comparing second-level details to other second-level details are components of quantity, as are measuring and comparing third-level details to other third-level details. Quantity then proceeds to the amount of comparative measurements of the first-, second-, and third-level details within, among, and between the details of the original features of the source. Any comparative measurement of the sequences, configurations, alignments, and positions of the details in images contributes to the quantity aspect.

Simple quantitative models have been offered in forensic comparative science. A number of ridge endings, bifurcations, and dots can be counted in fingerprints. The number of striae within tool marks can be counted. The number of cuts in a shoe print can be counted. There is much more to quantity than a number attached to a small component of the comparative process. The comparative measurements of area, shapes, sizes, alignments, distances, sequences, and configurations of details all contribute to quantity each time an image is examined.

RANGES OF LEVELS OF DETAILS

Each part of each image varies in quality and quantity of details with other parts of the same image. There is difficulty in defining the precise instant that the clarity of the details cross over from no details of an image to first-level general form, from first general form to second level-specific paths, or from second-level-specific paths to third-level details of textures upon those paths. There are also ranges of clarity, or qualities, within each of the three levels of details. Extremely poor-quality first-level details have less significance than very good-quality first-level details. This is true for the other two levels of details. As the quality of details improves within each level, the power or significance of the details within that level increases, improving the accuracy of the comparative measurements. As the quality of details worsens within each level, the power or significance of the details decreases, reducing the accuracy of the comparative measurements.

The textures of ridges in skin and gouges in shoes exist. A ridge path starts and stops in the skin, as does a gouge path in shoes. First-level clarity of these recordings will result in the examiner guessing the comparative measurements, which need accuracy. Science must go beyond guessing and into knowing and believing.

Figure 4-1 (Vanderkolk, 1999) depicts the significance of three levels of details in an image. The width of the bottom horizontal axis of the figure represents the quantity of details that are actually measured for sequences and configurations of details within an area of an image. As quality improves, more details can be measured. The left vertical line represents quality of details in the image, and the right vertical line represents significance of the quality of the detail. As quality improves, the significance of the detail increases. Quality approaches, but does not reach, 100% clarity or significance of details of the features of the source. No other values were placed on either axis, as quantifying quantity and quantifying quality are extremely complex. The figure represents measurements of details that result in more than none and less than all of the features of the source. Determining, describing, and listing of all the units of comparative measurements that take place in comparative examinations would be extremely cumbersome, if not impossible. The difficulties of describing what a unit is as quality varies and the cognitive processes that take place during comparative measurements restrict that ability.

The overall height within the three levels of details represents the various ranges of qualities that exist. The black line within the gray represents the actual threshold between the levels; the gray bordering the black represents the doubt or inability of the examiner to perfectly perceive that demarcated threshold when clarity of details transitions to the next level.

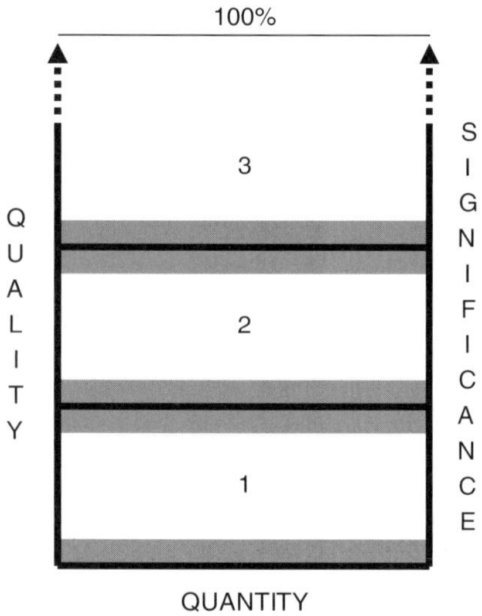

FIGURE 4-1
The Levels of Details. The quantity of units for comparative measurements is represented across the horizontal aspect of the figure. The quality, clarity, or significance of those details is represented along the vertical aspect of the figure. Quality of details can approach but never reach 100% or perfect recording of the features of the source of the natural image. There are no other numerical values attached to this representation as the general concept is presented.

The lower left corner of Figure 4-1 has the value of zero quality and zero quantity. There is no image at this absolute value of zero, whether zero represents quality, quantity, or both, as the lack of one aspect denies the existence of the other. The gray band above the value of zero quality represents the inability of the examiner to determine the significance of what the image represents within that quantity of details. The width of the gray represents examiner doubt. There is too much doubt at this insignificant level of clarity to even label what the image represents. A form that represents an object is not determined. As the clarity improves, first-level details of general form become apparent in the first level of white, or "1." The examiner can determine the general nature or form of what the image represents within this level. The examiner cannot make specific measurements.

As the quality of the image improves, the significance of the image approaches and enters second-level quality. As the quality of the image improves more, the significance of the image approaches and enters third-level quality. Notice how the top of the overall height of third-level details approaches but can never reach 100% quality of details.

Just as levels of clarities exist for details of unique features, levels of clarities exist for details of repeatable features. The transitions from zero to first, first to second, and second to third levels of clarities for details of repeatable features are similar to the transitions for clarities of details of unique features. The form of first level can depict an image of a shoe print or just one element of a tread, depending on the quantity of area of the image. First-level details of repeatable features can indicate the many types of tread that did not make the impression. The paths of tread as second-level details within the form depict a group of shoes that could have made the impression based on size, shape, sequences, and configurations of features among a group of shoes. The clarity of third-level details in impressions of manufactured texture along the tread can restrict that impression as a having been made by a sole that was manufactured in a uniquely textured mold among other molds that generate similar makes, models, and sizes of soles. This description of clarity as three levels of details of the recorded repeatable features of tread, or any manufactured object, can also be used.

Lack of clarity of details does not impart commonality with details of other images, whether the details are of repeatable features or unique features (Grieve, 1990; Vanderkolk, 1993). An image can contain both types of details if the source contains both repeatable and unique features. The examiner must avoid blending the details of unique and repeatable features together. When in doubt about the clarity of any detail, whether within a level or between levels, defer to lesser significance.

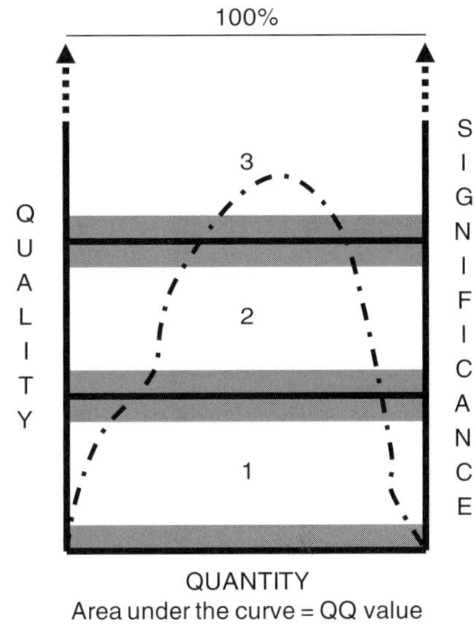

FIGURE 4-2
The levels of details are depicted with the segmented line across the figure. The line does not have a static value of quality across the quantities of details that are being measured in the image. Everything beneath the curve of the image supports the details at the upper threshold.

Figure 4-2 portrays the ranges of clarity throughout the area within an image. It also represents how first-level details support second-level details, and first- and second-level details support third-level details. The upper border of the enclosed area represents the ranges of clarity of the image throughout the image. The height of the border changes as the quality of the image varies throughout the area of the image. In the area under the upper border are also the lesser value details that support the maximum value of detail at that particular location within the image.

Figures 4-3 and 4-4 represent the corresponding relationship between two images known to be from the same unique and persistent object. Since neither image is a perfect recording of its source, nor each other, they possess differing quality and quantity of details. In Figures 4-3 through 4-9, the object that deposited the two images is represented by the largest circle. The two mid-sized circles represent the quality and quantity (QQ) value of the unknown and known impressions from its source. The QQ value of the relationship between the two images is represented by the smallest circle. A white interior of any circle represents sufficiency; black represents insufficiency; gray represents doubt about sufficiency.

Figures 4-5 and 4-6 represent the corresponding relationship between two images known to be from the same unique and persistent object but some different parts of that object, such as the left and middle parts of a finger for

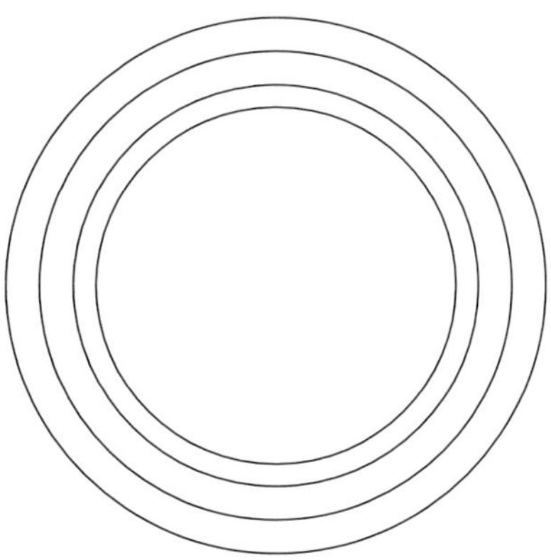

FIGURE 4-3
The QQ values of two images from the same source are represented by different circles in this figure. The source (largest circle), both images, and the relationship (smallest circle) are sufficient in this representation.

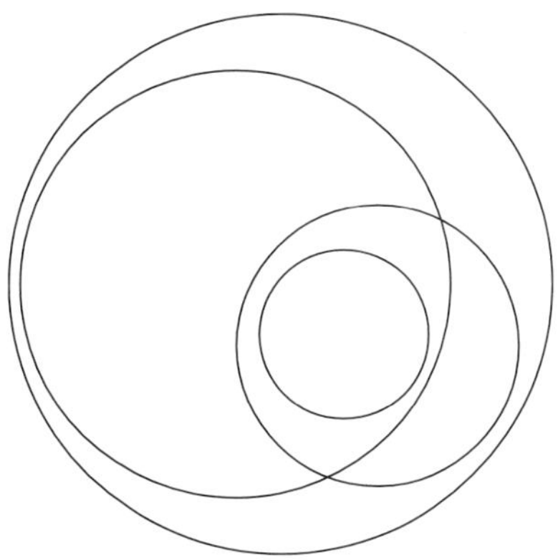

FIGURE 4-4
The QQ values of two images from the same source are represented by different circles in this figure. A part of the two images is from a similar location or source on the object. Other parts of the images are from different areas of the object.

the first image and the middle and right parts of the same finger. The QQ value of the relationship between the two images is represented by the corresponding area of the smallest circle. Gray doubt and black insufficiency are represented in the QQ value.

The upper threshold of the two images, in which the examiner is able to determine both actual agreement and disagreement of details from a unique object, is depicted in Figure 4-7. Parts of the source surface have endured some change due to trauma or aging within what had been the same area. A blister or scar might be represented in the second image of a finger and not the first image. A tack hole might be represented in the first image of a shoe sole and wear on the tread might have eliminated the presence of that hole, so the second image does not depict the hole. A chip might be represented in the second image of a gun's firing pin and not be represented in the first image. Persistencies of the features of the source have resulted in differences in the images that are understood due to the changes of the object's surface. The addition, loss, or change of some features that resulted in some different details in the images does not automatically invalidate the agreement of details of the remaining features of the unique and persistent source. This disagreement is understandable as a persistency issue of the source.

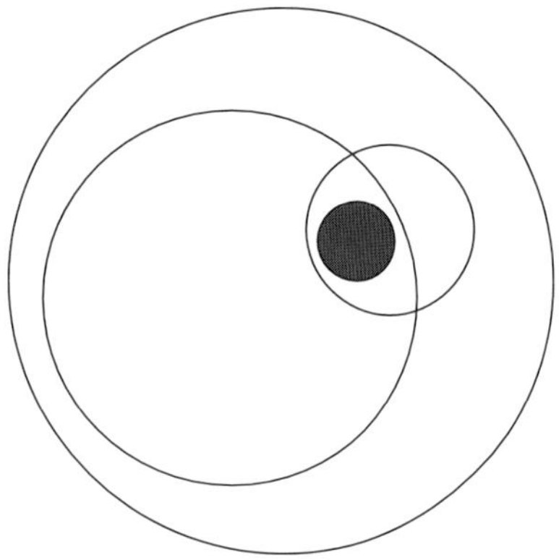

FIGURE 4-5
This figure is similar to Figure 4-4, except the QQ relationship might be insufficient, as represented by the small gray circle indicating doubt. The examiner would not determine these two images are from the same source, rendering an inconclusive result. Additional standards could be obtained for examination.

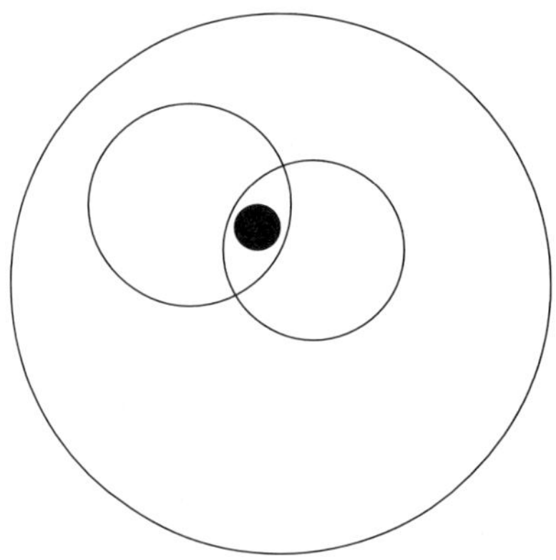

FIGURE 4-6
This figure is similar to Figures 4-4 and 4-5, except the QQ relationship is definitely insufficient, as represented by the small black circle indicating insufficiency. Both images are sufficient by themselves, but the relationship between them is insufficient. The examiner would not determine these two images are from the same source, rendering an inconclusive result. Additional standards could be obtained for examination.

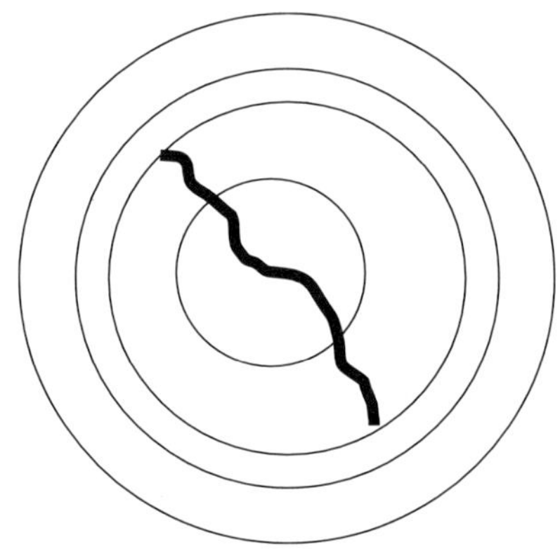

FIGURE 4-7
This figure represents two images from the same object, but some of the features have changed due to trauma or aging, resulting in differences between the first and second depositions of impressions. The jagged black line represents details of feature in the second image. These features were not present on the object when the surface of the source made the first impression. Enough other features have remained on the object to permit determination of common origin.

Figures 4-8 through 4-10 represent the relationships between two images known to be from different unique and persistent sources. The one large circle in Figure 4-8 represents one object as the source of two impressions. However, different surface areas of the object were the sources of the two impressions. The details in the two impressions are different. The smaller impression circles do not overlap because they share no common surface of the source that produced the images.

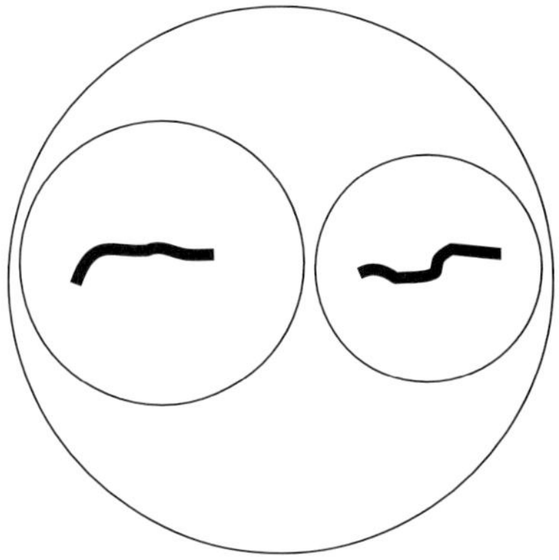

FIGURE 4-8
This figure represents two images from the same object but did not originate from any common area on that object. The surface of the source is different even though they came from the same object. Determining the same object as the source of these impressions cannot be made. Additional standards could be obtained for examination.

Figures 4-9 and 4-10 have two large circles as the objects are different. Different source areas from different objects produced the two images, thus, smaller QQ circles are within each larger object circle. The less dissimilar the two images, the closer they are, as represented in Figure 4-9. The images in the smaller circles in Figure 4-9 might both depict almost round shapes, but measurably different. The more dissimilar the details, the further apart they are, as represented in Figure 4-10. Nature has no straight lines or round circles. As one QQ comparative measurements are for nearly linear details and the other QQ comparative measurements are for nearly circular details, they are plotted further apart. The almost round feature on a source of a poor-quality image with only first-level details cannot be determined because of the QQ value. Because of the massive differences of increments of measurements between a line and circle, the examiner can determine an almost round feature in a source did not make the almost linear detail in an image with very little QQ details. The different details in the small QQ circles in Figure 4-10 are so different that very little QQ value is needed for determining the two images came from different sources.

If the examiner is unable to determine similarity or dissimilarity, agreement or disagreement, no relationship is determined. We, as examiners, are limited by our understanding of uniqueness, the persistency of the uniqueness on the

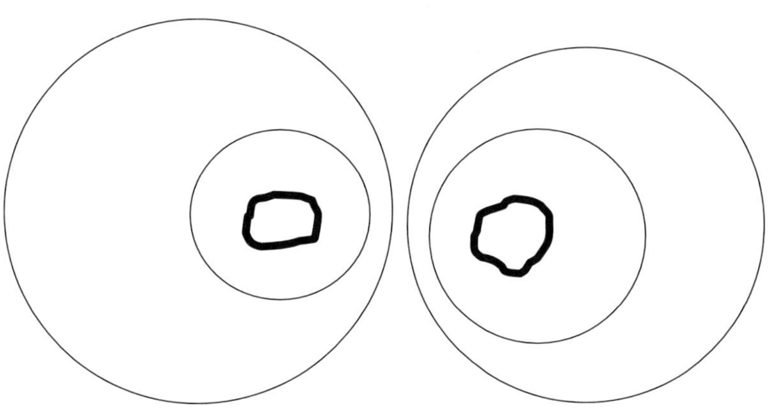

FIGURE 4-9
This figure represents two images from different objects that appear somewhat similar. The large circles of the objects are placed close to each other. Many comparative measurements are needed to demonstrate difference. The two impressions are sufficient to determine differences.

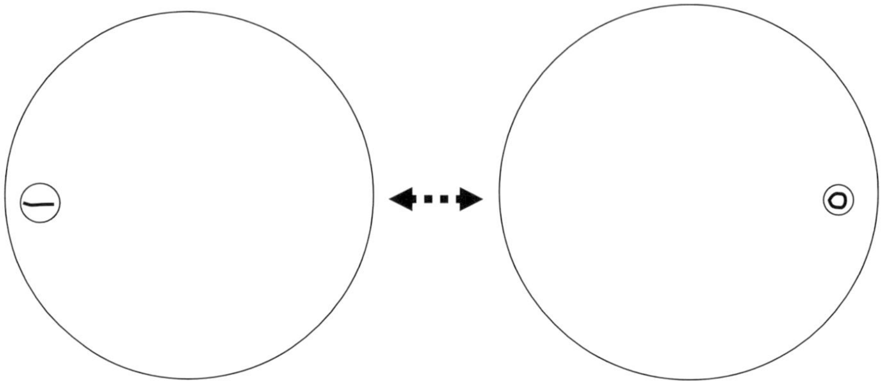

FIGURE 4-10

This figure represents two images from different objects that appear very different. The large circles of the objects are very far from each other. Very few comparative measurements are needed to demonstrate difference. The very small QQ value of the details as represented by the small circles are sufficient to determine difference as one impression has nearly straight lines and the other impression has nearly round circles as their details.

features of the source, the dimensions of the pattern of the structure, the clarity of the image of the source, and our ability to see or visualize it. Clarity of the image is a key. But this does not diminish the phenomenon of unique patterns in nature. Once it is a pattern in nature, whether animate or inanimate, it is morphologically unique.

Corresponding details of unique features of one source cannot occur in images of details of different unique features from other sources. The unique features of one source will never be accidentally or purposefully reproduced in another source. One source can be indistinguishable from another if clarity prevents a closer inspection or we do not look closely enough. The examiner might be confused if there is lack of clarity, but the examiner must always understand, lack of clarity of details of unique features in one image does not grant commonality of these details in the first image with details from other unique features in another image. Lack of clarity of details simply diminishes the power or significance of the details in images.

Figures 4-11 through 4-13 represent the variations in choices of metrics needed to accomplish a task of determining sufficiency of an image in the cognition and recognition processes. Figure 4-11 represents the early morning sun behind a mountain range. The silhouette of the mountains is distinct. How do I know which mountain range this is? Based on previous mountains I have seen and stored in memory, I comparatively measure the features of these mountains. I compare this viewing to what I have seen before. The measurements I take depend on the metrics I need to accomplish the task, as represented in Figure 4-12. The clarity of the silhouette and shapes in the mountains might restrict the quality of the metrics I can use. How many and what level of metrics do I need? I cannot predetermine the number of units and type of increments, so I combine a variety of metrics until I recognize the mountains in Figure 4-13. I do not use just the form of the general mountains. I include the general form with some paths and some textures along the paths. Then, I include the metrics of the relationships of each measurement to the other measurements through the comparative process. I use what is available and what I need. In the comparative measurements of images, the amount of comparative measurements, or quantity, depends on the quality or measurability of details that are present in the images. The maximum quantity of what is physically present and can be comparatively measured depends on quality, or levels of clarity, of what can be seen. So how much is needed to recognize mountains? The quantity depends on quality of what can be measured and what needs measured.

FIGURE 4-11
This figure represents the sun rising behind mountains creating a silhouette. How much QQ is needed to determine which mountains these are based on experience with mountains?

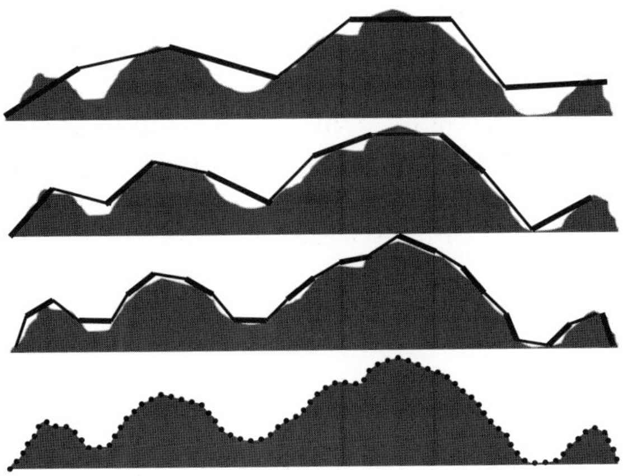

FIGURE 4-12
The clarity or quality of the silhouette and the quantity of metrics chosen to comparatively measure this scene cannot be predetermined. Four different sizes of units are depicted by a different length of a line or fine dots as the metric.

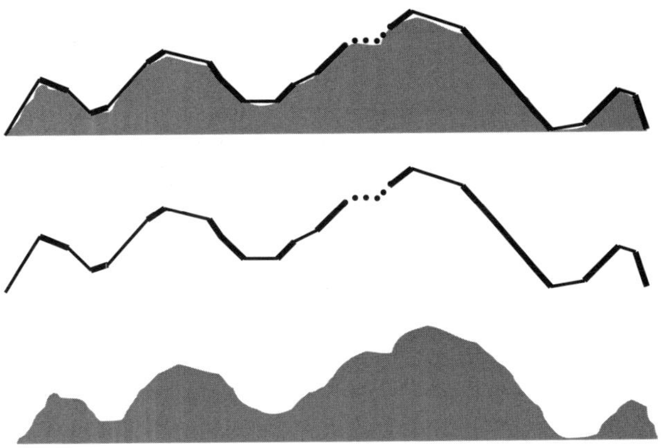

FIGURE 4-13
Different metrics were utilized to measure different areas of the mountain's silhouette. There is no requirement to predetermine how many units of different combinations of different metrics are needed. The quality and quantity of details required to make the determination which mountains these are depends on the clarity of the image, the metrics chosen, the quantities of those metrics, and the standard of mountains in the viewer's memory.

REFERENCES

Ashbaugh, David R. *Quantitative-Qualitative Friction Ridge Analysis: An Introduction to Basic and Advanced Ridgeology*. CRC Press LLC, Boca Raton, 1999.

Grieve, David L. 'Reflections on Quality Standards—An American Viewpoint', *Fingerprint Whorld*, April, 1990, 110.

McKasson, Stephen C., and Carol A. Richards. *Speaking as an Expert: A Guide for the Identification Sciences From the Laboratory to the Courtroom*. Charles C Thomas, Springfield, Illinois, 1998.

SWGFAST, Scientific Working Group on Friction Ridge Analysis, Study and Technology, 'Friction Ridge Examination Methodology for Latent Print Examiners' *http://www.swgfast.org/Friction_Ridge_Examination_Methodology_for_Latent_Print_Examiners_1.01.pdf*.

Vanderkolk, John R. 'Class Characteristics and "Could Be" Results', *Journal of Forensic Identification*, 1993, 43 (2), 119–125.

Vanderkolk, John R. 'Levels of Quality and Quantity of Detail', *Journal of Forensic Identification*, 2001, 51 (5), 461–468.

CHAPTER 5

Qualitative Quantitative Relationship of Details

CONTENTS

How many details of unique features of an object are needed to determine that two images are from the same source? In forensic comparative examinations, each image must have sufficient details of the features of the persistent source to enable the examiner to reach a significant conclusion. Because each unknown and known image varies in appearance from the source and between each other, the minimum needed amount of details depends on how clear the details are in each image and whether the details are of repeatable or unique features. Quantity requires quality as quality requires quantity. Each cannot exist without the other. A fixed-point standard of a quantity of limited types of details of unique features is irrelevant (Evett and Williams, 1996).

Can two independent images of one, and only one, unique feature of a source be clear enough to determine that they came from the same source? The answer is no, in theory, because the impressions of one feature of the source always have less quality and quantity than the one unique feature being depicted. Each image of the one unique feature will vary in appearance and have less value than the original feature. An aggregate of more than one unit of uniqueness in the lesser details is needed to form a value of at least one unit to determine the unique features of the source. Corresponding details of more than one unit of unique features must be captured in each image to determine they came from the same source.

The simplest, most general, and most accurate description of the minimum units of details of unique features needed to determine source is explained by the quality quantity (QQ) relationship of details between the two images, or the "qualitative quantitative theory of 1." When examining unique details of persistent unique features in two images, the clearer the details in images, the fewer details that are needed. The less clear the images, the more details that are needed. Yet one unit of detail is still the minimum needed. How can that be? How can one unit be singular yet require many details from the persistent unique features of the source? *Unique* means there is only one of its kind. *Unit,* also by definition, is singular or one. That minimum unit of uniqueness corresponds to the numerical value of one. In theory, if there is one unit of detail from the persistent unique features in agreement between two images, those images came from the same source.

All details will have less quality than the features they depict. Therefore, to have one aggregate unit of uniqueness in agreement in reality, there must be more than one unit of detail in the images for an examination to reach a definite determination of source of origin. More than the detail from one unique feature of the source is needed to equal the minimum of one aggregate unit of uniqueness in agreement between the images. The mathematical relationship that explains the minimum aggregate amount of details needed to reach sufficiency is based on $X \times Y = 1$, as presented in Figure 5-1. This relationship can also be expressed as the inverse relationship of $X \times 1/X = 1$. Since quality in every impression is less than 1, quantity must be more than 1 to reach sufficiency of 1.

FIGURE 5-1
The $X \times Y = 1$ or $X \times 1/X = 1$ graph and curves. The curves continue indefinitely along the X and Y axes.

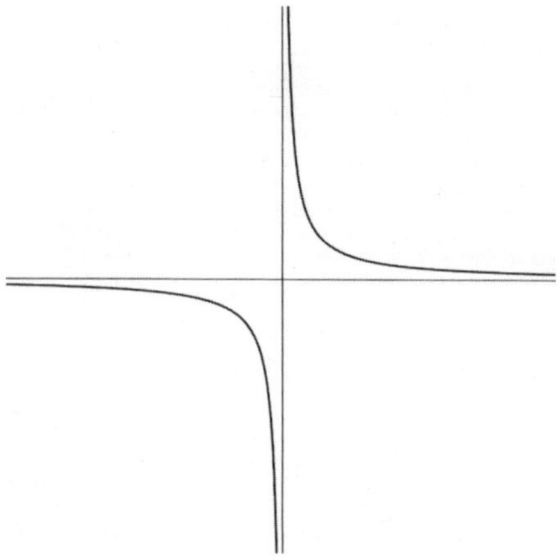

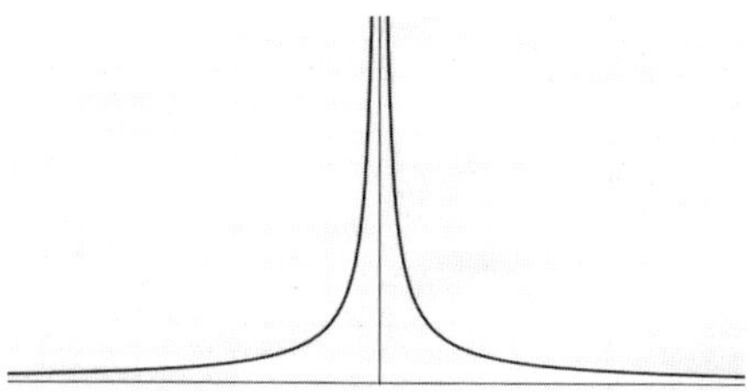

FIGURE 5-2
The $X \times Y = 1$ graph is then converted to represent only vertical positive value along the Y axis with the horizontal X axis as positive or negative value.

The mathematical relationship of $X \times Y = 1$ is converted to the QQ = 1 representation of the objective threshold of one cumulative unit of sufficiency in Figure 5-2, assuming there is no loss or change of features when considering persistency of the source. Figure 5-2 varies from Figure 5-1 by considering quality as always being positive, while quantities of comparative measurement metrics of similar details are to the right of the quality axis and quantities of comparative measurement metrics of dissimilar details are to the left of the quality axis. The metrics used in measuring very similar details that are not clear require many measurements to determine actual agreement or disagreement. For very different images, the comparative metrics used to measure obviously dissimilar details such as a circle and a line are extremely different. This is why very little area of QQ and measurements in two images are sometimes needed to determine actual disagreement. By determining just one aggregate metric of measurement is actually different, disagreement can be established.

Cognitive vision scientist Stephen E. Palmer (2002, 641–642) writes of visual awareness and objective versus subjective thresholds of awareness. His understanding of visual awareness led him to Figure 5-3, a simple, black to gray to white graph of sufficiency. Below the threshold of awareness is subliminal (black) and above the threshold is supraliminal (white). Between the black and white is gray.

We are left in a gray zone lying between two different thresholds. …
The gray area in between is bona fide subliminal perception to those
who advocate identifying consciousness with subjective thresholds but
bogus subliminal perception to those who advocate objective thresholds.
It appears that an impasse has been reached. Is there any way around it?

Palmer does not have an answer for the impasse.

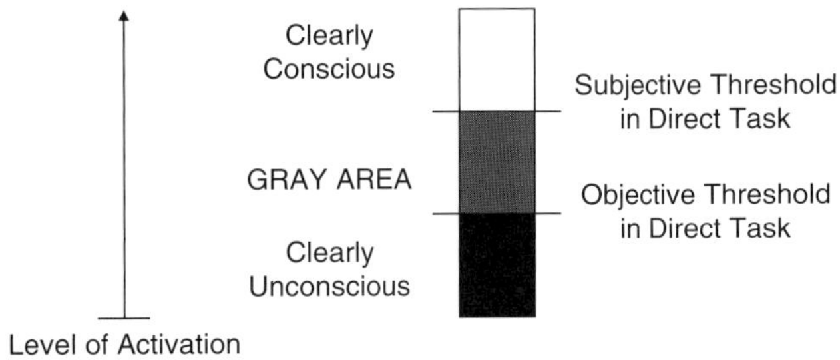

FIGURE 5-3
Cognitive vision scientist Stephen E. Palmer's depiction of a sufficiency threshold for awareness of a stimulus. "The gray zone between conscious perception and lack of visual information. There is a region of visual phenomena below the subjective threshold of awareness and above the objective threshold that some claim is subliminal and others claim is supraliminal." (Palmer, Stephen E. *Vision Science: Photons to Phenomenology*, Figure 13.3.2, with additional text from page 642. © 2002 Massachusetts Institute of Technology, by permission of The MIT Press.)

Awareness of stimuli in a visual image is similar to objective and subjective levels of sufficiency of uniqueness between two images. The theoretical QQ = 1 relationship will be explained in this chapter with a series of figures. When comparing the details of unique features in two images, objective insufficiency is represented in the black, below the interfaces of the two black and gray curves in Figure 5-4. On or above the two black at gray curves (QQ = 1) represent objective sufficiency. Figure 5-4 also introduces the concept of subjectivity in judgment of sufficiency in relation to the objective threshold of sufficiency in QQ = 1. The effort to eliminate the subjective irritation of doubt is represented by the addition of gray to the threshold value of one. In the white, above the gray subjective threshold, represents both objective and subjective sufficiency. Gray is also the color of the quality and quantity axes for the curves. This gray at the axes also represents the irritation of doubt that exists whether the judgment of insufficient details actually agree or disagree at minimal quality quantity (Vanderkolk, 1999, 2001). The examiner might decide the details are similar or dissimilar in the black, but actual sufficiency to reach a judgment of agreement or disagreement has not been met. If the examiner decides in the gray or black, levels of guessing occur. If the gray curves were to be moved below threshold of 1, the examiner would be guessing, as the data would not support the judgment of agreement or disagreement.

As random examples of the values along the axes and curves, if two images have an arbitrary equal value of 50% clarity in corresponding areas of the prints, 2 units of metrics of measurements of unique details are needed to objectively determine they came from the same source. If 10% clarity exists, a minimum of 10 units of measurements of unique details are objectively needed for source determination. If 20% clarity and 40 units of measurements of unique details are made, the determination of same source of origin might be considered easy as beyond both objective and subjective thresholds. This value of 8 would be above the curve in the upper right quadrant. If 10% clarity and 4 units of measurements of unique details are made, similarity might be decided, but insufficiency of agreement is objectively and subjectively determined in the black. For disagreement, if 10% clarity existed, 10 metrics of small straight lines would be needed to objectively determine difference existed between round details and straight details. A small arc of the circle could be measured using small straight line metrics. These straight lines could be extremely small. Little areas in images are sometimes needed to determine actual disagreement. More units of measurements are needed for less dissimilar details.

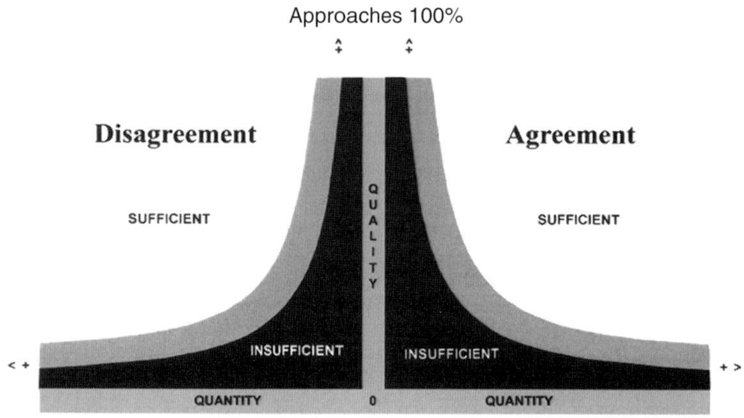

FIGURE 5-4
The Quality Quantity (QQ) curve based on $X \times Y = 1$, with objective (black to gray curve interface) and subjective (gray to white curve interface) sufficiency of agreement and disagreement of details from unique and persistent source(s). (Courtesy of the *Journal of Forensic Identification*, Vanderkolk, 2001.)

The black to gray threshold in Palmer's Figure 5-3 is similar to the objective value of 1 in the QQ curves in Figure 5-4. The gray to white subjective threshold in Figure 5-3 is similar to the gray to white subjective threshold that goes beyond the irritation of doubt in the QQ curves to white sufficiency. Figure 5-3 is similar to the QQ curves of Figure 5-4 in that both figures involve perceiving stimuli or details in images. When does that stimuli register in the brain as significant? When do details of unique features register as sufficient? Whether the models represent the perception for awareness of stimuli being present or for sufficiency of details in images, both figures represent a lesser objective threshold that interfaces with a gray area of doubt that interfaces with the white area of subjective awareness or sufficiency.

Examiners cannot objectively be aware of actual perceptual agreement or disagreement of unique details in QQ of less than the value of 1, as 1 is the absolute minimum of the objective threshold. Above the gray at its interface with white is the subjective threshold of awareness, the point at which examiners are willing to assert that they have determined sufficiency. The gray area between the black curve and the white is below the limit of sufficiency to those who advocate determining sufficiency with subjective thresholds but above the minimum to those who advocate using the absolute minimum objective threshold.

How do we measure uniqueness and actually place a value of 1 on it when each unique item is different? How would we subjectively know the universal minimum threshold, since we have not yet determined how to measure the absolute objective minimum QQ threshold? As Palmer (2002) stated, it appears that an impasse has been reached. The way around it is to acknowledge subjectivity and objectivity coexist within the examiners. Examiners must avoid guessing and conduct legitimate comparative examinations of the details within tolerance of the collaborating forensic comparative science communities. Tolerance is learned from participating in training and experiencing sufficiency in known impressions from the same source, known impressions from different sources, applying deductive and inductive reasoning during the training processes, and remaining tolerant of the dissimilarities and similarities experienced throughout the career of applying abductive reasoning.

The examiner must participate in a community that shares experiences and images of somewhat similar impressions from different sources and somewhat dissimilar impressions from the same source. The examiner must participate in regular testing and judging known source impressions within the community. Without community participation, the examiner will lose track of what is within tolerance of that community. The examiner needs must be refreshed about objective and subjective sufficiency within community tolerance on a regular basis. Longino (1990, 179) said, "Objectivity, then, is a characteristic of a community's practice of science, rather than of an individual's, and the practice of science is understood in a much broader sense than most discussions of the logic of scientific method suggest." As long as the subjective threshold of sufficiency is above the objective threshold of sufficiency, the threshold for sufficiency to judge is correct. If the subjective threshold is below the objective threshold, the examiner is in the area of guessing, if guessing could be measured. Guessing must be avoided. Without an ability to determine rational judgments considering similarities and dissimilarities in the black or in the doubt of gray, the examiner would be guessing when in or below the gray threshold. More research concerning features in source objects and their recorded details in images is needed to determine rational probabilities without guessing.

QUALITY AND QUANTITY

Quality is the measure of the reduction of data from the features of the source in a percentage between 0 and 100 percent. In Figure 5-4 and all of the QQ figures in this chapter, the vertical quality axis starts at zero, for there must be more than zero quality for there to be an image. The quality axis approaches but does not reach 100 percent (.999 ...) because no object can duplicate itself perfectly. The quantity axis represents the amount of metrics of measurable unique and persistent features of the source recorded as measurable details in areas of the images.

In a discussion of conducting many experiments to obtain data that can be plotted on a graph, philosopher Bernard Lonergan (1957, 58) states, "No doubt, it is possible to join the plotted points by a smooth curve, but the curve represents, not data that are known, but a presumption of what understanding will grasp." He also goes on to explain how the relations of the measurements and plotted points represent the awareness of grasping the potential law describing the general relationship of the data as a smooth curve.

The areas below, at, and above the smooth curves of QQ = 1 represent the data of reality that cannot be absolutely known. The pair of smooth curves of QQ = 1 is the theory, generalization, or formulation of the threshold of sufficiency to determine or exclude a unique and persistent source as having made an image. The value of "1" represents the understanding that is grasped of objective sufficiency in images to determine the source. The value of "1 + gray" represents the understanding that is grasped of subjective sufficiency in images to determine the source.

If one cumulative unit of agreement exists between the details in two images of features from unique and persistent sources, they have sufficient details to determine they originated from the same object. If one cumulative unit of disagreement exists between two images from persistent and unique features, they originated from different surfaces of sources, yet not necessarily different objects or items. If the objects are different with at least one repeatable unit on their surfaces that deposited the images, they are different sources of the two images. "Surface of the source" is used differently from "object" because the surface of the object becomes the source of the image. Many parts of the object did not make contact with a substrate to contribute to an image. If lack of persistency changes some of the features on the surface of the source, the remaining features must be sufficiently recorded in relation to their QQ to reach a judgment of sufficiency. This recording might not happen.

The QQ relationship of the images cannot be perfectly measured by the examiner. The comparative measurements do not and cannot use a fixed increment of a scale metric, as there are different sizes, lengths, or dimensions to each of the comparative measurements. With variation of appearances, there are different accuracies to each of the comparative measurements. A requirement for a number of specific types or levels of details of unique and persistent features cannot be predetermined.

Figures 5-5 through 5-9 are examples of depictions of the QQ objective and subjective relationship of unique details in images. The plot of each image relationship to other images is represented as a pinpoint value. The physical size of the black pinpoint is larger than the reality of the value, but the pinpoint must be seen to understand the concept. This pinpoint represents the objective reality of the value of the QQ relationship between images. The larger gray dot represents the examiner's subjective perception of measuring that QQ value. This gray dot is larger because the QQ measurement has subjectivity involved. Human perception is not perfectly objective because the human is involved, but perception is objective in that it comparatively measures object to object within tolerance for comparative measurements in science. As long as the examiner's subjective perception of objective comparisons is on the same side of the QQ axes as objective reality, the examiner is not wrong.

But how is support for the determination justified? Support is generated from the participation in the community and being open to review of the judgments. If objective QQ value is in the black area, the examiner cannot scientifically support the determination by guessing. Objective reality does not have gray doubt. If the examiner is in the gray area, the examiner has irritation of doubt and cannot scientifically support the determination. If the examiner is in the black, no support for actual source determination can be justified. The examiner must be in the white area above the curves for subjective QQ to be able to demonstrate support of judgment for determination of source for the images. The additional gray curve above the black curve also provides a conservative approach to comparative measurements by requiring more QQ value than what is objectively needed, while still remaining within tolerance for the community. All gray dots are plotted to have less QQ value than the black dots in Figure 5-5 through Figure 5-9. These depictions are intentional to also emphasize the need of the examiner to be conservative in sufficiency determinations. Being too conservative with a large gray curve and refusing to judge does not do justice to the science or courts. Being too reckless with a small gray curve below examiner's ability or guessing in the gray or black does not do justice to the science or courts. However, many times, insufficient or inconclusive is the proper answer. Sometimes the best answer is "I do not know."'

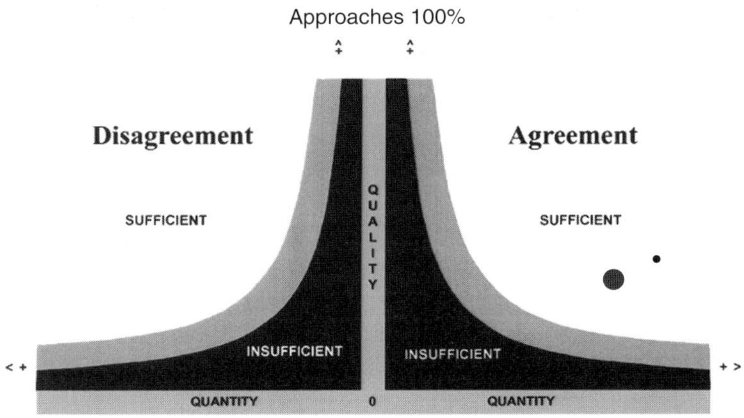

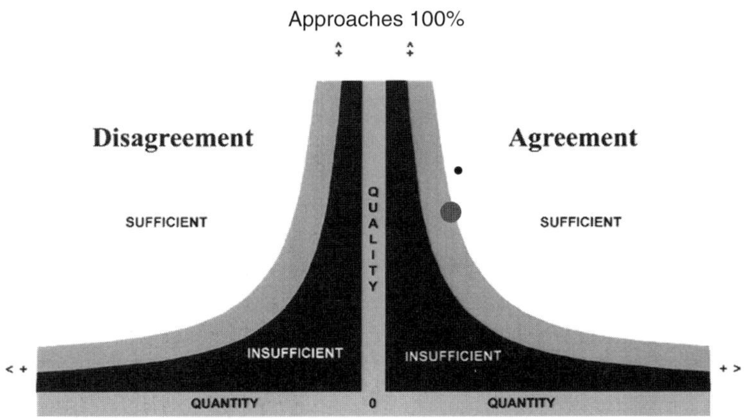

FIGURES 5-5 THROUGH 5-9

Reality of the value of the images is represented by the black dot. The examiner's perception of the value of the images is represented by the larger gray dot. The gray dot of judgment must be on the same side of the curve as the black dot of reality for the judgment to be correct. The gray dot is placed lower in the quality quantity value representing conservative judgment. If either dot is in the black or gray areas under the curves, the examiner needs to render an inconclusive judgment.

(Continued)

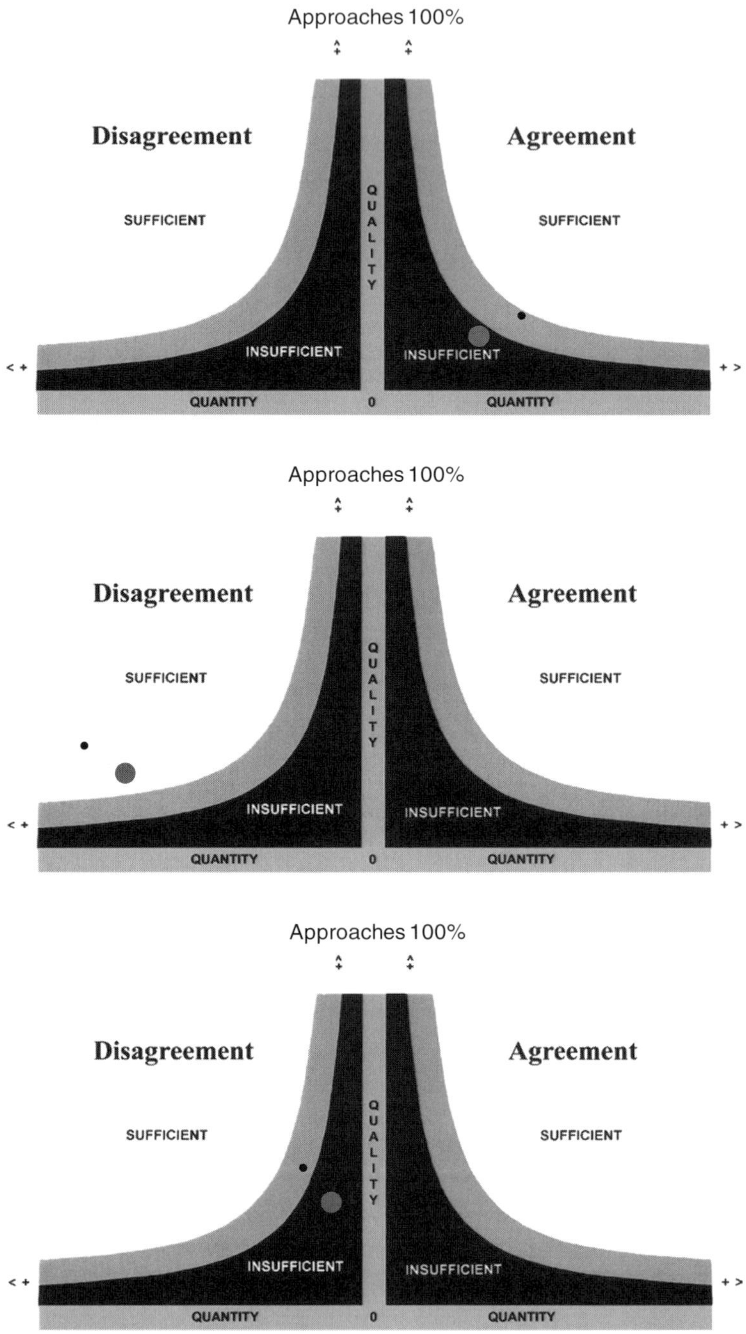

FIGURES 5-5 THROUGH 5-9—CONT'D

Being unable to absolutely know the QQ value of the pinpoint of reality, the examiner first strives to determine whether the details between two images are similar or dissimilar. Judgments, based on expertise, must be made. An object that varies in persistency also varies in differing quantities of details because some or all features of the source have changed. Persistency of the source, as discussed in Chapters 3 and 4, is an issue here. Lack of sufficient persistency of unique features is one of the reasons the details in the two images from the same object, yet different source surfaces, disagree. One other reason details from the same object might have the appearance of disagreement is because intervening residue or matrix was present when the source made contact with the substrate. The substrate with its textures and residues might also influence the variation of appearances in the images. Or intervening matrices or residues on the sole obstructed it from recording its features clearly by interfering as contamination and becoming part of the temporary surface of the source. Stones, dirt, and debris might contribute to a shoe's impression and then fall off the sole. A standard impression is later made. The sources of stones, dirt, and debris that had produced the image in conjunction with the sole have changed, even though the tread on the shoe sole remains the same. Persistency has changed the object's surface as the source of the impressions causing different details to be found in the impressions from the same shoe. The original stones, dirt, and debris were the sources of some details in the first impression. These features no longer exist on the sole when the second impression was made.

The black curves represented in Figure 5-4 depict the QQ relationship of sufficiency, a smooth curve, a theoretical explanation for the sufficiency of unique details between two images. The QQ curve represents not all of the data that can be absolutely known, for an examiner cannot perfectly measure all of the perceivable quality and quantity of uniqueness of the details in all items. All the actual measurements made by scientists will not generate a smooth curve as measurements are not perfect. These measurements will tend to generally depict a smooth curve. And that generalization of a smooth curve is represented by the relationship value of QQ = 1. These black curves are the theoretical model of sufficiency of 1 unit of needed uniqueness I am presenting. The additional gray curves are not part of the theory of 1 but represent examiner ability and doubt with a conservative approach to judging. There is no science without a scientist doing the measuring and judging. Ability of the scientist is part of science (Wertheim, 1996).

The smooth black curves of QQ = 1 represent this theory of sufficiency. This theory deals with unique details of unique features from any persistent source. There should not be many different theories of sufficiency for the immense variety of sources that produce images. The theory should not change among the many disciplines of comparative science. The theory should be general, simple, and adequate. Like laws, theories should not change until a better theory is determined. Laws of science should not change under different situations. Philosopher Bernard Lonergan (1957, 65) said the following about the invariance of laws that concern measurements:

> For, as has been remarked, observations give way to measurements; measurements relate things to one another rather than to our senses; and it is only the more remote relations of measurements to one another that lead to empirical correlations, functions, laws. Now clearly if laws are reached by eliminating the relations of things to the senses of observers and by arriving at relations between the measured relations of things to one another, then there exists an extremely solid foundation for the affirmation that principles and laws are the same for all observers because they lie simply and completely outside the range of observational activities.

The black curves are outside the range of observational activities. They exist because one unit of uniqueness is all that is needed to determine uniqueness, no matter the size or attributes of the unit. The black curves depict the threshold of object to object sufficiency and are the same for all observers. The gray curves incorporate observational activities and are greater than the objective threshold, beyond the theory. QQ = 1 is the required minimum relation of details in one image to details in another image from unique and persistent source(s) to determine whether the images originated from the same source. QQ = 1 does not change for the observers of details in images from unique and persistent features. The observer does not affect the law; the observer only affects the application of the law through his or her expertise of training, experience, understanding, and judgments of comparative measurements and decision making beyond the additional gray.

JUDGMENTS

Since the absolute QQ value of 1 cannot be absolutely determined by the examiner, judgments come into the decision making process. As discussed in Chapter 1, judgments are part of science. Figure 5-10 represents the QQ curve and the element of human judgments of comparative measurements. The interface between the black and gray curves represent the QQ = 1 curve. The black represents less than the value of 1, or insufficiency. Black also represents the certitude of ignorance where even the most liberal judgment would not be supported by the data between the images. The interface between the black and gray curves represents the value of 1, the minimum objective level of needed details. The widths of the gray curves vary with expertise and the examiner's ability to remove the irritation of doubt, as presented with the undefined size of expanding and contracting arrows in Figure 5-10. The bottom edge of the gray curved interfaces with black cannot change, as this value equals 1. The top edge range of the gray curved interface with white can change, as this edge represents expertise and the irritation of doubt. The white represents subjective sufficiency above the minimum absolute objective value of 1, beyond the gray irritation of doubt. The white represents certitude of knowledge while the black represents certitude of ignorance in which data is lacking to make a definite objective and subjective judgment of agreement or disagreement. The two gray curved ranges in Figure 5-10 represent the imprecise width of the divide between certitude of ignorance and certitude of knowledge. Gray represents doubt. The white areas represent the irritations of doubt and indecision that have been removed.

Scientific expert examiner judgments and refusals to judge oscillate around central means (Lonergan, 2005) of three locations in the QQ figure. The first location is the central mean of the gray QQ axes when initially determining similarity or dissimilarity between two images. This first oscillation of judgment continues until similarity or dissimilarity is decided, as represented in Figure 5-11. Once similarity or dissimilarity is decided, the second oscillation takes place within the gray curve whether sufficiency of similarity or dissimilarity exists. The oscillation takes place between the judgment of simple insufficient similarity and the judgment of actual sufficient agreement as depicted in Figure 5-12. Figure 5-13 presents the third oscillation that takes place between the judgment of simple insufficient dissimilarity and the judgment of actual sufficient disagreement.

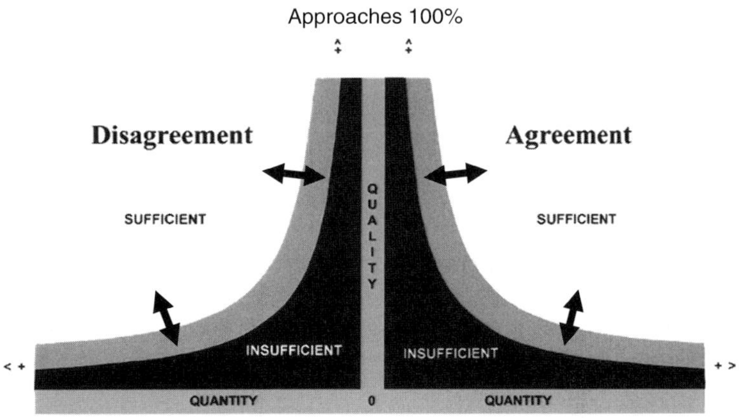

FIGURE 5-10
The two gray curved ranges with arrows represent the imprecise width of the locus of the divide between certitude of knowledge and certitude of ignorance, or doubt. The upper edge of the gray curves can vary as expertise varies. The lower edge of the gray curves at the black remains constant.

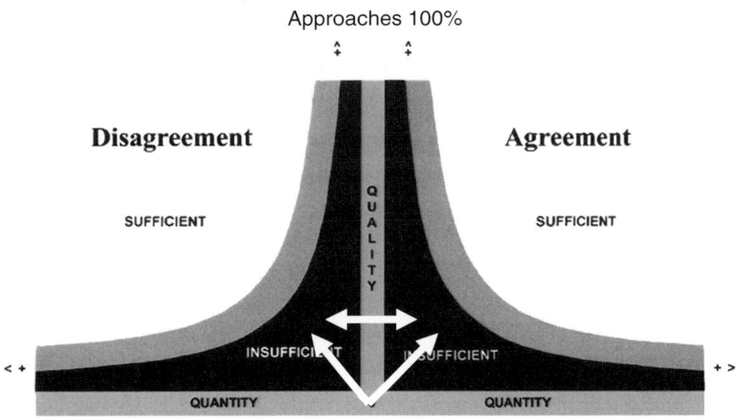

FIGURE 5-11
An early phase of the examination is represented by the white arrows oscillating between similarity and dissimilarity of details between two images.

What happens when the surface of the source changes? Both agreement and disagreement of details of different unique features can occur in two images that had been deposited by this same object. Figure 5-14 represents determinations made beyond the oscillating judgments within the areas of gray between similarity and dissimilarity then beyond the two gray curves resulting in agreement or disagreement of details from the same object, yet different conditions

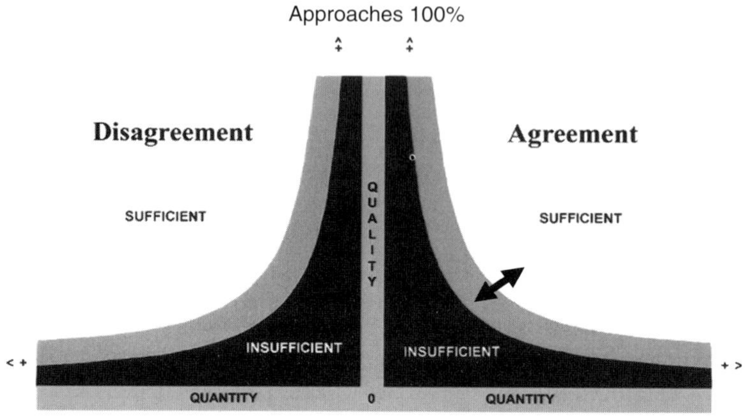

FIGURE 5-12
As the examiner approaches a determination of agreement of details, the oscillation of judgment between insufficient similarity and sufficient agreement takes place as represented by the arrow between doubt and certitude.

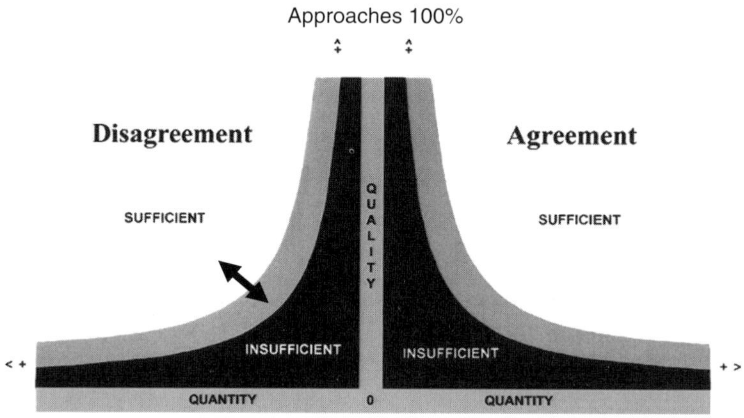

FIGURE 5-13
As the examiner approaches a determination of disagreement of details, the oscillation of judgment between insufficient dissimilarity and sufficient disagreement takes place as represented by the arrow between doubt and certitude.

of surfaces of a source. What judgments of conclusion will be reached when the oscillating decision making process results in a determination of agreement, disagreement, or both agreement and disagreement? These conclusions will be presented in Chapter 6.

Initially, the examiner starts at no knowledge of correspondence, or zero QQ similarity or dissimilarity, agreement or disagreement, at the axes intersection. No knowledge is represented in the gray intersection of the QQ axes at the value of zero quality intersecting with zero quantity. As the judgments of the analyses and the comparisons occur, evaluations come into the judgment process. Since nothing is recorded perfectly as images and there are variations in appearances between the images, the examiner can initially oscillate between similarity and dissimilarity of details, especially upon beginning

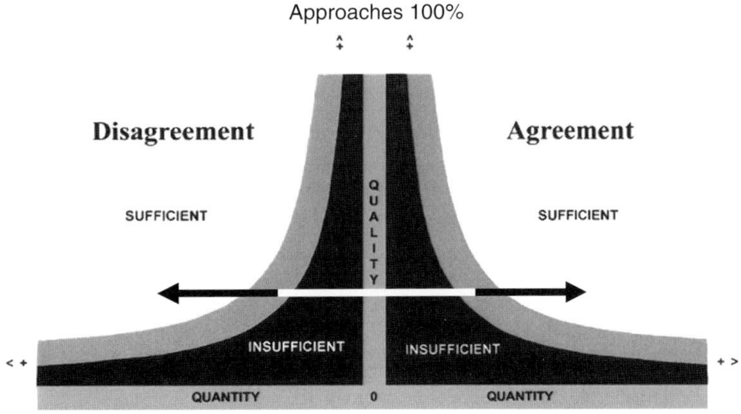

FIGURE 5-14
The examiner can determine both sufficient agreement and disagreement of details between two images. Changes in the surface of the source due to some lack of persistency can result in an object having some same and other different features on its surface between depositions of impressions.

the examination process. The first question asked is "Are the details similar or dissimilar?" No preliminary decision is yet made. More data is analyzed. Considerations for similarity and dissimilarity both occur. As more data is analyzed, compared, and evaluated, support is generated for a determination of similarity or dissimilarity, and then whether the details actually agree or disagree. As more support is generated, predictions occur. For demonstrative purposes, the tendency toward the judgment producing knowledge is that the details between two images are very similar. As this tendency of judging becomes stronger, as the overall supporting data becomes more robust, and predicted details are found, then eventually a reliable prediction (Wertheim, 2000) is made and more detail is found in similarity. This reliable prediction removes the irritation of doubt, resulting in a judgment of actual agreement of the sequences and configurations of details between the two images. No known further relevant and appropriate questions are available or needed. Oscillation has ceased. Judgment is rendered after the reliable prediction.

Prediction is part of trusting the laws of nature to make judgments within the community by the examiner. Carnap (1998, 682) said, "In addition to providing *explanations* for observed facts, the laws of science also provide a means for *predicting* new facts not yet observed." As similar details are observed and seem to correspond between two images, predictions occur that yet to be viewed details will be found in correspondence elsewhere in the images. Once these predicted new facts of details in two impressions are found to be correct, the examiner crosses the threshold of doubt and renders a judgment.

Throughout the examination, the scientific mind needs to ask and answer all relevant and appropriate questions and challenge those answers with critical reflection while oscillating between tentative judgments of similarity and dissimilarity. The examiner must challenge and confront the variations of appearances until all the questions have been asked and answered and reliable predictions have been determined as true. The determination is made that no new data would change the resulting judgment that the details of unique and persistent features actually agree or disagree. Challenging the judgments and asking and answering the relevant questions of comparative measurements take place by reexamining the images prior to concluding the examination. The human mind is much too complex to limit itself to a linear, one-time-through analysis of each image, one comparison of the two images, and one evaluation to make a critical judgment that is acceptable within the collaborating scientific community.

From the details that are in the images, the examiner must now make the correct judgments and determinations, avoid guessing, work through the irritation of doubt, and make judgments within tolerance of the collaborating communities of forensic comparative scientists. All data, or images involved, for making those judgments must be open and available to the community, as the complete thought processes of judgments are difficult, if not impossible, to record. The concluding judgments of the observable data must be open to the community.

Forensic comparative scientists seek the true relationship between images, realizing the approach and comprehension of truth. Truth is reached by experiencing a series of answers to relevant and appropriate questions, experiencing insights about the images, answers to more questions, developing further insights about the images, and moving towards a threshold when no further relevant and appropriate questions are needed. This is a self-correcting process of inquiring and knowing about the images. Learning through experiences, understandings, and judgments, the scientist becomes aware of the approach to a threshold of needed appropriate and relevant questions. Crossing the threshold to knowing, beyond that irritation of doubt, judgments are certain; as certain as critical, reflective, inquiring scientific judgment can be. When in the black or gray of the threshold while experiencing that irritation of doubt, judgments are at best probable. Additional training, experience, understandings, and judgments can reduce that gray area, but not the black. This is why there are two acceptable answers that result from the same details in images. The comparative measurement examinations of the same images by two examiners can result in one examiner reaching a definite determination of agreement and the other examiner reaching a determination of insufficiency. In a different examination, this is why there are two acceptable answers that result from disagreeing details that result in a one examiner reaching a definite determination of disagreement and the other examiner reaching a determination of insufficiency. A reckless examiner would reach definite determinations irrationally, while a hesitant examiner would be unwilling to determine with obviously sufficient data. Neither of the examiners serves the science properly. But no scientist can perfectly and infallibly remove the gray.

$X \times Y = 1$, or QQ = 1, is one of the simplest equations known. Since the forensic comparative examiner searches for agreement or disagreement of comparative measurements of uniqueness, once sufficiency of 1 is reached in the equation, sufficiently knowing and believing can also be reached. This is supported with the conservative addition beyond gray. The challenge to predetermine how much is needed to individualize depends on how clear the images are and how many details of corresponding unique features are present.

AGREEMENT AND DISAGREEMENT

In the QQ = 1 model, these are two separate and distinct positive black curves, mirror images of each other. The value of 1 is the same on both sides. The metrics used in comparative measurements change depending on the quality and quantity of details present in two images. The amounts and sizes of metrics used to measure similarity can be different than the amounts and sizes of metrics used to measure dissimilarity. Often, only small areas of two images are needed for measuring dissimilarities in poor quality images. Larger areas of impressions and different metrics might be needed to measure similarities in poor quality images.

The two black curves in the model must be separate and distinct. Actual agreement and disagreement of unique details in two images from unique and persistent source(s) cannot exist at the same time. This is for sources that do not lose measurable persistency of features. Two images from different unique and persistent sources cannot have two, four, six or any number of details of unique features that actually match. If an examiner states this is possible, the examiner is confused about uniqueness, confused about an image being one image without distortion, confused about actual agreement, confused about actual disagreement, or a combination of all four.

Tuthill (1994, 25) states the following:

> In fact, it would be quite correct to state that many years of experience have failed to disclose two fingerprints with any common characteristics, given sufficiently critical examination, because no two things, not even ridge characteristics, are the same. Occasionally, in the fingerprint literature, one sees a claim that two impressions from different fingers have been found to have six (or five or four) characteristics in common. Even a casual examination of the illustrations that accompany these revelations quickly reveals that the impressions are not the same. One wonders what some of these examiners are trying to prove.

Gray doubt exists between, or connects, the QQ axes below the insufficient areas under the QQ curves of agreement and disagreement. When confused, the examiner is unable to determine whether the details agree or disagree. No definite conclusion of source can be made as presented in Figure 5-15.

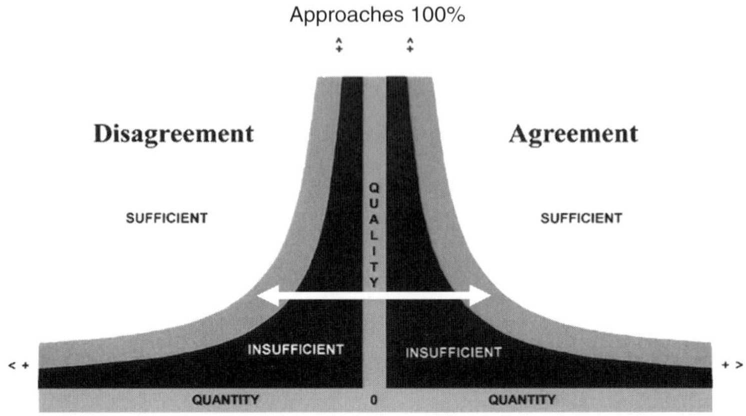

FIGURE 5-15

The examiner is unable to determine either sufficient agreement or disagreement of details between two impressions. Definite determination or exclusion of source of the impressions does not occur.

REFERENCES

Carnap, Rudolf. *The Value of Laws: Explanation and Prediction.* (From *Philosophical Foundations of Physics,* ed. Martin Gardner, Basic Books, New York, 1966; 12–16. Reprinted and edited by Martin Gardner, *An Introduction to the Philosophy of Science,* Dover Publications, Inc., 1995) in Curd, Martin, and J. A. Cover. *Philosophy of Science: The Central Issues*. W. W. Norton & Company, Inc., New York, 1998; 678–684.

Evett, I. W., and Williams R. L. 'A Review of the Sixteen Points Fingerprint Standard in England and Wales,' *Journal of Forensic Identification*, 1996, 46 (1), 49–73.

Lonergan, Bernard. *Insight: A Study of Human Understanding*. Longmans, Green & Co., London, 1957. Fifth edition, University of Toronto Press, Toronto, Canada, 2005.

Longino, Helen E. *Values and Objectivity,'* from *Science as Social Knowledge: Values and Objectivity in Scientific Inquiry*, Princeton University Press, Princeton, New Jersey, 1990, 62–82, in Curd, Martin & J. A. Cover, *Philosophy of Science: The Central Issues*, W. W. Norton and Company, Inc. New York, 1998, 'Values and Objectivity' 170–191.

Palmer, Stephen E. *Vision Science – Photons to Phenomenology*. Massachusetts Institute of Technology, Cambridge, Massachusetts, 1999. Third printing 2002.

Tuthill, Harold. *Individualization: Principles and Procedures in Criminalistics*. Lightning Powder Company, Salem, Oregon, 1994.

Vanderkolk, John R. 'Forensic Individualization of Images Using Quality and Quantity of Information,' *Journal of Forensic Identification*, 1999, 49 (3), 246–256.

Vanderkolk, John R. 'Levels of Quality and Quantity in Detail,' *Journal of Forensic Identification*, 2001, 51 (5), 461–468.

Wertheim, Pat A. 'The Ability Equation,' *Journal of Forensic Identification*, 1996, 46 (2), 149–159.

Wertheim, Pat A. 'Scientific Comparison and Identification of Fingerprint Evidence,' *The Print*, 2000, 16 (5), 1–8, originally published in *Fingerprint Whorld*, July 2000.

CHAPTER 6

Analysis, Analysis, Comparison, Evaluation, and Verification

CONTENTS

AACE+V

Lonergan (1957, 399) said the following:

> Human knowing is cyclic and cumulative. It is cyclic inasmuch as cognitional process advances from experience through inquiry and reflection to judgment, only to revert to experience and recommence its ascent to another judgment. It is cumulative, not only in memory's store of experiences and understanding's clustering of insights, but also in the coalescence of judgments into the context named knowledge or mentality.

The examination of evidence should be similar to the natural process of developing knowledge and belief. The examination method of analysis, comparison, and evaluation (ACE) followed by an independent ACE examination that results in verification (ACE+V) has been described in forensic comparative science as a method to perceive and know details in images and what those details signify based on knowledge and beliefs of self and others within the collaborating community of forensic comparative scientists (Huber, 1959, 1972; Cassidy, 1980; Tuthill, 1994; Ashbaugh, 1999; SWGFAST, 2002; Vanderkolk, 2004). Determinations made through the application of ACE are established by asking the appropriate and relevant questions of inquiry and answering them based upon training, experiences, understandings, and judgments with similar images.

A similar process is presented by McKasson and Richards (1998) of a recurring method of discerning detail and making decisions as examination, comparison, evaluation (ECE) followed by verification (V). Stephen Palmer (2002) provides in the cognitive psychology study of vision science a similar description of a method to perceive and categorize objects as object representation, category representation, comparison process, and decision process. These phases of perception are very similar, no matter how they are described.

Actually, ACE should be AACE, becoming more similar to Palmer's description of a four stage process. In order to compare two things, an analysis of the first and second things needs to occur. Since there are two analyses, analysis becomes analyses (AA). The application of each analysis depends on the critical needs of the viewing and the complexities of the two images. *A*nalyze the first or unknown image, *a*nalyze the second or known image, *c*ompare the first image to the second image, and then *e*valuate the significance of the analyses and comparisons. In forensic comparative science, two images are studied by the examiner in consideration of each other. The process does not require long term memory of details as both images are present for the current examination using working memory. The process of analyzing the first and second image is similar. The actual process of analyzing each image should not be different. Both images need to be analyzed prior to the actual comparison because comparison requires one object for comparing to another object using the same criteria. Since both objects need to be analyzed before comparison starts, I am converting ACE to AACE in these writings.

Describing the examination process of gathering data from visual detail in images and converting that data to knowledge is a challenge. Not all data that are processed by the vision system can be written in notes, as terminology cannot do justice to the complexity of the images and the mental processes of comparative examinations. AACE enables the examiner to separate the phases of perception into simple steps for better understanding and explaining. AACE allows the expert to better understand information gathering, to document the details found in the analyses and comparison phases, and with this documentation, demonstrate what led to the concluding judgment in the evaluation.

This is analogous to scientific method of critically observing details in images, determining similarities or differences in the data, performing comparative measurements to experiment whether the details in the images actually agree or disagree, analyzing the data in the experiment of the comparison to determine sufficiency of data, determining whether actual sufficient agreement or disagreement exists for making a judgment of evaluation, using the awareness of experiential and empirical data to assist in formulating the judgment, and being open to retesting by self or others to determine whether the judgments of the examination can be replicated. AACE is not a linear, one-time-through-each-phase method of examination. The individual phases of AACE recur during the process. The direction of application of the phases can also reverse to a previous phase. At times, the phases occur so quickly they appear to blend. The complexity of the human mind negates a process of one-directional linear, single application of each phase.

The examiner needs to ask and answer appropriate and relevant questions during each phase of the examination to reach the conclusion. Consciously or subconsciously being biased, or failing to ask and answer the appropriate and relevant questions, can lead to improper conclusions. By knowing the potential biases, the examiner can be aware of the appropriate and relevant questions that the community makes known, and then ask and answer these questions about the images in the examination.

The relevant and appropriate questions include anything that can be considered about the images, such as, is the source naturally or humanly made? Does the source have only unique morphology, or does it have both repeatable and unique morphology? What are the persistencies of the repeatable and unique features of the source? What effect does the substrate that receives the image have on the image? What effects do the matrices or residues that are transferred, the manner of impressing or striating the substrate, the manner of motion, distortion of the source or substrate have on the image? What effects do the overall environmental conditions, collecting, processing, preserving, viewing, and examination strategy have on the conclusion? The examiner needs to study impressions within the community and understand comparative measurements of images that vary in appearance. There is no such thing as a perfect match and the examiner must develop experiences, understandings, and judgments to learn tolerance for the comparative measurements.

The examination must be conducted so that the details in the images are accurately analyzed, compared, and evaluated. The analyses are conducted to determine the components of the images: the substrates, matrices, processes used to visualize, lighting technique, printing technique, or anything to help understand the nature of the variations of appearances. The analysis phase of the examination entails scrutinizing both images, usually the questioned or unknown image first. Both images are scrutinized to determine the paths, sequences and configurations of the recorded details of the features of its source.

After analyses, the details are comparatively measured between both images and noted for later evaluation. This comparative measurement determines the similarity, sequences, and configurations of details between the two images. The comparison phase is conducted to determine if the comparative measurements can determine whether details in the two images actually agree or disagree. Upon conducting the comparison phase, any inappropriate or biased adjustments from the decisions made during the analyses and comparisons of the two images are not acceptable.

Changing comparative measurements without asking and answering what caused the distortions and measurement change is improper. Adjusting measurements in opposing directions by making neighboring details longer and shorter, closer and farther, just because that is the way the details appear in the other image is not appropriate. Explanations or justifications that force details to correspond between the two images should bring up concerns and doubt about the judgment. Explanations of distortion should be consistent throughout the images. If confused, admit it and give little or no significance to the comparative measurements. Circular reasoning to force the details to seem as if they correspond is not acceptable. However, recurring and reversing application of the method is acceptable if the bias of circular reasoning is avoided. Stepping aside from the examination and starting over is a strategy to challenge maintaining or adjusting the comparative measurements. The justifications of comparative measurements of sequences and configurations of details must be consistent throughout the areas of variations in appearances. If adjustments have been made to the understanding of the details in the images, the answers to the appropriate and relevant questions must be reviewed.

After comparison, an evaluation of the significance of the similarities and dissimilarities of details occurs. This evaluation must be supported by the training, experience, understanding, and judgments of the examiner's knowledge and beliefs within the community of collaborating scientists.

RECURRING, REVERSING, BLENDING APPLICATION OF AACE

The human mind is much too complex to describe the process simply as independent and linear phases of singular applications of analysis of the first image, analysis of the second image, comparison of the two images, and evaluation. Figure 6-1 represents a model to help illustrate the complexity of the phases that occur, recur, reverse and might appear to blend during an examination.

FIGURE 6-1
An AACE model for the examination process.

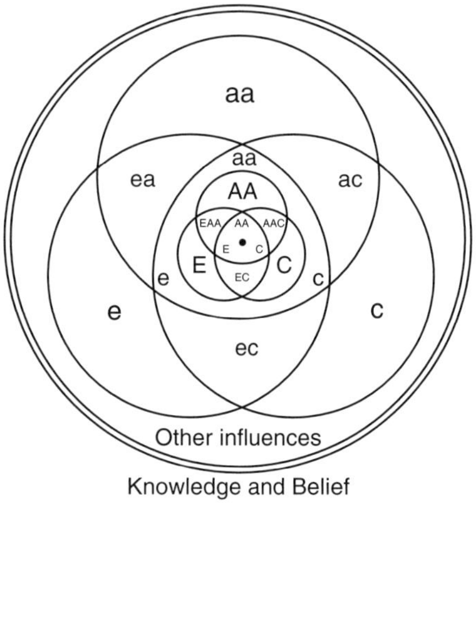

The black dot in the center of AACE represents the axis of all processing of details in the images. The independent phases of AACE cannot separate from the core axis that holds the processes together as all phases interact. The black dot also represents the inattention given to the images or the lack of awareness of perception that can occur in the examination. The examiner needs to scrutinize the details that can be perceived within the images and move away from the black center dot to the outer parts of each phase where attention is more focused. The outer area of each phase represents the effort by the examiner to critically examine the image or images while specifically concentrating and attending to the examination within that phase. The overlapping of phases within AACE represents rapid processing of details in which analyses, comparisons, and evaluations happen quickly and seem to have occurred with little effort.

The current examination of AACE takes place within the larger circles of examiner expertise within the relevant community. Expertise is represented by the larger interlocking circles represented by "aa, c, and e" of the previous trainings, experiences, understandings, and judgments of the examiner. The examiner analyzes, compares, and evaluates (ace) each analysis, comparison, and evaluation within each phase of AACE, based on previous experience, understanding, and judgments, or expertise. The examiner may not consciously recall specific previous knowledge but is aware of the previous experiences that lead and justify this particular examination.

Encompassing the aace and AACE circles are the daily variables of perception, pressures, biases, or other knowledge that might influence the examination. The examiner must be aware of these variables so that the current examination is conducted as objectively as possible within the subjective human expert. The final encircling of the entire model represents the awareness that is generated once a judgment decision of knowing within beliefs of the forensic comparative science community has been determined.

The examination starts with analyses, then comparison, then evaluation. However, the examiner easily changes the process to another phase. These phases often recur. Since both images are available for reconsideration throughout the duration of the examination, a natural tendency of scrutiny is for the examiner to reanalyze, recompare, and reevaluate throughout the working memory processing of the examination. If unable to determine the significance or sufficiency of details within a particular phase of the examination, the examiner can return to a previous phase.

One phase of the examination cannot be completely isolated from the other phases. There is no point in analyzing the first image if nothing further will occur. After analyzing the first image, the examiner begins the analysis of the second image. The examiner should not try to eliminate the awareness of the details in the first image. It would be extremely cumbersome to try to analyze all standard images with no awareness of the details in the unknown image. While discerning details in the second image, a mental comparison to the details of the first image occurs. The analysis of the second image seems to start a comparison of the details in the two images. The comparison phase has begun, even though the second analysis is still taking place. The extent of analysis needed during this second analysis is considered during the blending of the comparison phase with the analyses. Even while analyzing the second image and then comparing the second image to the first, an evaluation of the analyses and comparison phases begins. The evaluation is blended into the two analyses, which had been blended with the comparison. This happens within all phases of the examination. The blending of phases is most apparent when quickly excluding a source as having made both images when the first-level details are extremely different (Tuthill, 1994; Ashbaugh, 1999).

During the comparison phase, reanalyzing takes place. As critical comparative measurements are made between the two images, the detail is reanalyzed and rescrutinized in consideration of the previous analysis. During the comparison, evaluations begin. During the evaluation phase, reanalyzing and recomparing take place. This is represented in the overlapping of the phases. The examiner needs to critically attend, contemplate, and reflect upon the images while in each phase. Rapid blending of the phases can hinder the reflective pondering needed for reaching the correct understanding and judgments within each phase.

The examiner must seriously apply each independent phase of AACE while scrutinizing the images. This critical application of AACE is represented in the model by the specific locations of the capital A, A, C, and E, away from the black dot of inattention. Critical attention, perception, reflection, and decisions need to take place within these A, A, C, and E locations of the phases of examination.

The larger overlapping circles labeled with lower case letters of a, a, c, and e that encompass the smaller current examination of the AACE circles represent the expertise of the examiner. The expert has more knowledge and beliefs of the process of comparative examination of images than simply the available visual data present in the two images. The current AACE examination happens within the blended phases of previous experiences, understandings, and judgments of the analyses, comparisons, and evaluations (aace) of expertise. That is why the model represents the current AACE examination taking place within the completely overlapping area of the larger expert aace phases of the model.

VERIFICATION

According to the Scientific Working Group on Friction Ridge Analysis, Study and Technology (SWGFAST, 2002), "Verification is the independent examination by another qualified examiner resulting in the same conclusion." Another independent AACE examination of the images that results in the same conclusion as the first examiner's decision results in a verification of the determination. If a differing conclusion is reached, verification does not occur. There are different strategies of conducting a reexamination of the images in a case. The images can be presented to the second examiner with no suggestions of any processing of the images by the original examiner. Or, some indications of evaluation, such as two aligned images on a screen, are provided to the second examiner. Possibly, only one candidate is provided for the reexamination. Maybe two enlarged and charted images are provided by the original examiner. There are many methods of applying the re-examination phase of the original images beyond these examples. The manner applied to seek re-examination by another examiner must be selected so that the second examiner is not improperly influenced or biased by the original examiner's decisions or work products. This second examiner must be able to reach an unbiased conclusion.

JUDGMENTS WITHIN AACE

Figures 6-2 through 6-4 are depictions of the paths taken when judging within AACE. The judgments occur within consideration of the phases of AACE in Figure 6-1. The decision to begin the process must ask questions of the substrate, matrices, distortions, images, details, and the features of the source.

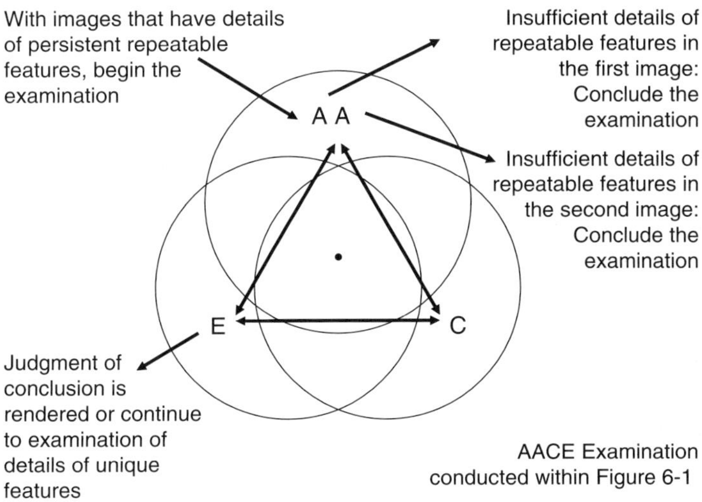

FIGURE 6-2
The AACE model while conducting comparative measurements of details of repeatable features. The AACE examination process takes place within the model in Figure 6-1.

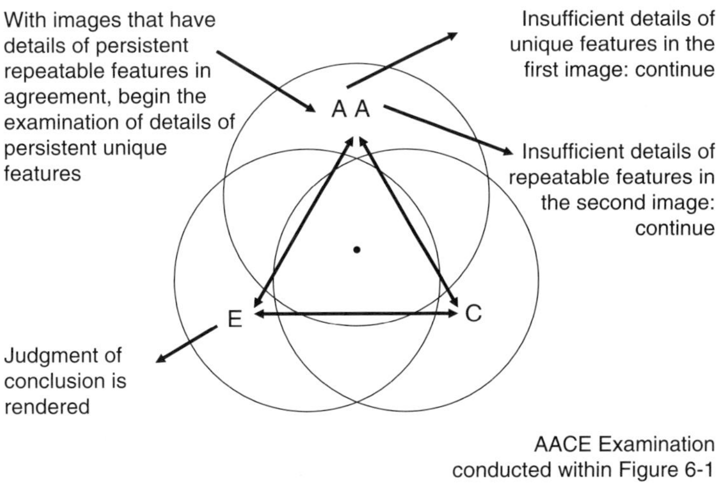

FIGURE 6-3
The AACE model while conducting comparative measurements of details of unique features after the examination of repeatable features. The AACE examination process takes place within the model in Figure 6-1.

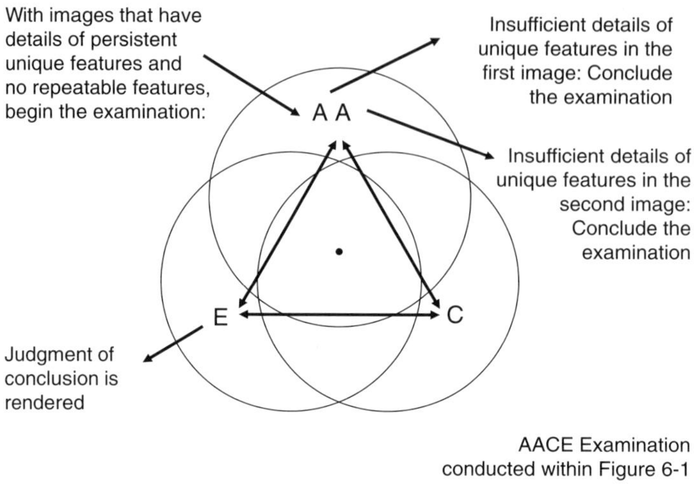

FIGURE 6-4
The AACE model while conducting comparative measurements of details of unique features in which the source does not possess repeatable features. The AACE examination process takes place within the model in Figure 6-1.

The questions that follow in the process are "Are there details of repeatable features?" "Are there details of unique features?" "How persistent are those features?" "Is there sufficient quality and quantity of those details?"

ANALYSIS

Analysis is the assessment of the image details as they appear on the object or an impressed, marked, or striated substrate. The substrate, residues, deposition pressure, motion, distortions, damage, development, or processing technique used, the image capture technique, lighting, and viewing are all considered during the analysis of the each image.

The first image is examined to determine whether its details represent persistent repeatable features or unique features. For images of details that have persistent repeatable features, if the details are obviously insufficient to reach a conclusion, the examination is concluded within the analysis phase. If the details are sufficient, or there is doubt about sufficiency, the details of persistent unique features are examined. The quality and quantity (QQ) within and among the three levels of details are considered in the aggregate to determine the overall assessment of the image. Based on expertise of sources, images, and the substrates that are marked with the images, the examiner determines whether the images are sufficient to warrant continuing to the next phase. If the unknown image is obviously insufficient, the examination ends with a judgment of insufficiency.

If the known or standard image is obviously insufficient, additional standards can be obtained. If there is doubt about the value of either image, the examiner should continue to the comparison phase. This judgment of sufficiency of either image is presented in the right side of Figure 6-5, as only one image is being considered for sufficiency to warrant continuation with the examination. The same quality quantity (QQ) curve as presented in the previous chapter is used as each image must be considered for sufficiency independent of the other current image yet based on the experiences, understandings, and judgments of previous examinations with other images. So in effect, the examiner is actually comparing the image in this analysis to the experienced knowledge of sufficiency of other images in previous trainings, examinations, and collaborations. Not having previously viewed these particular images or their sources, the experience factor with other images helps the examiner judge the merit of whether to continue the examination. At this phase, if the details of an image are insufficient, make the judgment and stop the examination. If in doubt about sufficiency, continue to comparison. If doubt continues in the comparison or evaluation phases, re-analyses can occur. Doubt can be reinforced with inaccurate comparative measurements or dispelled with unbiased and precise measurements in comparisons. The examiner can reverse from the comparison phase to the analysis phase and reanalyze either or both images. The reanalysis must avoid biases and analyze, while continuing to ask and correctly answer all appropriate and relevant questions.

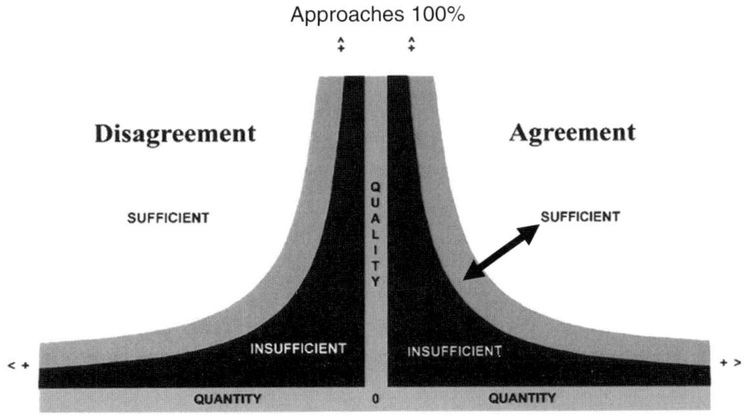

FIGURE 6-5
The black arrows between the gray curve and the white represent examiner doubt about sufficiency or obvious sufficiency. If the image is possibly sufficient or sufficient, the examiner should continue to the next phase of the examination with the option of reverting to this phase.

COMPARISON

Comparative measurements of similarity, sequences, and configurations of the details in the two images take place in the comparison phase. The details within the similar range of levels of clarity are measured, with the understanding that tolerance for variation of appearance must be observed for all comparative measurements. A fixed scale with no variation of measurements within tolerance for distortions is not practical in forensic comparative science.

Comparative measurements of the details of the persistent repeatable features of the source(s) are normally conducted first. The measurements start at the simplest, first-level general directions, shapes, or the broad range of shared groupings or categories of details. If needed, the examiner proceeds to the second level of specific paths of details, and then if possible or needed, proceeds to the third level of textures and edge configurations. If sufficiency of measurable dissimilarities or disagreement of details of persistent repeatable features of the sources is determined, the evaluation of the examination is warranted. If the sufficient measurable details of the persistent repeatable features of the source(s) are in agreement, the examiner proceeds to comparatively measure the details of the unique features of the source(s). The comparative measurements of the details of the unique features start at the simplest, first level of general direction, if possible or needed, proceed to the second level of specific paths, sequences and configurations, and then if possible or needed, proceed to the third-level sequences and configurations of textures and edges. The sequences and configurations of details are all compared. If sufficient measurable disagreement is determined, within tolerance for variation of appearance in images of persistent sources, the evaluation of the examination is warranted. If sufficient measurable agreement is determined, within tolerance for variation of appearance in images of a persistent and unique source, the evaluation of the examination is warranted.

If the comparison results in doubt about the significance of details in the images, such as whether the details actually exist as first analyzed, the examiner can revert back to the analysis phase and reanalyze the images. Caution must be used to not improperly adjust the analyses. All the appropriate and relevant questions must be asked and answered. The examiner must avoid biases from influencing the judgments.

Predictions are made throughout the comparison phase. As the predictions that are determined to be correct become stronger, a reliable prediction is made, and when it is found to be correct and without the irritation of doubt, evaluation is warranted.

EVALUATION

Evaluation is the conclusion of judgment made from the knowledge generated in the analyses and comparison phases of the examination, within the beliefs of the collaborating community of forensic comparative scientists, and the expertise of the examiner.

After analyses, comparisons, and evaluations result in the determination that the details of the repeatable features of the source(s) agree, the details of the unique features of the source(s) are examined. The details of the unique features of the source(s) are analyzed, comparatively measured, and evaluated whether the similarities or differences are sufficient to determine actual agreement or disagreement of details.

With items that only have unique features, such as any natural pattern like volar skin, the issue of details being of repeatable features is disregarded. Categorization, classification, or taxonomy does not require features to have specifically repeated patterns. Determining an impression is within the generality of being a fingerprint is not the same as determining whose fingerprint it is. Since the structures, sequences, and configurations of natural patterns cannot be repeated, there is no purpose in considering a persistent repeatable features conclusion.

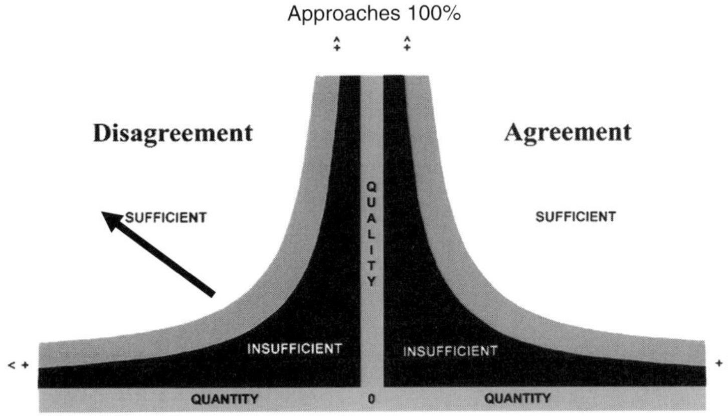

FIGURE 6-6
The examiner determined sufficient disagreement of details between two images of persistent and unique features.

When the determination is made that the details of the features of a unique source disagree, persistency of the features in the source can be established as sufficient, and the examiner is satisfied the source sufficiently recorded its features, an evaluation of exclusion is warranted, as shown in Figure 6-6. If the examiner cannot establish the persistency and sufficient recording of the source, an inconclusive determination is warranted.

Excluding a specific surface of a source as having made the unknown image is not the same as excluding an object as having made that image. The examiner needs to know if the source being excluded can be present on the surface of that object, whether that object is a person, shoe, or tool. Excluding a person is more complete than excluding a person's hand or foot, finger or toe, or specific section of skin. Sufficient complete and clear recordings of sufficient detail on the volar surfaces might be needed to exclude all parts of a person, or a hand, finger, foot, toe, ridges, or a ridge as possessing the surface of the source that made a particular unknown image. When excluding, the examiner must be accurate in describing what is being excluded and not exclude too much.

When the determination is made that details of the features of a persistent unique source agree, an evaluation of individualization of that one source as having made both images is warranted, as shown in Figure 6-7.

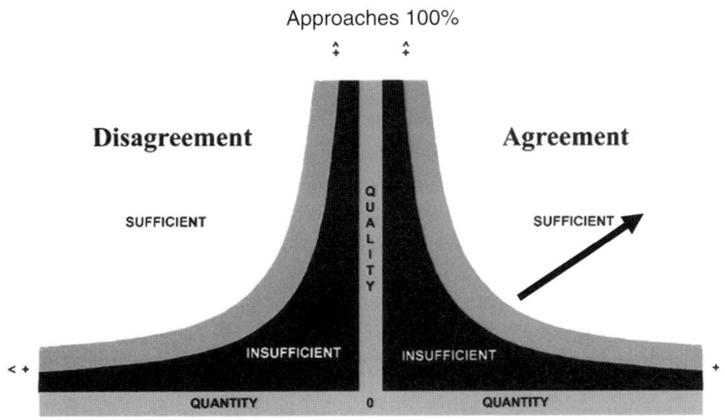

FIGURE 6-7
The examiner determined sufficient agreement of details between two images of persistent and unique features.

If, after analyses and comparisons, no determination of sufficient agreement or disagreement of details can be made, an inconclusive determination is warranted. The details might seem like they could agree, but there is doubt whether they actually do. The details might seem like they could disagree, but there is doubt whether they actually disagree. The examiner cannot determine whether the sequences and configurations of details are

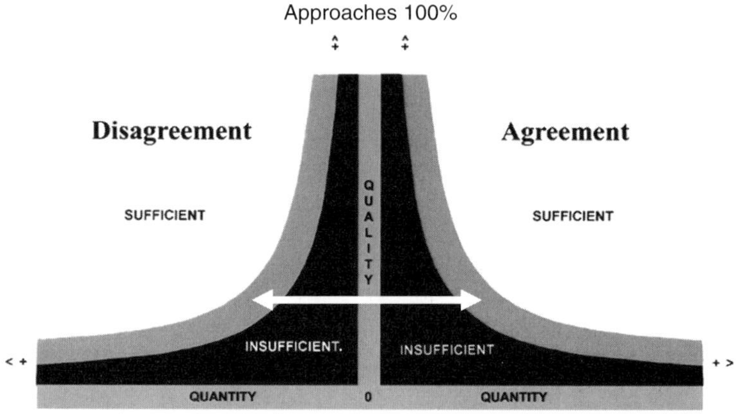

FIGURE 6-8
The examiner determined insufficient agreement or disagreement of details between two images of persistent and unique features. The details might appear similar or dissimilar, but the examiner is unable to judge whether the details actually agree or disagree.

sufficient to decide. This could be due to insufficiency of the unknown image, insufficiency of the known image, inability by the examiner to make a determination, or a combination of any of these factors. The examiner cannot determine which factor is insufficient and defaults to an inconclusive determination. This results in a determination of "no exclusion or individualization was effected." Figure 6-8 represents this judgment.

The judgments of evaluation might result in a conclusion of "no exclusion was effected." In this scenario, the examiner did not determine disagreement with the standard. The examiner is concerned with persistency of the source or the application of the source to the substrate, resulting in many variations in the recordings of details. Disagreement of details of persistent features might actually exist between the two images but the examiner did not find it. The examiner is unwilling to exclude the candidate as the source of the image. Often the source cannot be excluded by the examiner as the source of impressions. The value of the images might be close to the threshold of sufficiency. The examiner was willing to try the examination and did not want to rule either image as insufficient. Figure 6-9 represents this conclusion.

FIGURE 6-9
The examiner did not determine sufficient disagreement of details between two images of persistent and unique features.

Also, depending on the questions the examiner asked, the judgments might result in a conclusion of "no individualization was effected." In this scenario, the examiner did not determine agreement with any of the standards. Agreement might actually exist between the two images, but the examiner did not find it. The examiner is concerned with persistency of the source or recordings of details. The examiner is unwilling to determine the candidate as the source of the image. Often, firearms, tools, shoes, tires, or volar skin cannot be determined as the source of impressions. The value of the images might be close to the threshold of sufficiency. The examiner was willing to try the examination and did not want to rule either image as insufficient. Figure 6-10 represents this conclusion.

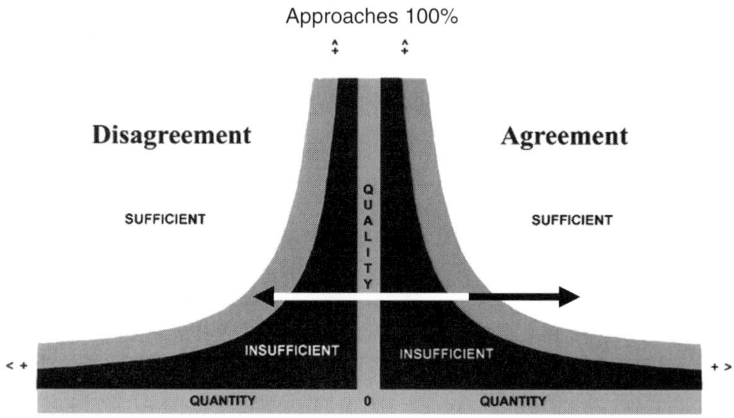

It is possible to have sufficient agreement and sufficient disagreement of details of unique features of the

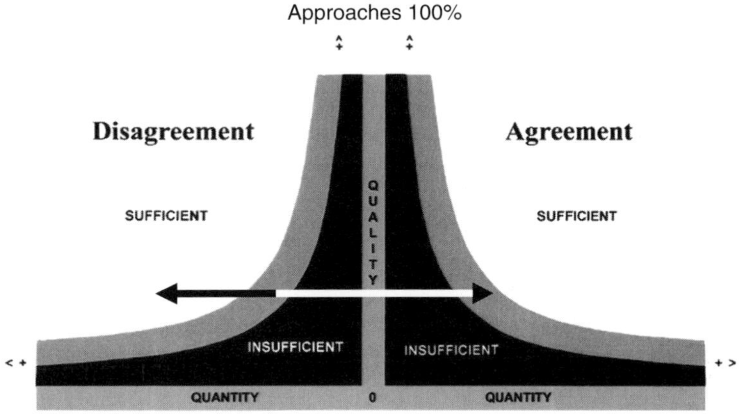

FIGURE 6-10
The examiner did not determine sufficient agreement of details between two images of persistent and unique features.

source. This is possible because of persistency issues with the source. Nothing is perfectly permanent. Skin ages, is damaged, and heals. New scars and imperfections could be generated. Tools and shoes receive wear and damage. The examiner must consider persistency of the source(s) when deciding the significance of the agreement or disagreement and making a judgment whether an object made an impression. Changed sources can generate agreeing and disagreeing details of unique features from the same object. Figure 6-11 represents this scenario. Since actual agreement was determined, even with disagreement elsewhere between the impressions, an individualization judgment occurs.

CONCLUSIONS

During the analyses, if one of the images is determined to be insufficient to warrant a comparison and evaluation between the two images based on experience, understanding, and judgments of similar images, the examination can conclude the process with a determination of insufficiency of that image. If the standard is the insufficient image, additional standards could be sought. After analyses, comparisons, and evaluations within the critical examination process of two images, the following conclusions can be reached after examination of images from persistent sources that sufficiently record details of repeatable and unique features or only unique features.

In this model, the following conclusions correspond to the oscillations below, at, and above the gray thresholds of judgment in the quality quantity curves. These are the various results of the examination of impressions, marks, or objects:

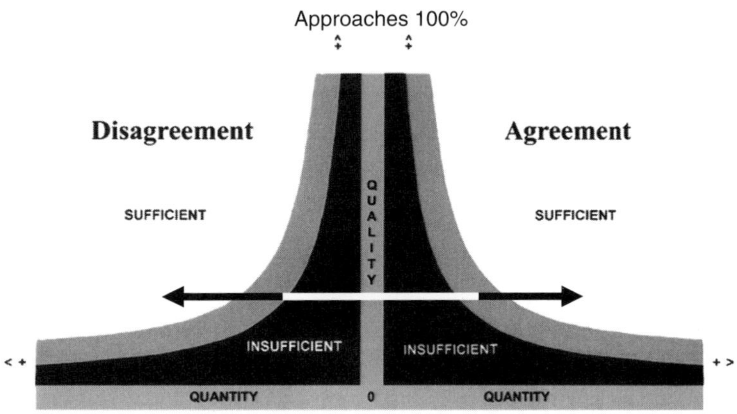

FIGURE 6-11
The examiner determined sufficient agreement and disagreement of details between two images of persistent and unique features. Some features changed on the source possibly due to trauma, wear, aging, or healing.

1. *Exclusion:* The two images have different sources of origin. Actual disagreement of details from persistent repeatable or persistent unique features of different sources has been determined. Do not exclude if persistency cannot be determined or if the recording of details from the source is insufficient.

2. *Inconclusive:* No determination was made whether the two images have different origins. Sufficient disagreement of details of persistent repeatable or persistent unique features was not determined.
3. *Inconclusive:* No determination was made whether the two images have common origin. Sufficient agreement of details of persistent unique features was not determined. If details of persistent repeatable features exist, they agree.
4. *Inconclusive:* No determination was made whether the two images have different or common origin. The examinations that resulted in conclusions 2 or 3 continued. More questions were asked and answers sought. The examiner reconsiders the analyses of the two images. Each of the two images might be sufficient. The examiner tried the examination but was unable to determine sufficient agreement or disagreement of the details of the persistent features of the source(s).
5. *Individualization:* The images share common source of origin. Actual agreement of details from persistent and unique features of the source has been determined.

REFERENCES

Ashbaugh, David R. *Quantitative-Qualitative Friction Ridge Analysis: An Introduction to Basic and Advanced Ridgeology*. CRC Press, Boca Raton, 1999.

Cassidy, Michael J. *Footwear Identification.* Public Relations Branch of the Royal Canadian Mounted Police, Ottawa, Canada, 1980.

Cowger, James F. *Friction Ridge Skin. Comparison and Identification of Fingerprints.* Elsevier, New York, 1983, CRC Press LLC, Boca Raton, Florida, 1993.

Huber, R. A. 'Expert Witness,' *Criminal Law Quarterly*, 1959-60, (2), 276–295.

Huber, R. A. 'The Philosophy of Identification,' *RCMP Gazette* July/August, 1972, 9–14.

Lonergan, Bernard. *Insight: A Study of Human Understanding*. Longmans, Green & Co., London, 1957. Fifth Edition, University of Toronto Press, Toronto, Canada, 2005.

McKasson, Stephen C. and Carol A. Richards. *Speaking as an Expert: A Guide for the Identification Sciences From the Laboratory to the Courtroom*. Charles C Thomas, Springfield, Illinois, 1998.

Palmer, Stephen E. *Vision Science – Photons to Phenomenology*. Massachusetts Institute of Technology, Cambridge, Massachusetts: 1999. Third printing 2002.

SWGFAST, Scientific Working Group on Friction Ridge Analysis, Study and Technology, 'Friction Ridge Examination Methodology for Latent Print Examiners,' *http://www.swgfast.org/Friction_Ridge_Examination_Methodology_for_Latent_Print_Examiners_1.01.pdf, 2002*.

Tuthill, Harold. *Individualization: Principles and Procedures in Criminalistics*, Lightning Powder Company, Salem, Oregon, 1994.

Vanderkolk, John R. 'ACE+V: A Model' *Journal of Forensic Identification* 2004, 54 (1), 45–51.

CHAPTER 7

Fractures, Tears, and Separations

NATURAL AND UNNATURAL FRACTURES AND SEPARATIONS WITHIN NATURAL AND UNNATURAL OBJECTS

Forensic comparative scientists are often faced with the task of determining whether two objects once shared a common origin. The scientist studies the common and unique features of two broken, torn, cut, or separated objects, such as might be found at crime scene, to ascertain whether they were once connected to or parts of one another. After analyses, comparisons, and evaluations, the examiner makes a judgment whether the items had at one time formed a continuous object based on the quality and quantity and levels of clarity of the repeatable and unique features of the objects.

The belief in the law "natural patterns are unique" carries over to the natural alignments and bonds of molecules and cells within objects. Studying the fracture patterns that are generated in natural objects reinforces this belief throughout the forensic comparative science disciplines. As noise is involved in the construction of an object, noise is involved in its destruction. The noisier a separation, the more data for consideration that is usually available.

The best way to start a study of fractures is to examine the generation of natural unique patterns and unnatural repeatable patterns, as was done in Chapter 3, and then begin breaking, tearing, cutting, and separating objects and putting them back together as a practice of puzzle solving in science. Using the process of deductive and inductive logic of breaking known objects and reassembling the correct pieces and excluding the incorrect pieces leads the examiner to the awareness that abductive logic can be used to accomplish case work involving broken, torn, cut, or separated items.

CONTENTS

NATURALLY UNCONTROLLED SEPARATIONS OF NATURAL OBJECTS

Natural objects such as wood, leaves, stones, and soil are unique in their surface and internal structures of patterns of cells and molecules and the bonds that hold them together. As these objects are subjected to sufficient natural or uncontrolled forces, they break apart naturally. Because nature generates unique patterns in creating objects, it must also form unique patterns as it fractures the original objects. Thus, these broken edges and surfaces of natural patterns are unique.

Figures 7-1a–7-3c depict a variety of natural patterns after being broken. These objects were broken or fractured either by myself or by nature, without the use of any type of cutting tool. Since I am part of nature and used only myself or another natural object to apply uncontrolled forces to the original item, the break was a result of nature impacting nature's objects, resulting in naturally broken parts.

Figures 7-1a and b are pictures of a broken wood board. The grain pattern colors reveal unique natural patterns. As I break each piece, the direction and application of the external uncontrolled natural forces cause the bonds between molecules or cells to separate, resulting in a unique break. Each board that I break results in unique natural patterns of separation because I cannot naturally recreate the applications and directions of forces needed to break another piece of wood the exact same way. These unique forces, combined with the unique patterns of cells and molecules and their bonds, result in a unique separation pattern for each board. Notice the wood grain and fractured edges that are in these naturally unique patterns in Figures 7-1a and b.

FIGURE 7-1
(a) and (b) Broken wood board.

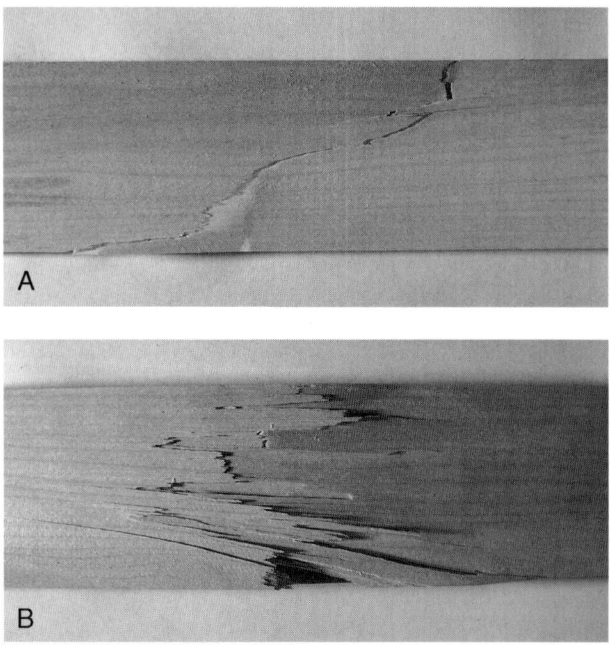

Figures 7-2a and b are leaves taken from one branch of a tree and then torn. The surface dimensions, textures, and colors portray unique natural patterns. Leaves often have symmetry of general form but not symmetry of specific pattern. Examining each leaf in areas that appear to have bilateral symmetry of form reveals that the specific patterns of textures are different. These torn leaves depict naturally unique patterns.

Figures 7-3a and b show a stone broken into two pieces. As I break the stone by prying apart

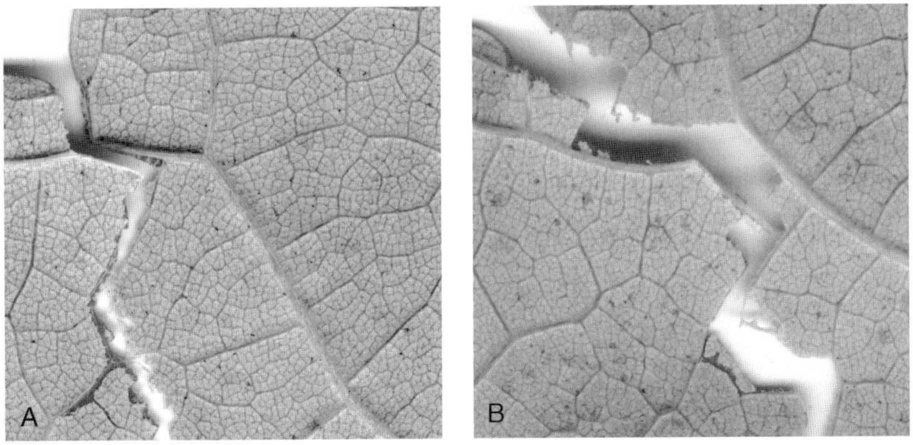

FIGURE 7-2
(a) and (b) Two different torn leaves.

an already present crack, the direction and application of the external natural uncontrolled forces cause the uniquely shaped and bonded molecules to separate. As with the wood and leaves, I cannot naturally recreate the applications and directions of forces needed to break another stone the same. Figures 7-3a and b depict naturally unique patterns of a broken stone, while Figure 7-3c is a cast of one of the separated surfaces of the broken stone next to the interfacing surface from corresponding piece of the original stone. A cast was made of the first piece to represent a negative image of it, becoming an image of the corresponding second piece. The shadows generated from oblique lighting assist

FIGURE 7-3
(a) and (b) Cracked stone with alignment of two pieces. There is more separation in (b) to demonstrate the broken edge with more shadow. (c) Cast of one piece of the stone next to the corresponding surface of the other broken piece.

FIGURE 7-4
(a) and (b) Two examples of drying and cracked soil.

the examiner in determining correspondence. The first stone-cast image is very similar to the second piece of stone.

Figures 7-4a and b are pictures of soil samples in the earth. As each sample of moist soil dries, the external natural uncontrolled forces of moisture leaving the samples result in natural patterns of soil fracture along its weaker bonds in relation to the stresses and pressures of the environment.

UNNATURAL SEPARATIONS OF NATURAL OBJECTS

Unnatural separations of natural objects are caused by human efforts or machines using a controlled cutting device, such as saws, scissors, lasers, or other devices. The separations can be managed by using a specific type of cutting tool and choosing a specific location on the objects and cutting to specific dimensions. The resulting unnatural separations can still be examined based on the remaining features of the newly cut items. Natural objects, such as wood, have visible unique patterns on and within themselves. As humans use some tool to cut or separate these items, the separated surfaces of the side-by-side inner cross-sectional edges might be destroyed, but the remaining surface patterns of the objects might still be sufficient for examination.

Wood can be cut with a saw, making a kerf, or destroyed area of cross section of material. The remaining natural patterns within the wood are visible in the pictures in Figures 7-5a–c. If the cut is not too wide, the natural specific pattern can indicate to the examiner that the wood had been part of the same piece. However, once the cut becomes large enough, resulting in too much kerf, the shapes deviate, resulting in an inability to determine whether the wood shared common origin.

NATURAL SEPARATIONS OF UNNATURAL OBJECTS

Humans design and create unnatural objects, such as sheets of paper, glass, plastic lenses, tapes, and metal tools. These items can have many repeatable features, but they also must have unique features because nature still uses its

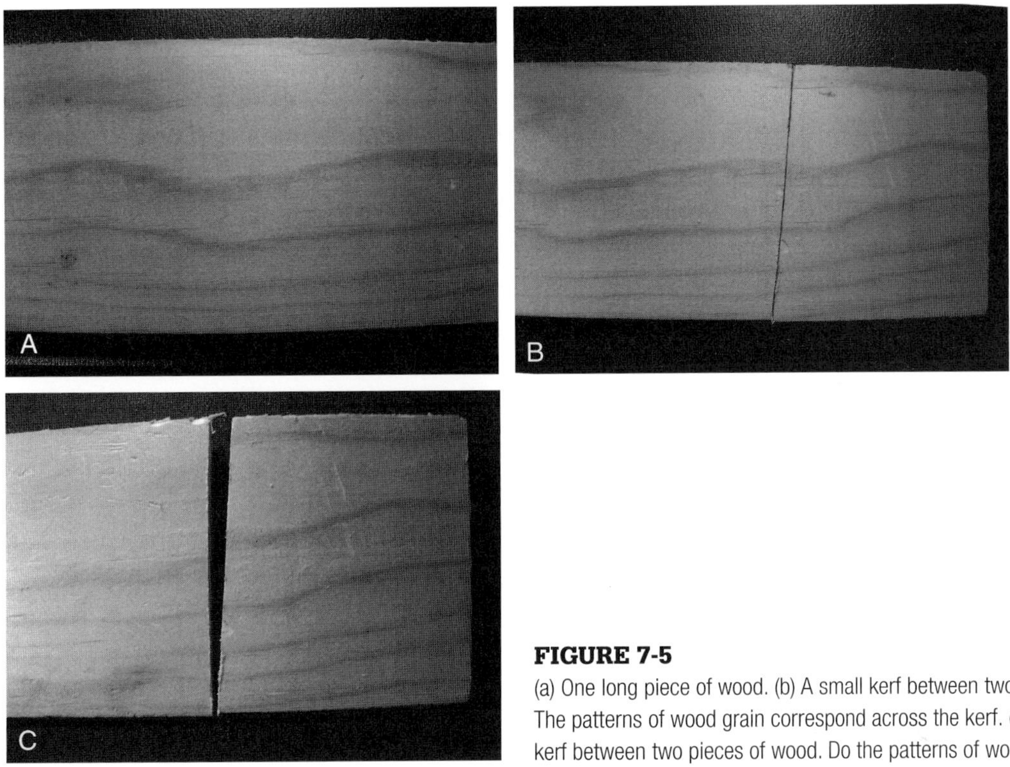

FIGURE 7-5
(a) One long piece of wood. (b) A small kerf between two pieces of wood. The patterns of wood grain correspond across the kerf. (c) A much larger kerf between two pieces of wood. Do the patterns of wood grain agree?

processes of unique pattern formation, even as humans strive to create repetition through mass production. Separations from uncontrolled forces of nature result in naturally unique patterns.

As I naturally tear a piece of paper that has repeatable unnatural features of dimensions, colors, and spacing of lines, I am also tearing apart the bonded paper fibers. The surface of the paper is not smooth because it is composed of many intertwined fibers and components. The surface of a glossy white piece of magazine paper is dramatically presented in Figure 7-6a. There had been no control over the alignments of the individual paper fibers within each section of paper.

The individual fibers and their patterns within paper are unique. Also, an examination of paper sheets reveals the variability in repeatable features, as the spacing of the lines within one pad of paper often do not align. This can be easily determined by flipping through the papers while they are still bound and watching the lined border alignments related to each other and to the edges of paper, as depicted in Figures 7-6b and c. Even the repeatable features vary. For this particular exercise, from one pad of still bonded sheets of lined

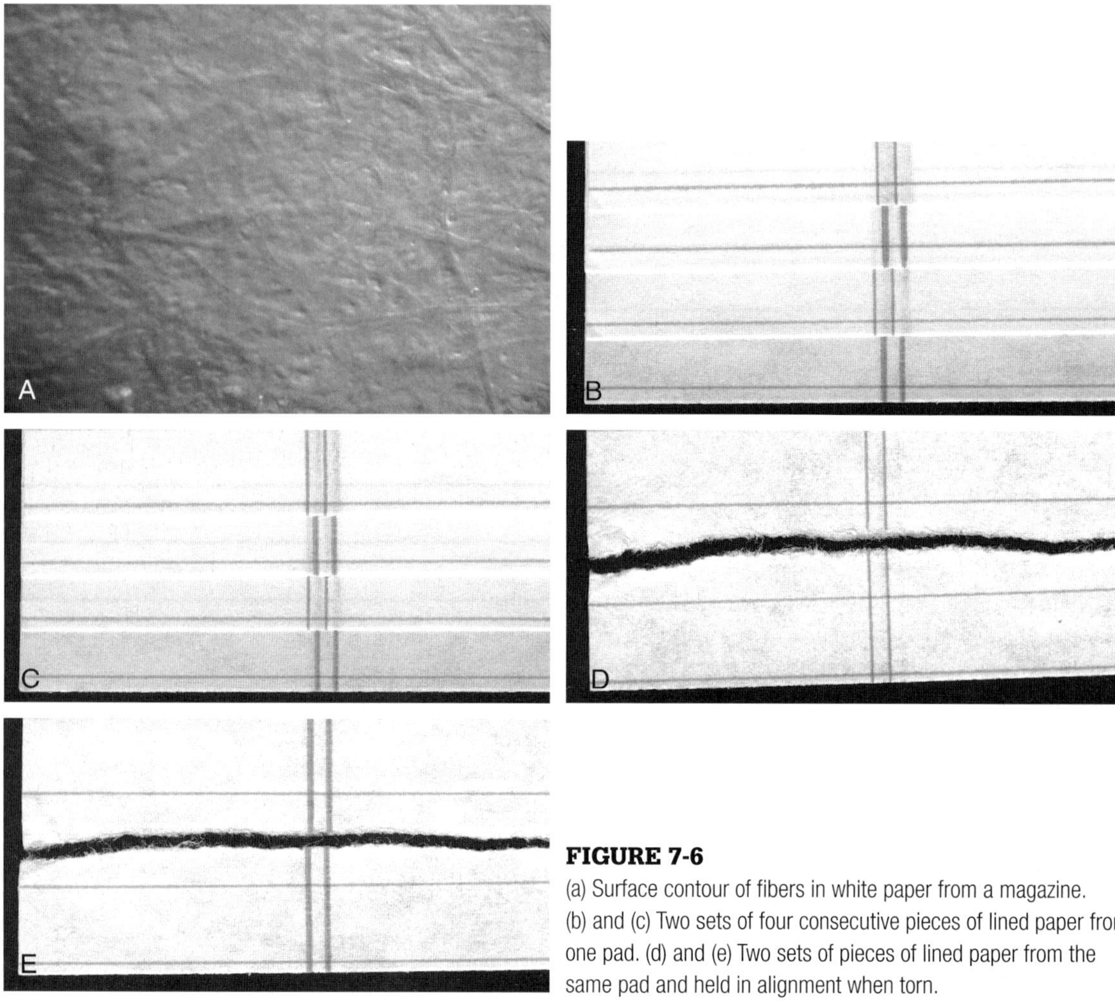

FIGURE 7-6
(a) Surface contour of fibers in white paper from a magazine. (b) and (c) Two sets of four consecutive pieces of lined paper from one pad. (d) and (e) Two sets of pieces of lined paper from the same pad and held in alignment when torn.

paper, I held the top four sheets tightly in alignment as I tore them. I attempted to tear them simultaneously along one path between the lines of the sheets of paper. Surface markings of manufactured inks, both repeatable and unique, are examined in conjunction with the torn edges of paper. As paper is torn, these fibers will separate uniquely as the shapes and alignments of the fibers are unique. Each naturally torn edge of paper will be unique as demonstrated in Figures 7-6d and e.

As I break a sheet of glass, each fractured edge of glass will be uniquely patterned. The manufacturing of glass might result in repeatable dimensions of a sheet of glass. Even these dimensions are within tolerance of acceptability. However, the molecules within the glass are uniquely arranged, thus the naturally broken edges of glass are uniquely patterned. Surface markings, both repeatable and unique, are examined in conjunction with the broken edges. Figures 7-7a and b depict broken glass without the surface markings.

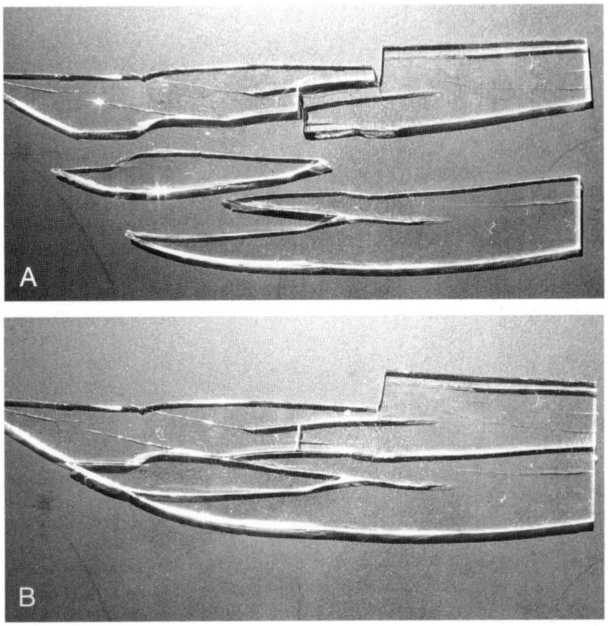

FIGURE 7-7
(a) Broken separated pieces of glass. (b) Broken pieces of glass in corresponding position with other pieces.

A hit-and-run traffic accident may result in a request to determine whether broken pieces of automobile parts found at the scene share a common origin with parts found on a suspect's or victim's vehicle. Often, these parts are broken plastic lenses. The manufacturing of plastic might result in repeatable visible dimensions of a turn signal lens. However, the unique arrangement of molecules within the plastic and the random forces cause the broken edges of plastic to be uniquely patterned. The examiner's early judgments determine whether the manufactured repeatable features are different between the broken pieces. Shapes, colors, dimensions, or designs that are different are very valuable for eliminating the pieces as having been connected. If the repeatable features are similar, an examination continues to the unique breaks. Figures 7-8a–c depict broken plastic.

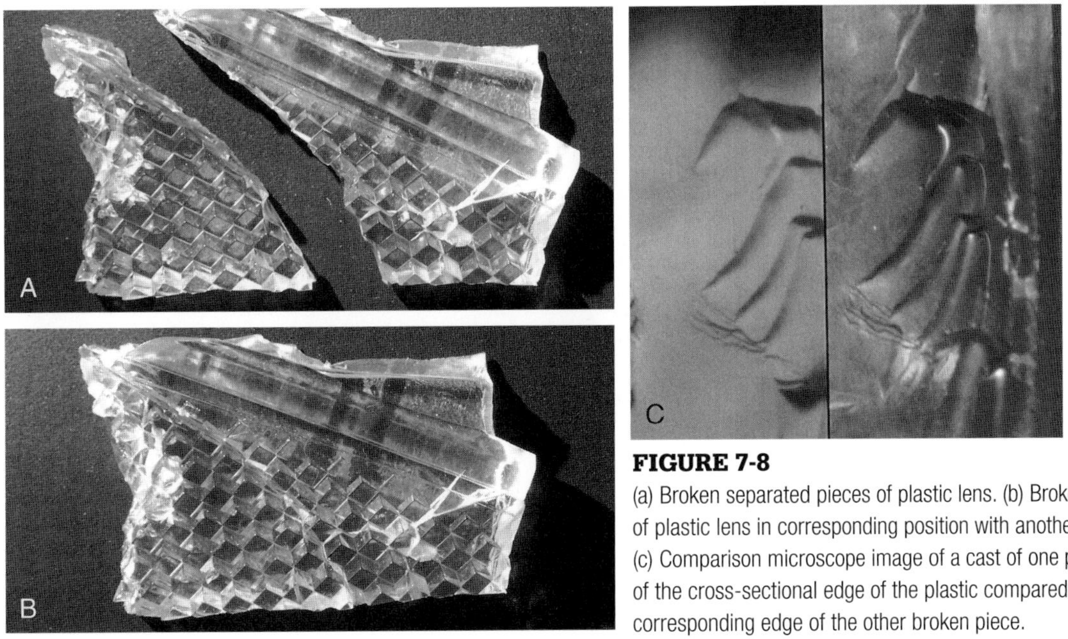

FIGURE 7-8
(a) Broken separated pieces of plastic lens. (b) Broken pieces of plastic lens in corresponding position with another piece. (c) Comparison microscope image of a cast of one piece of the cross-sectional edge of the plastic compared to the corresponding edge of the other broken piece.

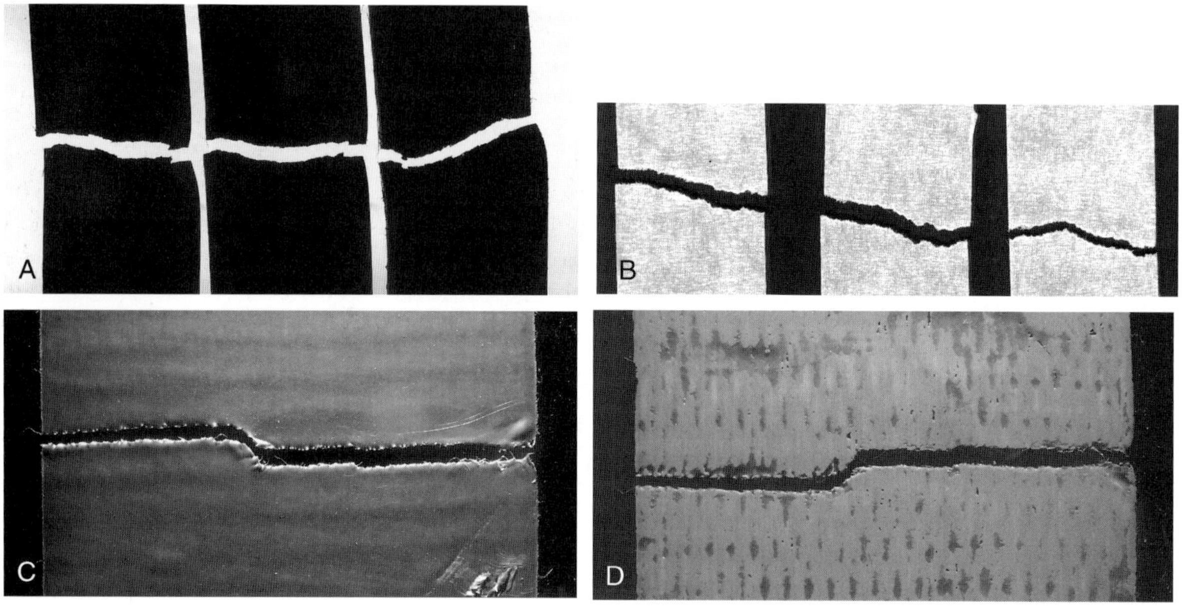

FIGURE 7-9

(a) Torn pieces of black vinyl tape. (b) Torn pieces of tan masking tape. (c) Torn piece of duct tape. (d) Adhesive side of torn piece of duct tape.

In crimes, tape is often used to bind victims, build bombs, or cover packages. Electrical tapes, duct tapes, and masking tapes all have repeatable features within their surfaces, but they also have the unique features within. There are variations within the tapes, especially the variety of patterns of fabric, weave, adhesive, and backing in duct tapes. As I tear these tapes, unique patterns form along the tears. Figures 7-9a–d depict torn tape.

Knives are often used as weapons or tools in crimes. The blade is designed to manufacturing specifications; however, the finished edge of the blade is unique. The tip of the blade might break off during a stabbing of a victim. The naturally uncontrolled forces result in a unique pattern along the cross-sectional edges of a broken metal blade. Random surface marks on the original blade will continue from one side of the fracture to the other. Figures 7-10a and b depict broken metal blade.

UNNATURAL SEPARATIONS OF UNNATURAL OBJECTS

Unnatural separations of unnatural objects are caused by human efforts or machine design using a cutting-type device that is controlled. The use of saws, scissors, lasers, chisels, or other devices can create controlled separations of

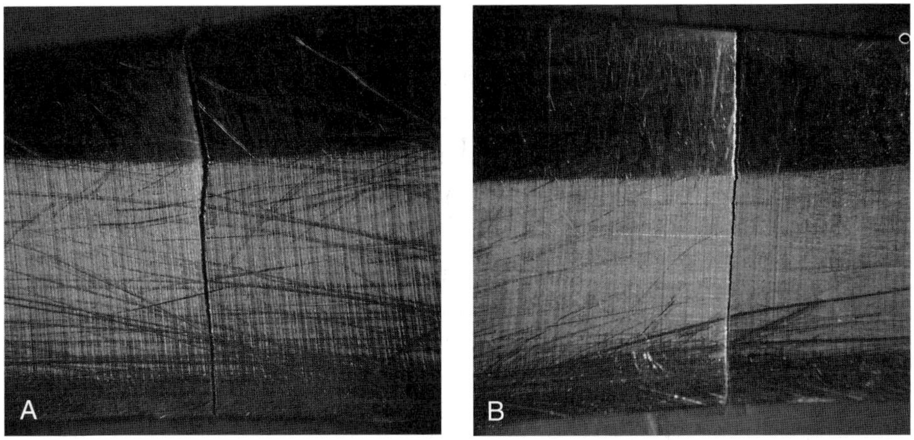

FIGURE 7-10
(a) One side of a broken knife blade and tip. (b) The other side of the broken knife blade and tip from (a).

unnatural objects such tapes, sheets of paper, and plastic bags, which have visible unique or repeatable patterns on their surfaces and unique patterns within themselves. As humans use some tool to cut or separate these items, the separated surfaces of the side-by-side cross-sectional edges might be destroyed, but the remaining surface patterns of the objects might still be sufficient for examination. Controlled unnatural separations normally result in fewer features that are available in the examination process.

As I cut tapes, fewer measurable patterns emerge. It is difficult to determine variability in straight lines. Original surface dimensions and imperfections in the material might carry over from one side to the other side of the cut and contribute to the judgment. Figures 7-11a–c depict cut tape.

A sheet of paper can be cut with scissors. The number and randomness of the cuts contribute to the judgment. The cut separation can be too large, or the width of missing paper varies too much to determine whether the papers share a common origin. Any markings on the surface of the paper are also used in the examination. Handwriting, inks, and colors are some factors studied to determine whether they carry over from one surface to the other. The examination of limited features might result in the inability to determine common origin. Figure 7-12a–d depicts cut paper.

Plastic bags are normally mass-produced with repeatable design features. Many uncontrolled unique features are also present in and on each bag. As one bag is cut or separated from the next bag, the controlled unnatural separation of the bags might not destroy the features needed to determine two bags had at one time been directly connected to and a part of each other or produced as part of the same film of plastic. Figures 7-13a–c depict plastic garbage bags that had once been directly connected to each other. The various uncontrolled unique patterns of pigment variations, the sizes and arrangements of random materials

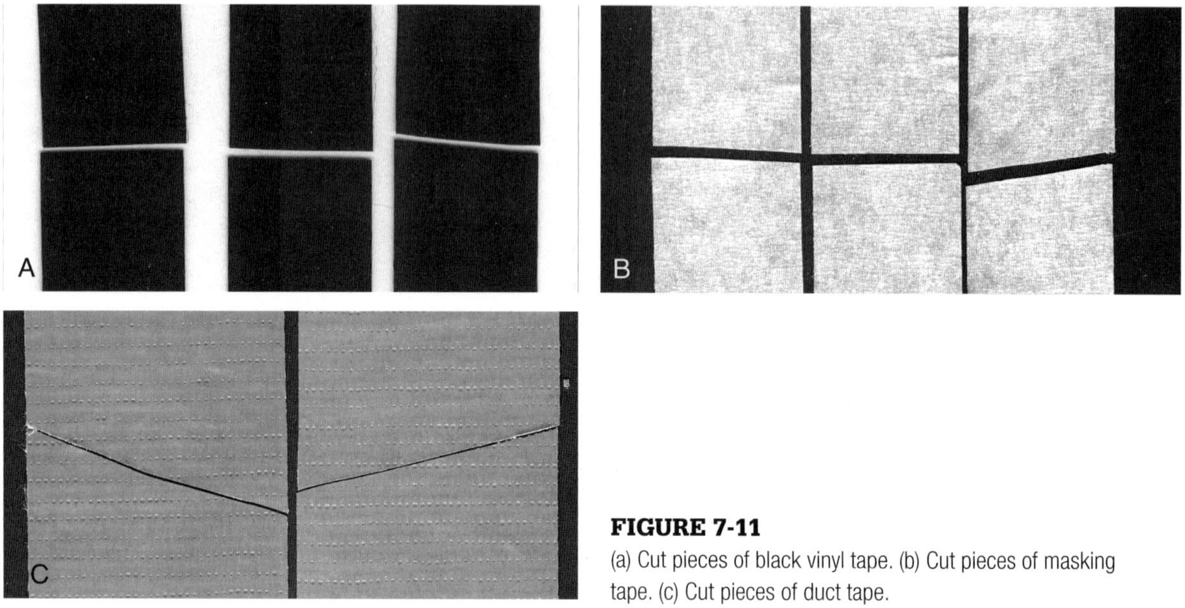

FIGURE 7-11
(a) Cut pieces of black vinyl tape. (b) Cut pieces of masking tape. (c) Cut pieces of duct tape.

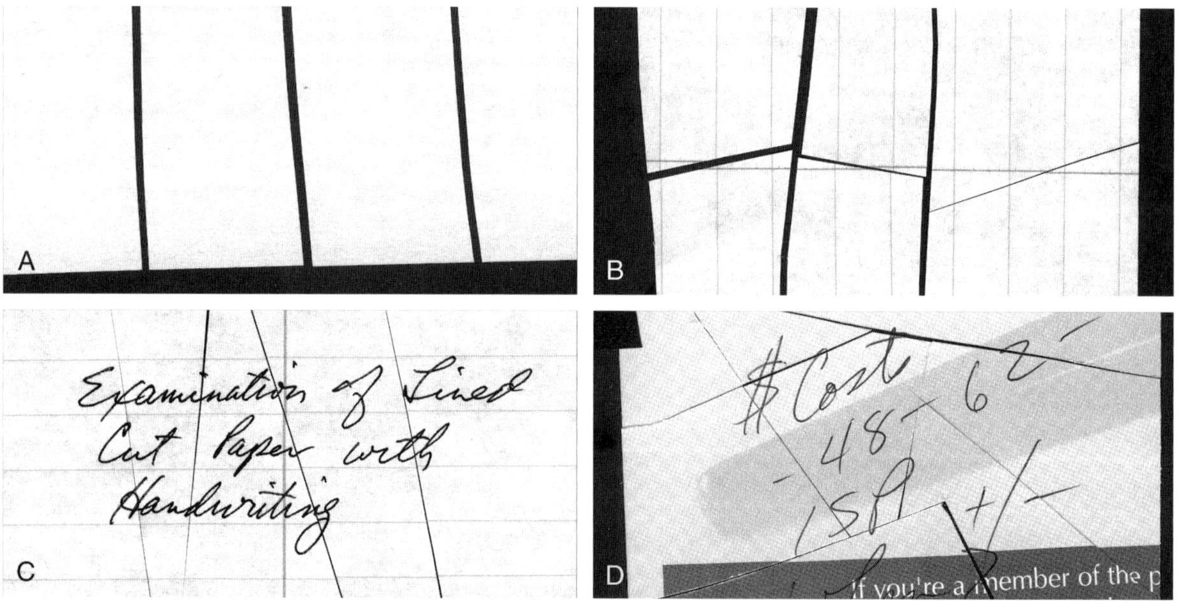

FIGURE 7-12
(a) Cut pieces of white paper. (b) Cut pieces of lined paper. (c) Cut pieces of lined paper with handwriting. (d) Cut pieces of magazine paper with writing and a variety of marks.

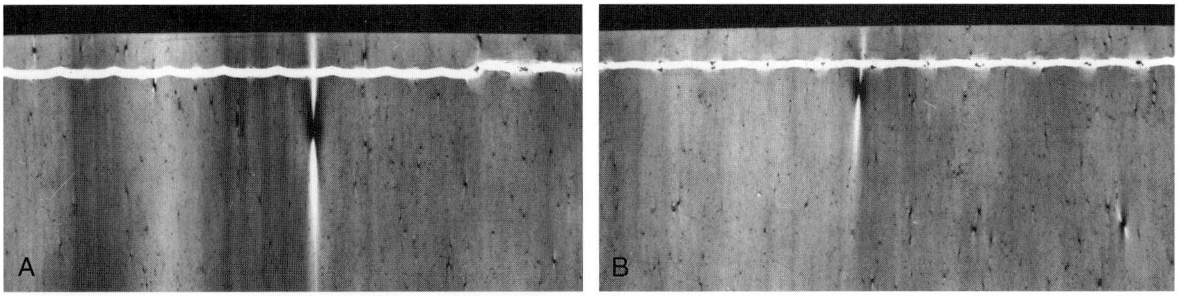

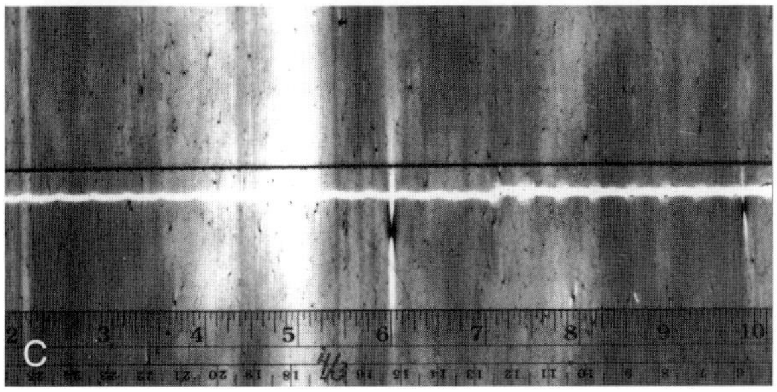

FIGURE 7-13
(a) Light shining through one layer of plastic bag film below the bottom heat seal of one bag and the top of the next bag. (b) A different location on the same bags in (a). Light shining through one layer of plastic bag film below the bottom of one bag and the top of the next bag. (c) Light shining through a wider view of both sheets of plastic film of the same two flattened bags in (a) and (b). The black line is the heat seal at the bottom of one bag. (Courtesy of the *Journal of Forensic Identification*, 1995, 45 (1), 38–50.)

and their associated stretch marks, the stretch marks at the separations at the bonds, all within the repeatable features of tool marks generated during the manufacturing of the plastic bags, enable the examiner to determine that both bags had been directly connected to each other.

THE EXAMINATION

Fractured, torn, cut, or separated items are examined using the process of analyses of items, comparisons of the items to one another, and evaluations of the analyses and comparisons. Levels of clarity are utilized when studying the repeatable features of the items and the unique features of the items. Many lighting, enlarging, and visualization techniques have been presented in this chapter. For repeatable features, first-level general design, second-level specific paths of structures, and third-level textures along the paths and surfaces of structures are scrutinized to determine similarity or dissimilarity between the two items. If sufficient agreement is found in the repeatable features, and the items cannot be excluded as having once been connected to and a part of one another through any differences of manufactured designed structures, the unique features of the items are then examined.

The unique features are also analyzed, compared, and evaluated on the outer surfaces and inner cross-section edge surfaces of the items. For the unique features of the items, first-level general shape, second-level specific paths, and third-level textures along the paths and surfaces of natural structure are scrutinized to determine similarity or dissimilarity between the two items.

A visual examination of the juxtaposed pieces can be supplemented by a tactile examination. The feel that is generated when two pieces of broken substance such as metal or plastic interlock in place significantly emphasizes the correspondence of the formerly connected surfaces. The feel of fitting and locking pieces is part of the examination processing of rigid broken pieces. Soft material can be easily damaged during a fracture examination when forced to conform to the other piece. Examiners must realize the importance of experience with materials when examining a wide variety of evidence.

The persistency of the features must be considered when determining a conclusion of the examination. The condition of the surfaces can deteriorate through additional use, abuse, wear, or decomposition. If the edges and surfaces have worn further and are additionally damaged, the examiner usually cannot determine whether this condition is a result of additional damage or the pieces had actually originated from different sources. These variations do not warrant a determination that the two pieces had not been directly connected. After tearing pieces of paper, I added more damage to their edges by rubbing the edges with my fingers. I exposed the edges to high humidity. Figures 7-14a and b depict the original tear and then the damaged edges. These papers had been directly connected, but the damage has changed the second- and third-level details to the extent that a determination of common origin is not possible, but exclusion would be incorrect. An inconclusive finding is the only alternative.

FIGURE 7-14
(a) Two pieces of torn paper. (b) The same two pieces of torn paper in (a) after additional damage inflicted upon the two pieces.

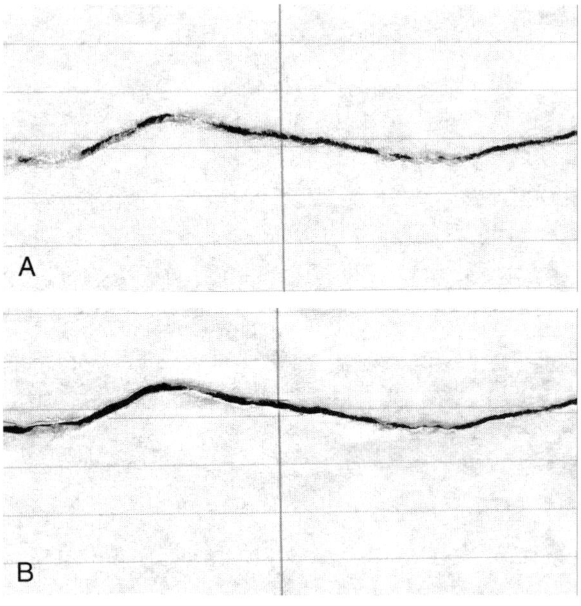

There will never be a perfect fit of two items. Once an object is separated into two items, it can never be perfectly returned to the original nature of the original object. There must always be variations in appearances between the two items; hence, judgment is part of the examination. The determination of common origin must be supported by sufficient quality and quantity of agreement of repeatable and unique features of the items.

CONCLUSIONS

This chapter emphasizes the unique natural patterns in all objects, whether the objects and their patterns are formed by nature or by human-designed manufacturing processes. The resulting natural patterns of components of atoms, molecules, and cells, within all objects, are not controlled in their arrangements. No matter how an object is broken, cut, or separated, its resulting parts can be examined to determine whether they had once been connected to and a part of each other. With insufficient information, this examination could result in an inconclusive determination. I chose to have this as the first chapter of specific types of examinations. As the examiner studies fractures, and original whole objects, he or she will become aware of the actual uniqueness around us. Breaking objects can teach us so much about uniqueness.

The separated objects in this chapter represent a limited number of the vast quantity of objects in the universe that can be examined to determine whether they had once been connected to and a part of each other. The discussion here indicates the simplicity of understanding and explaining the process of forensic comparative examination of broken, torn, cut, or separated objects.

No matter the natural object, fractures or separations caused by the uncontrolled forces of nature will result in unique patterns. Likewise, no matter the unnatural object, fractures or separations caused by the uncontrolled forces of nature will result in unique patterns. Unnaturally separated natural or unnatural items can also be examined for common origin. As long as the edges and surfaces of the pieces placed in juxtaposition are sufficiently preserved between the fracturing and the examination, and if sufficient quality and quantity of first, second, and third levels of both repeatable and unique features are present and observable in the two items, the examiner should be able to reach a conclusion, as expressed in Chapter 6.

BIBLIOGRAPHY

'A Crime Scene Manual for the Identification Specialist,' Canadian Police College, March 1986, 75–86, 150–155.

Agron, Nicki and Bernie Schecter. 'Physical Comparison and Some Characteristics of Electrical Tape,' *AFTE Journal*, 1986, 18 (3), 53–59.

Barton, B. C. 'The use of an electrostatic detection apparatus to demonstrate the matching of torn paper edges,' *Journal of the Forensic Science Society*, 1989, 29 (1), 35–38.

Berx, Veerle and Jan De Kinder. '3D Measurements on Extrusion Marks in Plastic Bags,' *Journal of Forensic Sciences*, 2002, 47 (5), 976–985.

Dixon, Kent C. 'Positive Identification of Torn Burnt Matches with Emphasis on Crosscut and Torn Fiber Comparisons', *Journal of Forensic Sciences*, 1983, 28 (2), 351–359.

Ford, K. N. 'The Physical Comparison of Polythene Film,' *Journal of the Forensic Science Society*, 1975, V.15, 107–113.

Gerhart, F. James, and Dennis C. Ward. 'Paper Match Comparison by Submersion,' *Journal of Forensic Sciences*, 1986, 31 (4), 1450–1454.

Kirk, Paul L. *Crime Investigation – Physical Evidence and the Police Laboratory*, Interscience Publishers, Inc. a division of John Wiley & Sons, Inc. New York, 1953, 116–121, 232–243, 257–262, 269–271, 676–679.

Kirk, Paul L. edited by John I. Thornton. *Crime Investigation: Second Edition*, John Wiley & Sons, New York, 1974, 12, 13, 246–247, 261–266, 316.

Kopec R. J., and C. R. Meyers. 'Comparative Analysis of Trash Bags—A Case History,' *AFTE Journal*, 1980, 12 (1), 23–25.

McKinstry, Edward A. 'Fracture Match—A Case Study,' *AFTE Journal*, 1998, 30 (2), 343–344.

Mishoe, David C. 'Identification of a Suspect by Skin Fragment: Comparison of Shape, Size, and Ridge Flow,' *Journal of Forensic Identification*, 1993, 43 (3), 234–239.

Moenssens, Andre A., Carol E. Henderson and Sharon G. Portwood. *Scientific Evidence in Civil and Criminal Cases – Fifth Edition*. Foundation Press, New York, 2007, 496–497, 757–758,

O'Hara Charles E. and James W. Osterburg. *An Introduction to Criminalistics – The Application of the Physical Sciences to the Detection of Crime.* The Macmillan Company, New York, 1949 fourth printing 1960, 227–228, 290–291, 294, 301–302.

Osterburg, James W. *The Crime Laboratory – Case Studies of Scientific Criminal Investigation* Clark Boardman Company, Ltd. New York, 1982, 13, 14, 54, 55, 58–61, 68, 69, 107–109, 115–133, 140–143.

Pierce, D. S. 'Identifiable Markings on Plastics,' *Journal of Forensic Identification*, 1990, 40 (2), 51–59.

Shor, Yaron, and Robert B. Kennedy, Tsadok Tsach, Nikolai Volkov, Yehuda Novoselsky, and Asya Vinokurov. 'Physical Match: Insole and Shoe,' *Journal of Forensic Sciences*, 2003, 48 (4), 808–810.

Stanko, Richard F. and David W. Attenberger. 'The Evidentiary Value of Plastic Bags,' *FBI Law Enforcement Bulletin* June 1992, 11–13.

Thornton, John I. 'Fractal Surfaces as Models of Physical Matches,' *Journal of Forensic Sciences*, 1986, 31 (4), 1435–1438.

Vanderkolk, John R. 'Identifying Consecutively Made Garbage Bags Through Manufactured Characteristics,' *Journal of Forensic Identification*, 1995, 45 (1), 38–50.

von Bremen, Ulf G. and Lorne K. R. Blunt. 'Physical Comparison of Plastic Garbage Bags and Sandwich Bags,' *Journal of Forensic Sciences*, 1983, 28 (3), 644–654.

Zugibe, Frederick T. and James T. Costello. 'The Jigsaw Puzzle Identification of a Hit-and-Run Automobile,' *Journal of Forensic Sciences*, 1986, 31 (1), 329–332.

Tools and Guns

CONTENTS

TOOLS

Any object that is capable of having a mechanical advantage over another object can be considered a tool. The sufficient contact of a tool on a softer object can leave its markings, impressions, or images on the surface of that other object. These markings can be impressed, striated, or a combination of both.

Studying the surfaces of tools and the receiving substrates assists the examiner in the process of determining whether the known tool made the questioned mark. The manufacturing processes of screwdrivers, pry bars, wire cutters, scissors, hammers, knives, guns, or other tools often produce blades, surfaces, or edges that bear repeatable features such as size and shape that result from design specifications of mass production. Unintended variations in the tool used in forming an object can produce repeatable features in that object. However, the finishing processes used on the edges or surfaces of the tools, blades or jaws, produce unique microscopic variations in the edged surfaces of each tool. No two screwdrivers, pry bars, guns, or bolt cutters are microscopically alike. Likewise, edges or surfaces of all finished metal tools, even consecutively manufactured tools and guns, are microscopically different.

Figures 8-1a–h show the surfaces of screwdriver tips, wire cutters, a knife, and a razor blade. The features along the length of each surface vary. The features at similar locations along each surface vary. Also, one side of each blade varies from the other side of the same blade.

TOOL MARKS

If a screwdriver had been used to pry open a victim's window and striae remain in the metal frame, the screwdriver needs to be examined before its surface is damaged. The correct screwdriver can be found and examined, but if the

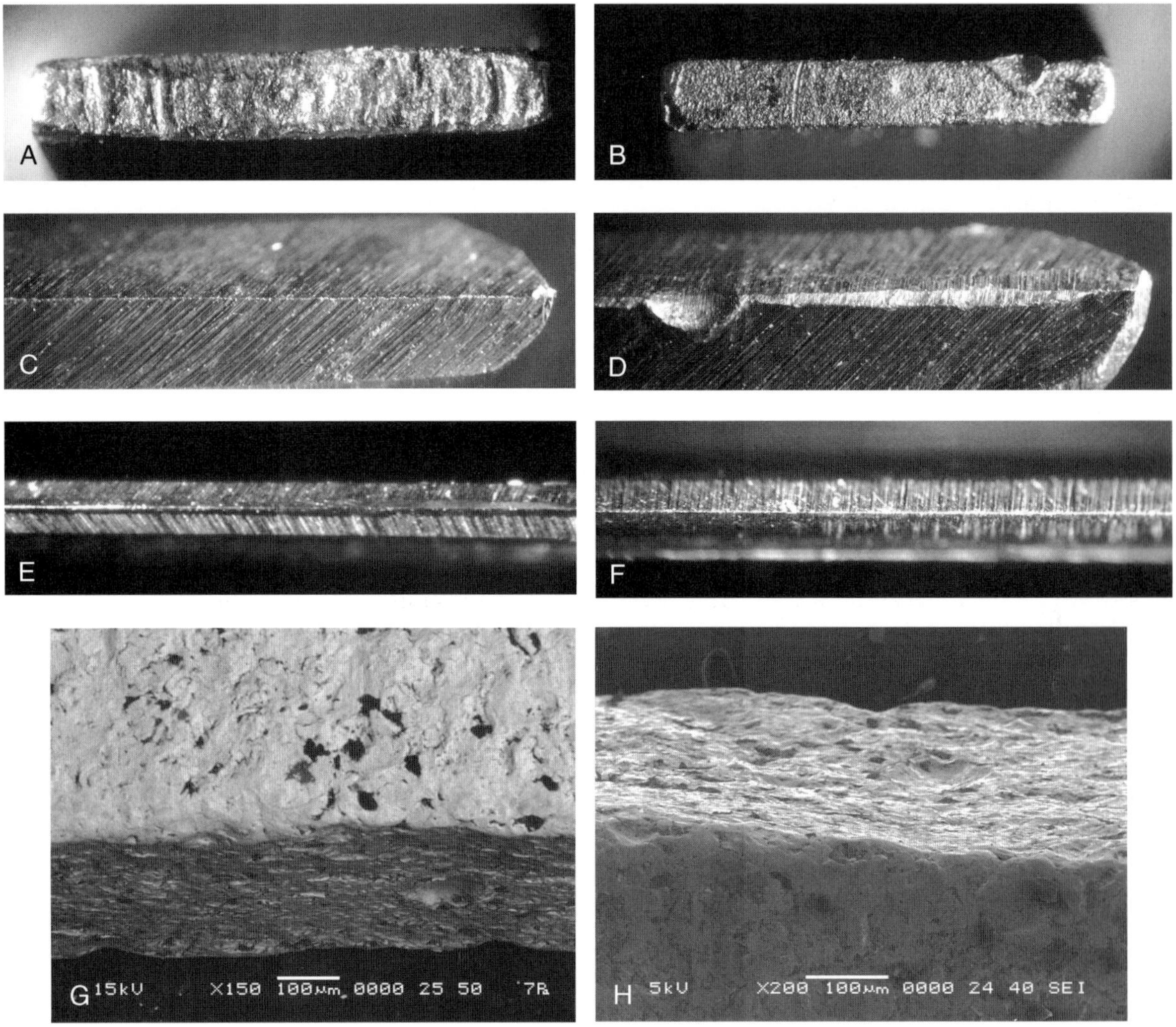

FIGURE 8-1
(a) and (b) Screwdriver blades. (c) and (d) Wire cutter jaws. (e) Knife blade. (f) Razor blade. (g) and (h) Scanning electron images of a screwdriver blade. ([g] and [h] provided by Damon Lettich, Indiana State Police Laboratory.)

surface that had been the source of the striae is sufficiently destroyed through use, abuse, or environmental wear, the resulting striae produced by the screwdriver will not correspond to the questioned tool mark, even though it is the same screwdriver.

Many marks from tools are presented in the figures in this chapter. The features of the tool can be recorded as first-, second-, and third-level details in the impressions. For repeatable features of a screwdriver, the first-level details indicate the general manufactured design of the specific blade. Second-level details are the recorded dimensions of the component, and third-level details indicate the designed contours and textures within the manufactured dimensions of that piece. The unintended repeatable features, often called subclass characteristics, can record first-, second-, and third-level clarity like the intended repeatable features. Once a feature is repeatable, it does not make a difference whether it was intentional or not.

The unique features of the tool can be recorded as first-, second-, and third-level details. For the unique features, the first-level details indicate the general appearance and locations of the unique imperfections. Second-level details record the paths and dimensions of the uniqueness, and third-level details are the contours and textures within the paths and dimensions. The levels of clarity for the repeatable and unique features are distinct.

I will use screwdriver marks as the primary images to show striae patterns generated from tools as the example of screwdriver marks in aluminum carries over to any other tool mark in any other substrate. Many screwdriver striae marks are depicted in the following figures to demonstrate the variation of appearances caused by (1) the application of the tool to a wide range of substrates and (2) the critical lighting involved in viewing the original marks or their casts. Usually the tool marks at crime scenes are captured with a silicone rubber–type casting material. These casts will depict a negative impression of the original mark. When conducting tool mark examinations of known tools, the standard marks from the known tools are normally recovered with a similar casting method. Thus, negative impressions are compared to negative impressions. Figures 8-2a and b depict casts of striated tool marks made by the same source, and Figures 8-3a and b depict casts of striated tool marks made by different sources.

Figures 8-4a–d show sections from one continuous sliding application of a screwdriver blade to aluminum foil. The angle of applying the blade to the aluminum foil varies from oblique to almost perpendicular while striving to maintain a similar pressure of applying the tool to the foil. As the microscopic contour of each side of the blade varies throughout its edges, the resulting striae pattern varies throughout the length of the tool mark. The beginning of the tool mark is somewhat different than the end of the tool mark, even though the same side of the blade made the one continuous impression. This represents the variability within one tool.

Another screwdriver mark is depicted in Figures 8-5a–d. This mark is also a continuous mark in which I attempted to maintain an approximate 45-degree angle of application, so the same position of the blade of the tool made the mark throughout the length of the striae pattern. However, starting with heavy pressure and slowly lessening the pressure results in variations of appearances in striae patterns from the same blade.

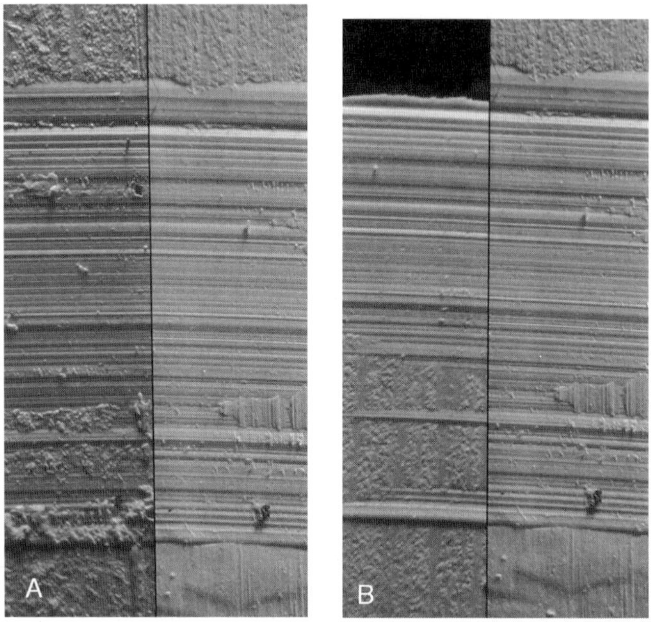

FIGURE 8-2
(a) and (b) Casts of screwdriver marks viewed under the comparison microscope. These marks were made by the same blade.

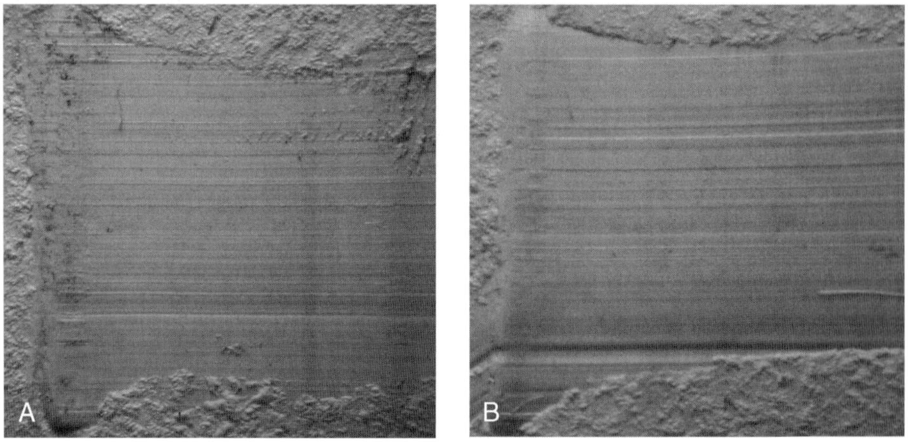

FIGURE 8-3
(a) and (b) Casts of screwdriver marks viewed under the comparison microscope. These marks were made by different blades.

A third screwdriver mark is shown in Figures 8-6a–d. These are the same tool marks but viewed using different lighting techniques. By changing the applications or directions of light, the mark appears differently. This emphasizes the need to use similar lighting for the examination of the questioned and standard tool marks. Variation caused by different lighting will also result in images of tool marks from the same source that vary in appearances. This emphasizes vision starts with the light.

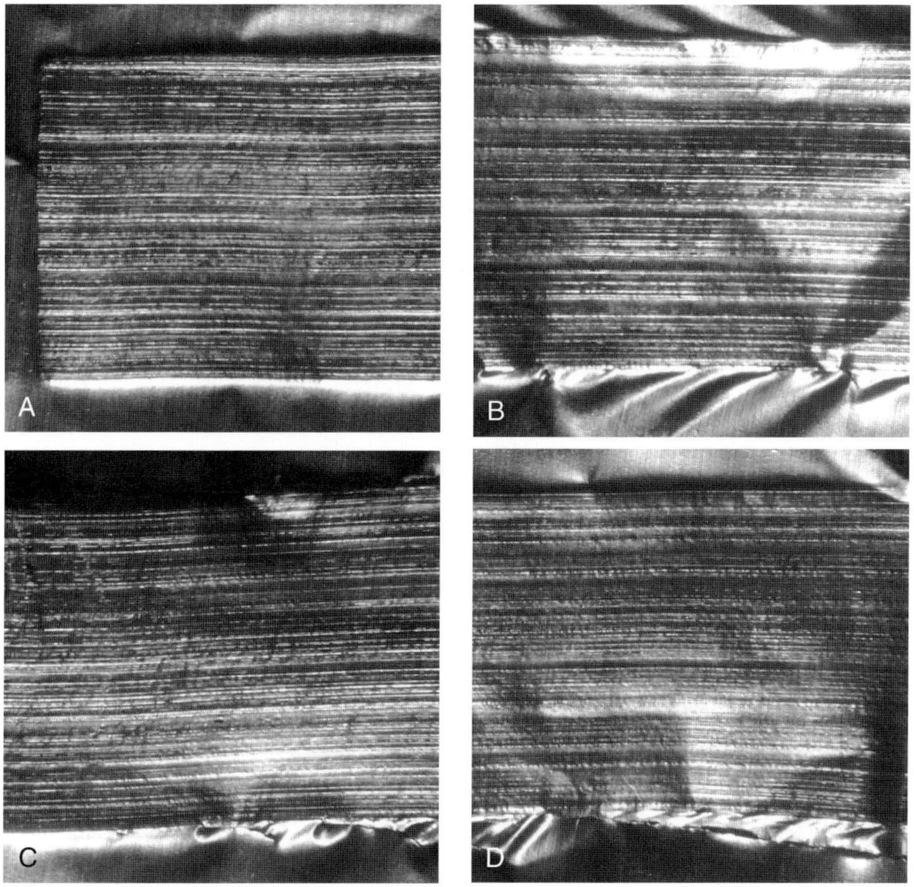

FIGURE 8-4
(a)–(d) Sections of one continuous application of a screwdriver blade to aluminum foil while varying the application from oblique to almost perpendicular.

Figures 8-7a–d show the same screwdriver mark with the same lighting, but there is a slight change to the angle of the striated foil as it is held in the stage or tray below the objective lens of the microscope. Changing the angle of the substrate bearing the mark varies the appearance of the striae patterns. The angle of presentation will vary the appearances of the widths of the striae and the reflected light. It is not possible to perfectly align two different tool marks from the same source, under two objectives of the forensic comparison microscope, using exactly the same lighting. There will always be variations in the appearances of two tool marks from the same source.

Many applications of the same screwdriver blade to different substrates generate variations of appearances because the receiving substrate will not accept the tool markings in the same way. Different pressures are involved in leaving a sufficient mark. Different substrates will have different amounts of materials

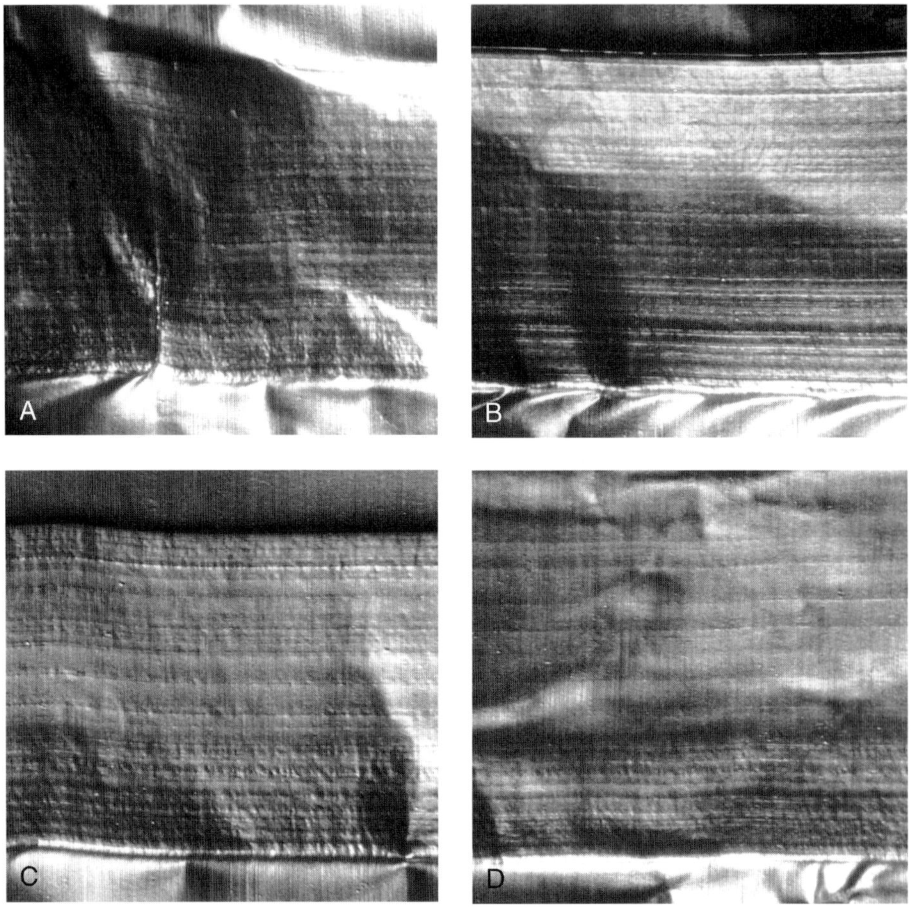

FIGURE 8-5
(a)–(d) Sections of one continuous application of a screwdriver blade to aluminum foil while varying the application from heavy to light pressure.

that are crushed or gouged out. Figures 8-8a–d represent these variations. Even though the substrate varies, sufficiency might still exist between the two marks to determine that the striae had been produced by the same tool.

Figures 8-9a and b show a set of screwdriver marks as viewed through the comparison microscope. The image on the left represents the unknown mark, and the image on the right represents the known standard mark. The marks in these figures were made by the same screwdriver blade. However, I lightly applied a sander to the blade between markings, simulating the use and abuse that might occur to a tool during many applications. The wear on the surface of the edge of the blade produced different uniqueness. The sources of the marks changed through use or abuse of the blade, even though the same side of the same blade made the marks.

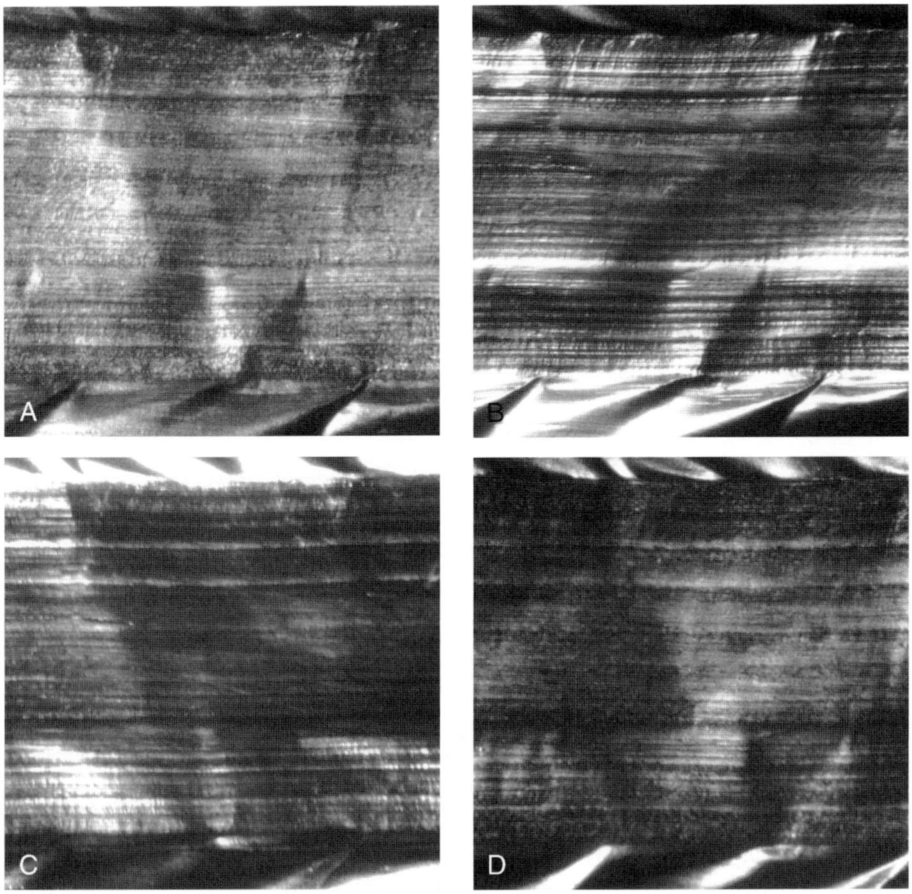

FIGURE 8-6
(a)–(d) The same tool mark with different applications of light.

Figures 8-10a–d depict the striae patterns generated from different screwdriver blades possessing similar manufactured dimensions. Although the dimensions are similar, the striae patterns generated within are unique to the specific source.

Figures 8-11a–d show striae patterns from the same edge of a screwdriver blade as viewed through the comparison microscope. The challenge of determining sufficiency of agreement of striae patterns is evident here. Differing quality and quantity of details are presented in these pictures that demonstrate the variation of appearances in tool marks from the same source. Figures 8-12a–c are casts of the striae generated from two applications of the jaws of the same wire cutter in lead. These figures show the correspondence of tool marks generated from the same wire cutter. These striae, like other

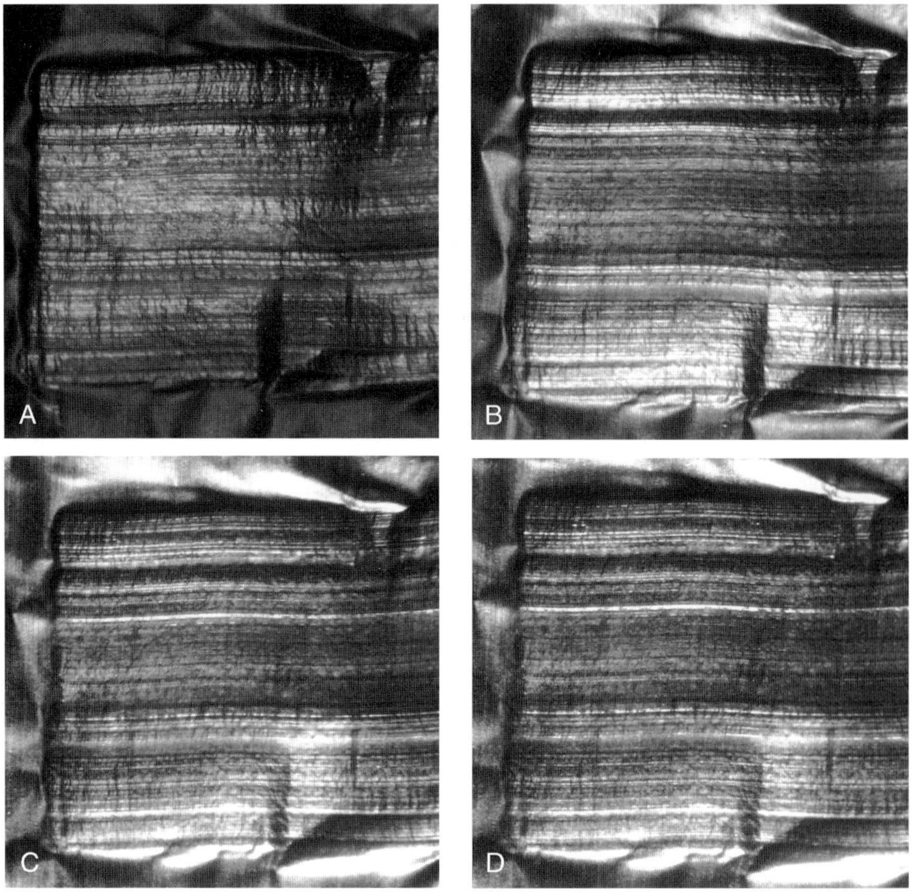

FIGURE 8-7
(a)–(d) One tool mark with its angled position adjusted under the lens of the microscope.

tool marks, do not repeat in their patterns generated from any other part of any wire cutter. All the same reasons for variations in appearances of striated screwdriver marks carry over to variations in appearances of cutting marks and any other tool markings.

First-, second-, and third-level details of unique features of a screwdriver are shown in the images of marks in Figures 8-13a–c. These images were captured by a profilometer with a confocale detector, measuring the three-dimensional microscan profiles of striations at nanofocus. First-level general direction, second-level paths and widths of striae, and third-level depths, angles, and relative textures of sequences and configurations are captured with this technology.

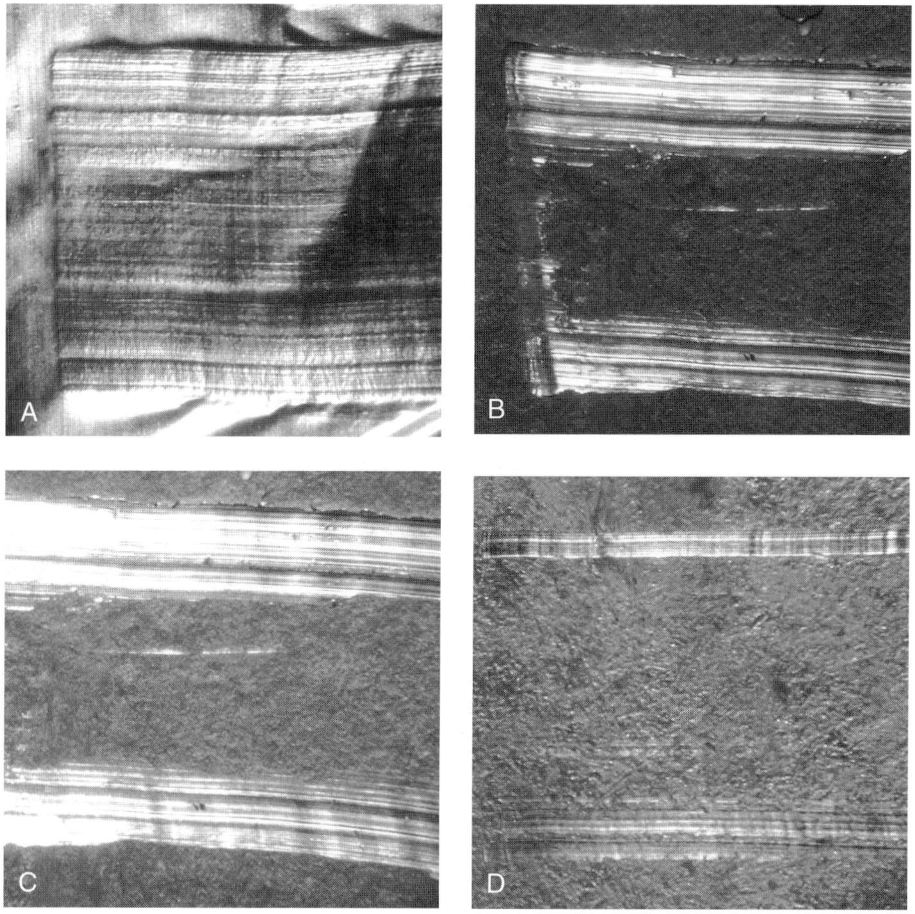

FIGURE 8-8
(a)–(d) One tool making marks in four different substrates.

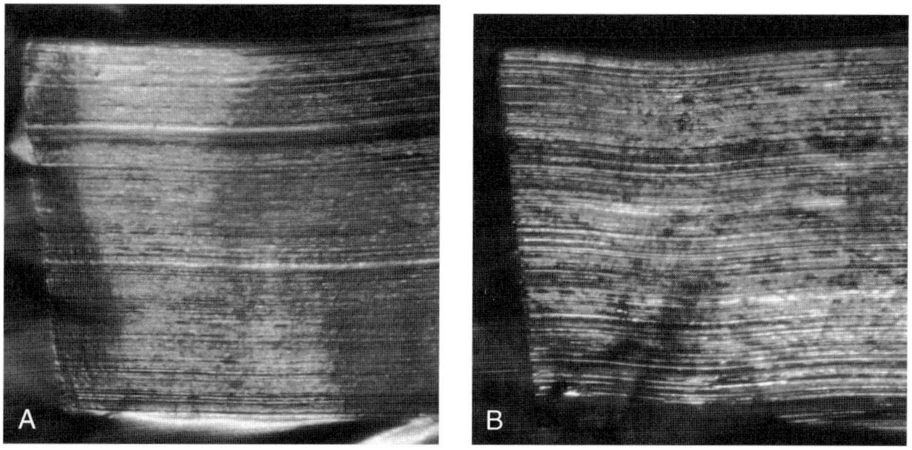

FIGURE 8-9
(a) and (b) Tool marks after applying a sander to the blade between markings.

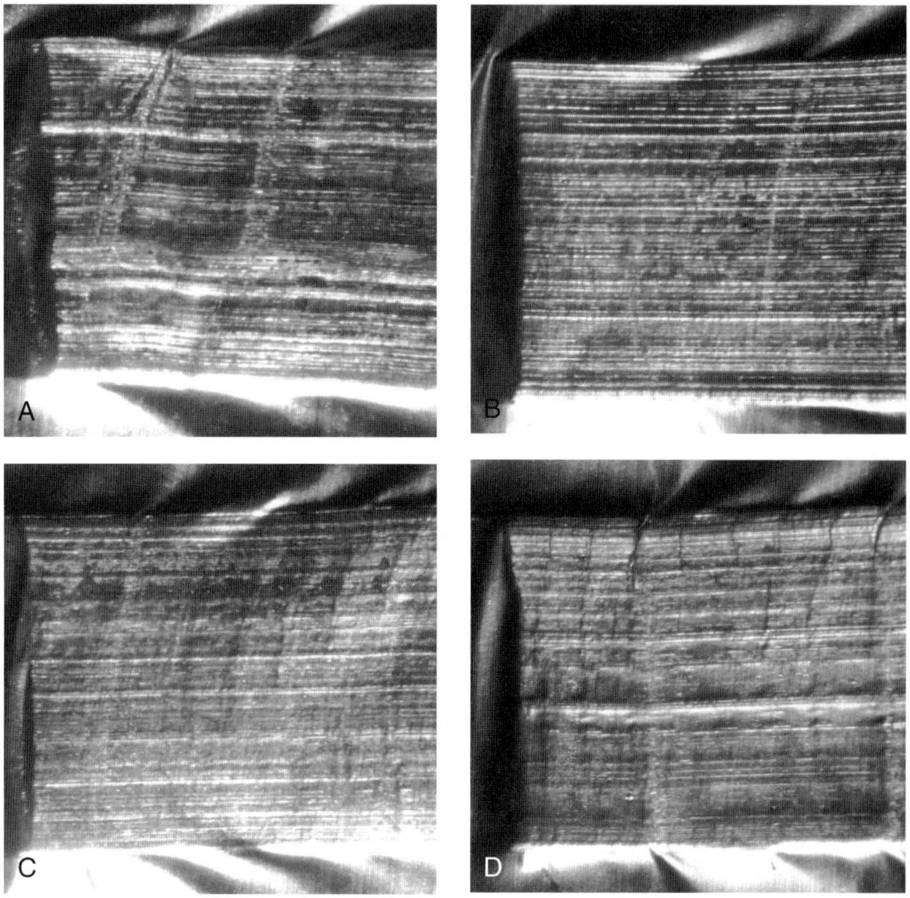

FIGURE 8-10
(a)–(d) Tool marks made by different screwdriver blades with the same manufactured dimensions.

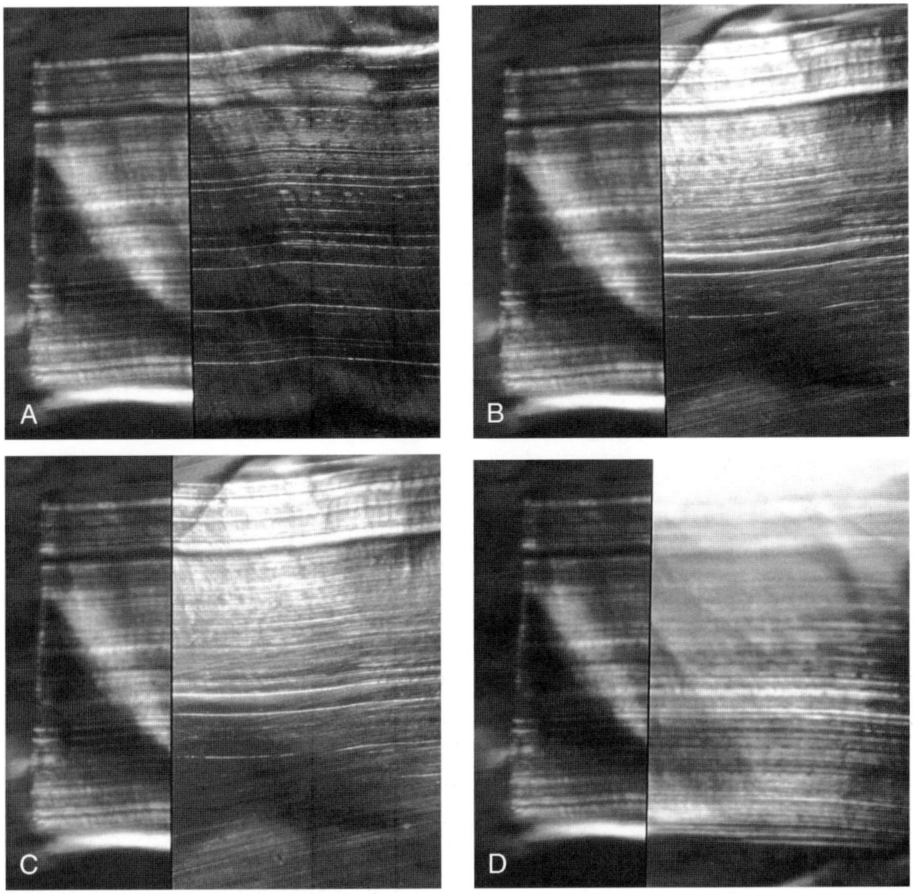

FIGURE 8-11
(a)–(d) Different tool marks made by the same blade. When is sufficiency of correspondence achieved? The lack of clarity in the images might make it more difficult to reach sufficiency.

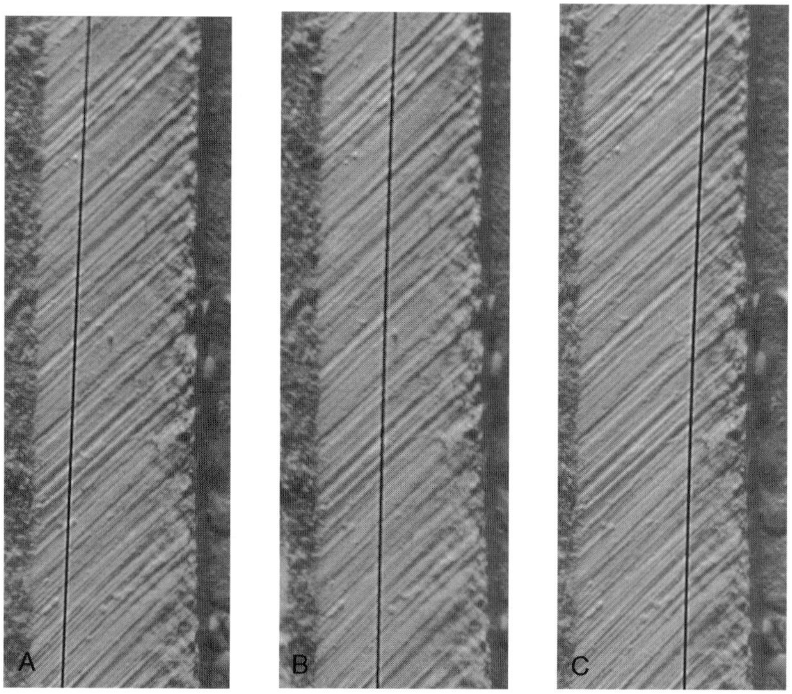

FIGURE 8-12
(a)–(c) Sets of two cast tool marks from the same wire cutter. The hairline of the comparison microscope is adjusted to demonstrate the continuation of the marks across the two casts of striated marks.

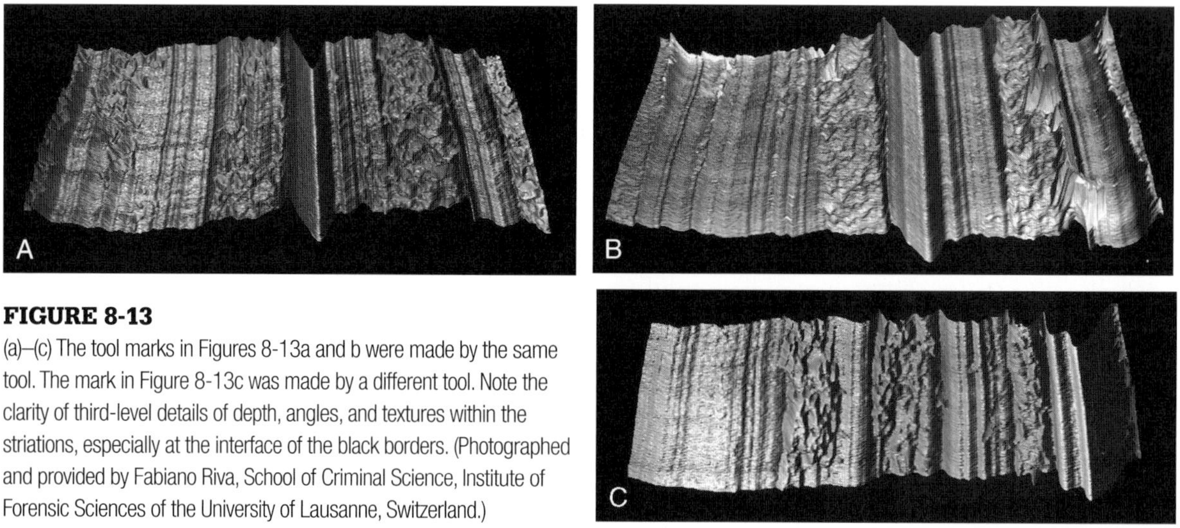

FIGURE 8-13
(a)–(c) The tool marks in Figures 8-13a and b were made by the same tool. The mark in Figure 8-13c was made by a different tool. Note the clarity of third-level details of depth, angles, and textures within the striations, especially at the interface of the black borders. (Photographed and provided by Fabiano Riva, School of Criminal Science, Institute of Forensic Sciences of the University of Lausanne, Switzerland.)

GUNS

The sufficient contact of a component of a gun on softer objects such as bullets, cartridge cases, or primer caps can leave markings, impressions, or images on that object. These markings can be impressed, striated, or a combination of both. Guns are tools that leave marks of their features on the bullets and cartridge cases. Studying the surfaces of guns and the receiving substrates of cartridge components of bullets, primer caps, and cartridge cases assists the examiner in the process of determining whether the known gun had fired the component of the cartridge.

Manufacturing processes result in repeatable dimensions of design specifications of the chambers, bores, breeches, firing pins, extractors, and ejectors. The similar sizes, shapes, and dimensions of the guns and their components put them into similar categories such as make, model, and caliber. However, the finishing processes used on the edges or surfaces of the components produce unique microscopic variations within each gun. No two breeches, firing pins, extractors, ejectors, chambers, or bores are microscopically alike. No other edges or surfaces of any finished metal gun, even consecutively manufactured guns, are microscopically alike. If a component is manufactured by casting in a mold without a finishing process, the comparative measurer must not confuse these repeatable features of the component as being unique features. The examiner must study the surfaces of guns and ammunition and their manufacturing processes to determine whether the features of a specific component are repeatable or unique.

MAJOR COMPONENTS OF A GUN

Pictured in the following figures are some major components of a variety of guns. The breeches of four different guns are shown in Figures 8-14a–d. The breech in the gun supports the cartridge case head during the firing process. The finishing of hard metal of the breech results in microscopically unique patterns in the breeches. The textures and contours of microscopic imperfections on the breech can be impressed into the softer cartridge case head and primer cap during firing.

Firing pins are shown in Figures 8-15a–d. Depending on two common designs of guns and cartridges, the firing pin strikes the primer cap or cartridge rim during the firing of the gun. Many smaller caliber guns use rim-fire cartridges and firing pins. A variation of the firing pin would be a hammer nose found in many revolvers. The tips of firing pins often share repeatable dimensions of size and shape. The finishing of hard metal results in microscopically unique patterns in the surfaces of the firing pins. Wear and tear on the firing pin results in additional unique features. The textures and contours of designed repeatable features and microscopic unique imperfections on the tip of the firing pin or hammer nose can be impressed into the primer cap or cartridge case rim during firing.

FIGURE 8-14
(a)–(d) Breeches of guns. Note the variations in surface markings.

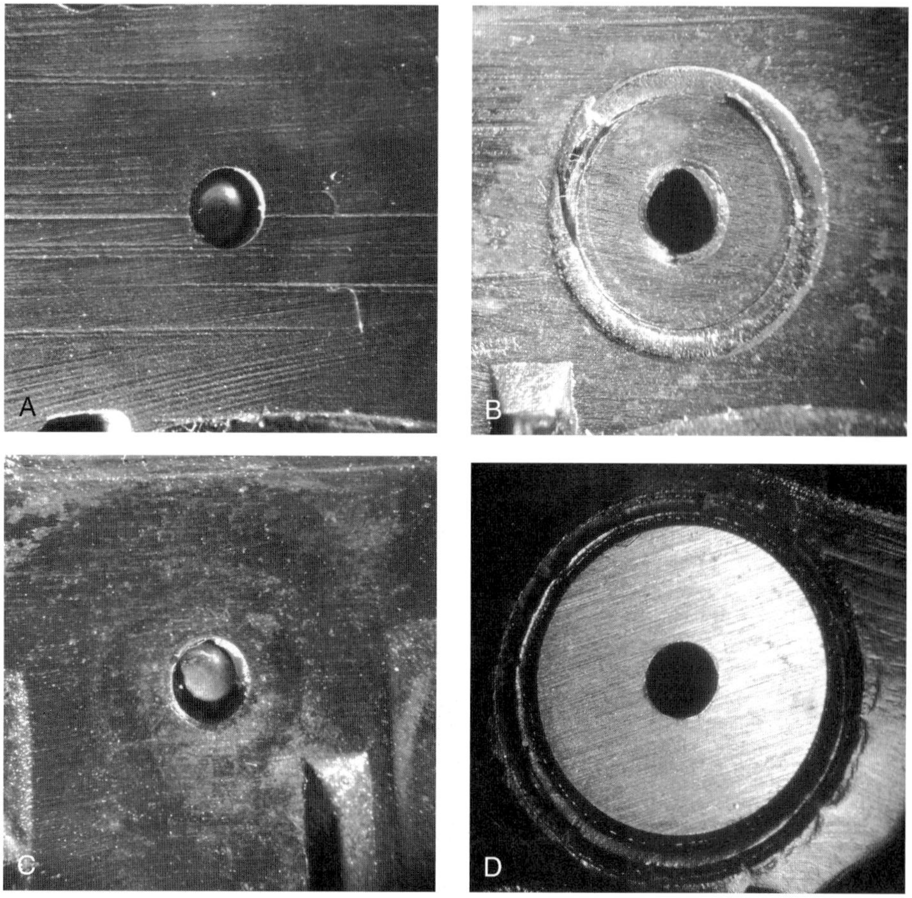

FIGURE 8-15
(a)–(d) Firing pins shown through the firing pin hole in a breech of the gun.

An extractor hooks under the rim of the head of the cartridge case and is designed to pull or push the fired or unfired cartridge case out of the chamber. This hard metal tool often scratches or impresses the area under the rim of a case during the firing and cycling of the gun. The cycling is the designed action of the gun to remove a case or cartridge from the chamber of the gun during firing or manual unloading. The markings can be examined to determine whether the cartridge case had been marked by the extractor. Extractors are shown in Figures 8-16a–d.

An ejector pushes or kicks the fired or unfired cartridge case out of the opening in the slide or ejection port of the gun after being extracted from the chamber. Instead of an independent ejector, a firing pin might be designed to also act as an ejector. This hard metal tool often impresses the head area of a case during the firing of the gun and cycling of the action. The patterns on the

FIGURE 8-16
(a) The back side of an extractor near the breech and firing pin. (b) A bottom view of an extractor near the breech. (c) A top view of an extractor on the left side of the image. The firing pin is protruding through the firing pin hole near the center. (d) One set of five extractors from a revolver.

cartridge case can be examined to determine whether it had been marked by the ejector. Ejectors are shown Figures 8-17a–c.

The chamber of the gun holds the cartridge in place during firing. The walls of the chamber can impress or scratch the surface of a cartridge case during loading, unloading, or firing. Figures 8-18a and b show various chambers in guns.

The rifled barrel of a gun has a series of spiraling lands and grooves in its bore. Shotguns are smooth bored. Figures 8-19a–d show rifled bores. Note the manufacturing processes produce repeatable features of design, number, and dimensions of lands and grooves in the bore that is formed in a spiraling manner to impart a series of recessed grooves among the remaining lands. The lands grip the bearing surface of the bullet and cause the bullet to rotate or spin around its nose-to-base axis as it travels through then leaves the bore. The processes of forming and finishing the lands and grooves within the bore

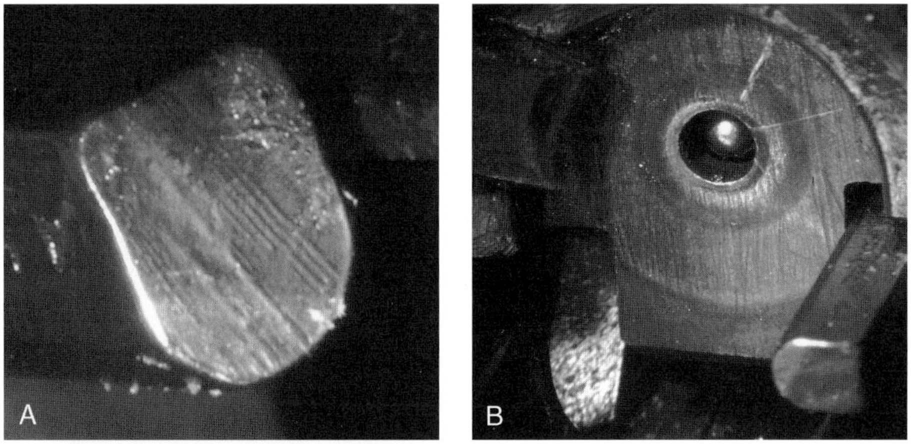

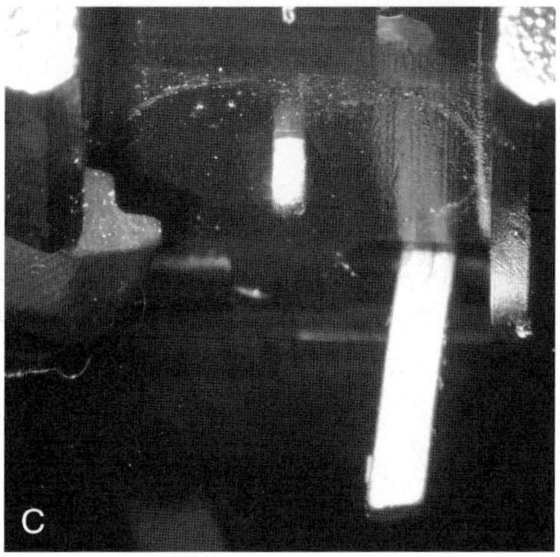

FIGURE 8-17
(a) The surface of an ejector. (b) The ejector in the lower right with the extractor in the upper left and firing pin recessed in the firing pin hole of the breech. (c) A different gun with the ejector in the lower right, extractor on the left, and firing pin protruding through the firing pin hole of the breech.

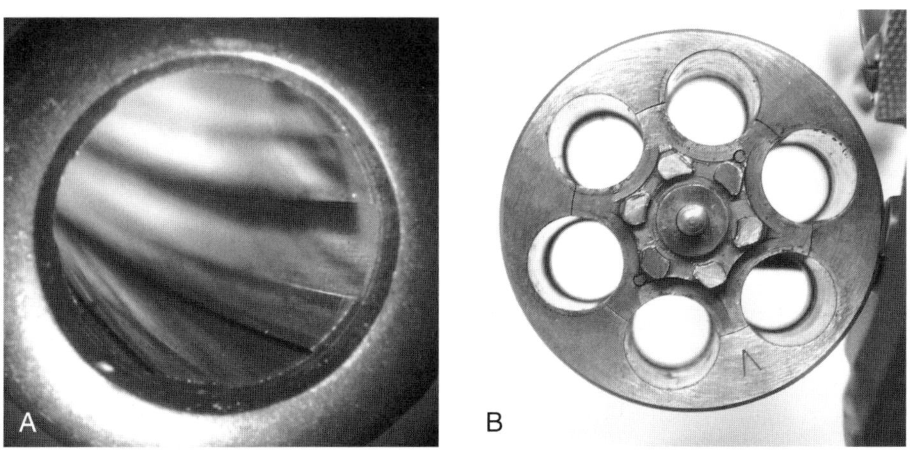

FIGURE 8-18
(a) A chamber from a pistol barrel leading to the lands and grooves of the bore. The raised surfaces of the lands and grooves keep the cartridge in the chamber and from entering the bore. (b) A set of six chambers from a revolver.

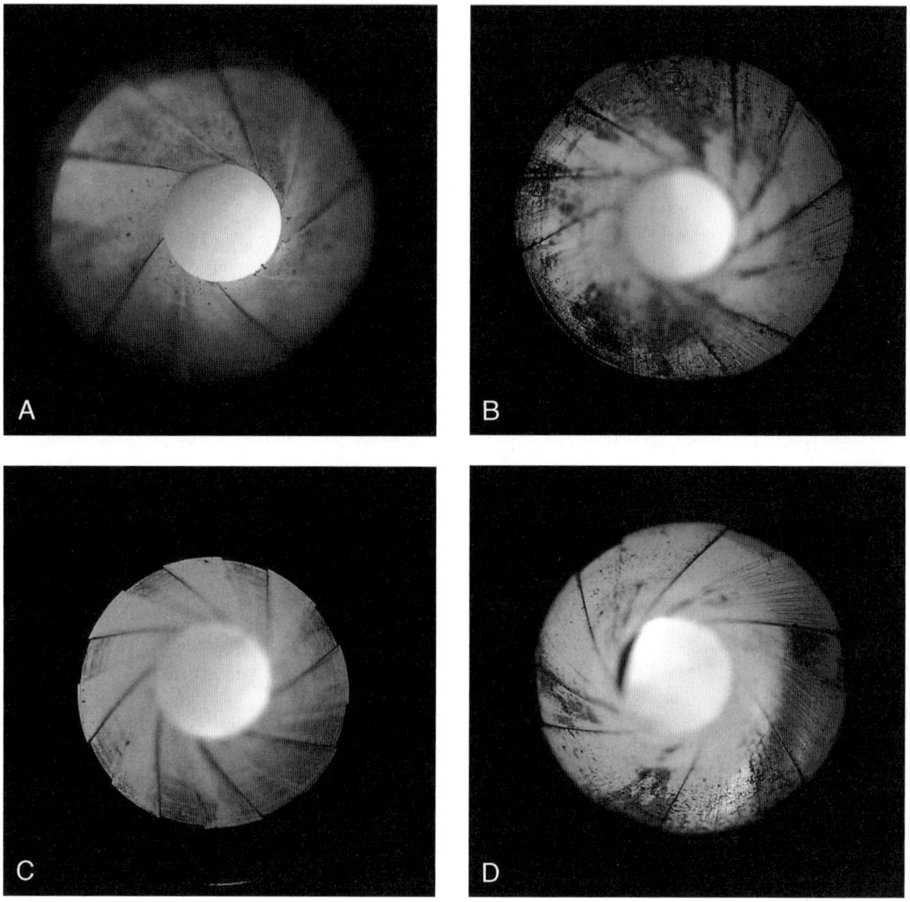

FIGURE 8-19
(a)–(d) Rifled bores depicting the variations in manufactured dimensions of lands and grooves.

produce microscopic variations of uniqueness. Each section within each land or groove varies from every other section of the same land or groove. Each land and groove varies from every other land and groove in their unique features. Figures 8-20a–d demonstrate the uniqueness found in lands and grooves.

Many marks from firearms are shown in the remaining figures. The features of the gun can be recorded as first-, second-, and third-level details. For repeatable features of a gun, the first-level details indicate the general manufactured design of the specific component of the gun. Second-level details are the recorded dimensions of the component, and third-level details indicate the designed contours and textures within the manufactured dimensions of that piece. The unique features of the components of a gun can be recorded as first-, second-, and third-level details. For the unique features of a part of the gun, the first-level details indicate

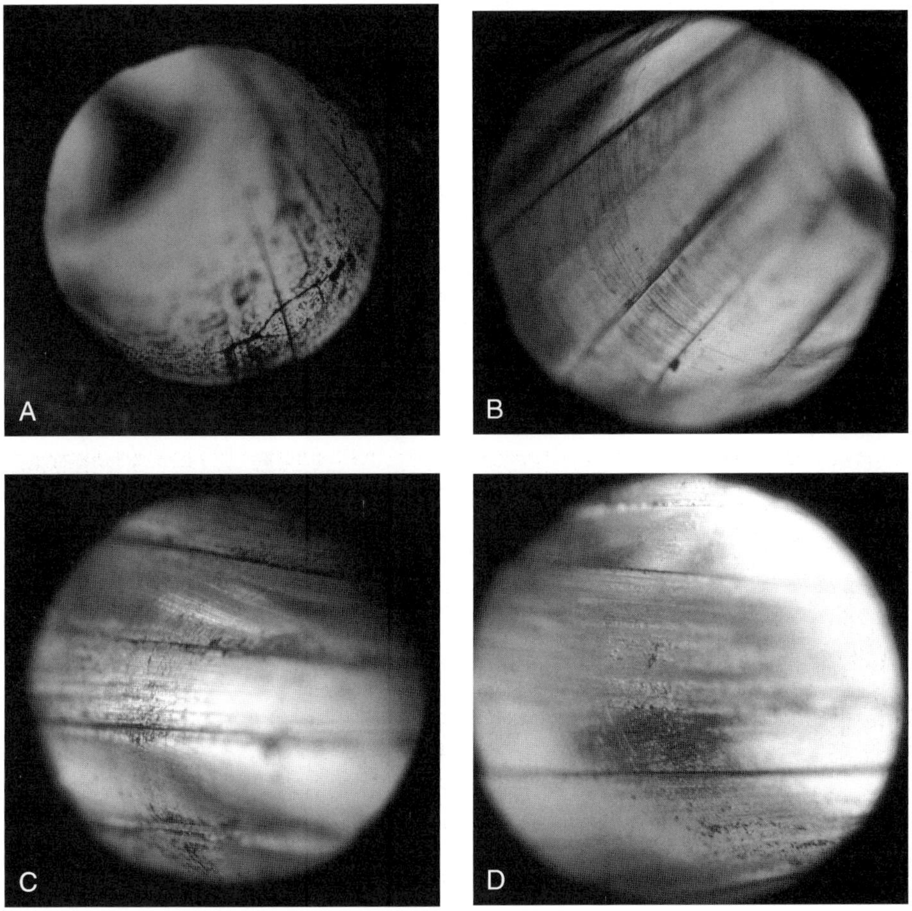

FIGURE 8-20
(a)–(d) Rifled bores depicting different lands and grooves demonstrating the variety of uniqueness found within a bore.

the general appearance and locations of the unique imperfections. Second-level details record the paths and dimensions of the uniqueness, and third-level details are the contours and textures within the paths and dimensions.

STRIATED MARKS

Viewing bullets is similar to viewing tool marks, as engravings on a fired bullet and cartridge case are marks from the tool or gun. Fewer examples of firearm tool marks are presented than the marks earlier in this chapter, because tool marks are tool marks. Figures 8-21a–d show one continuous application of a bullet passing over one land within a bore. The initial contact near the nose of the bullet with the land generates variations of appearances as those striae patterns found at the base of the bullet along the same land impression. Different forces of engraving the striae are generated as the smaller nose makes contact with the

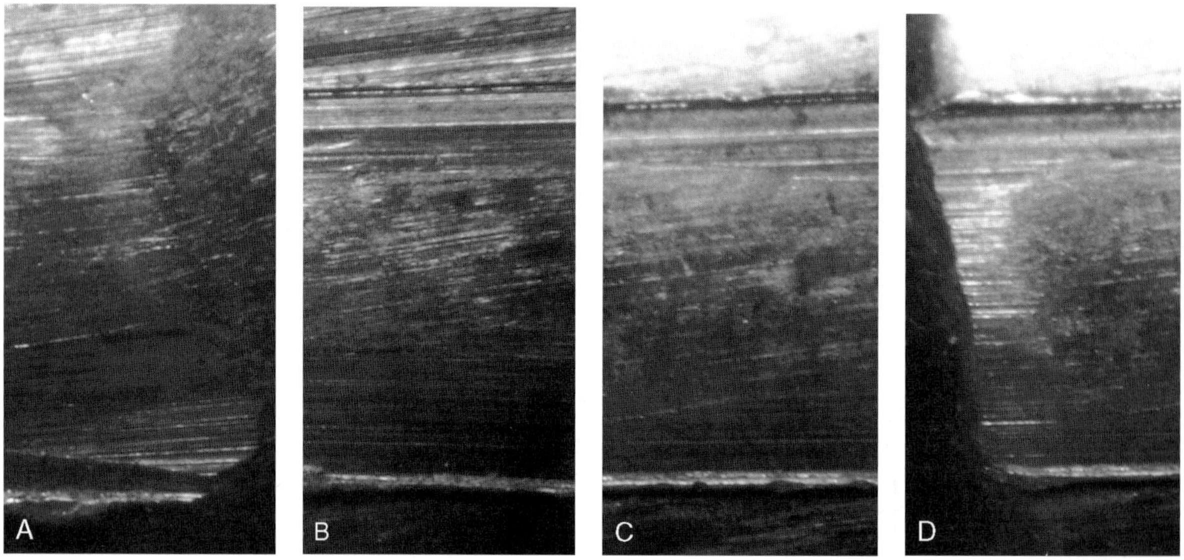

FIGURE 8-21

(a)–(d) One series of a variety of striations along one land impression on a bullet.

lands and then the wider base of the bullet expands from the forces of the generated gases. The base is designed to seal the expanding gases behind it. This represents some of the variability of engraving striations within one land of one gun.

Applying the lands and grooves of a bore to different substrates of lead or jacketed bullets will generate variations of appearances because the receiving substrate will not accept the markings the same. Figures 8-22a–c represent these variations. These images do not necessarily represent impressions from the same land. Ideally, similar ammunition as the unknown bullet is used when obtaining standards for examination.

Figures 8-23a–b depict the striae patterns generated from different lands possessing similar repeatable manufactured dimensions. Although the details of the repeatable dimensions are similar, the striae patterns generated within the repeated dimensions are unique to the specific land. These figures show sets of land impressions as viewed through the comparison microscope. The marks in each of these figures had been made by different lands. The striae patterns do not agree even though the details of the repeatable dimensions are similar.

Figures 8-24a–d show sets of deposited marks from four different corresponding lands of two bullets viewed through the comparison microscope. Different levels of quality and quantity of details are presented in each figure. Sufficient correspondence of the unique striae patterns within the repeatable features of the

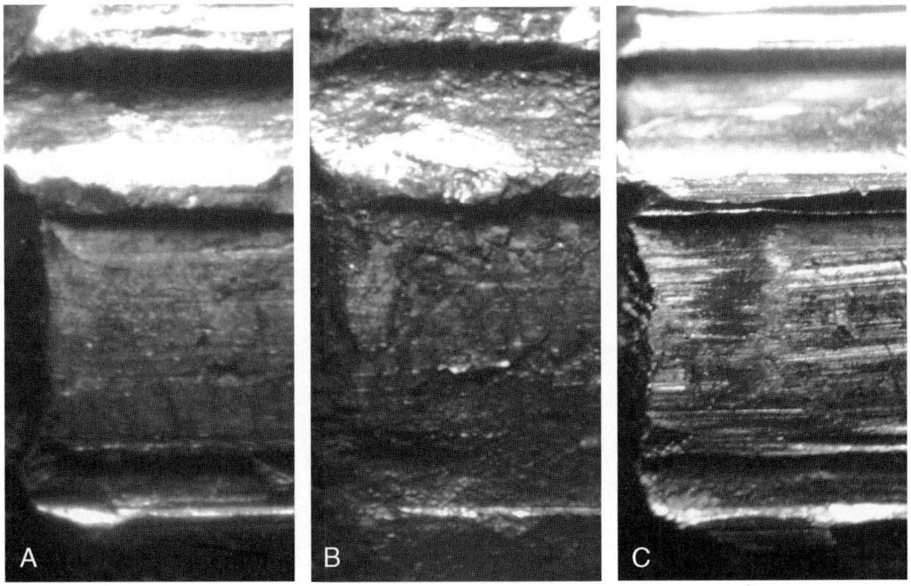

FIGURE 8-22
(a)–(c) Lead, coated lead, and jacketed bullet fired though the same gun.

land and groove design is considered to reach a conclusion whether the bullets had been fired in the same gun. Sometimes the striae patterns within one land or groove impression are sufficient and sometimes the aggregate quality and quantity of striae patterns of more than one land or groove impression is considered.

FIGURE 8-23
(a) and (b) Sets of impressions from different lands on two bullets fired from the same gun.

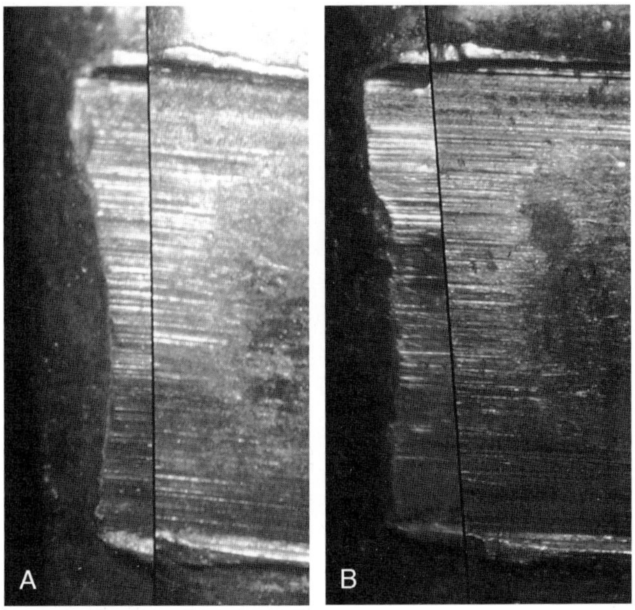

IMPRESSED MARKS

Impressed marks from the breech are often found in the head of a fired cartridge case or its primer cap. Figures 8-25a–d and Figures 8-26a–d are comparison microscope images of two sets of two cartridge case heads showing breech marks. A grinding tool can be used in finishing the breech and will generate somewhat circular, arcing, or straight marks depending on the selected process. Many guns might impress their features into the cartridge case head and primer cap resulting in first-, second-, or third-level details of uniqueness from the finished engravings found on the breech. Any designed repeatable features on the breech can also be recorded in the head or primer cap. Caution must be used when examining the details to not blend repeatable features into unique features.

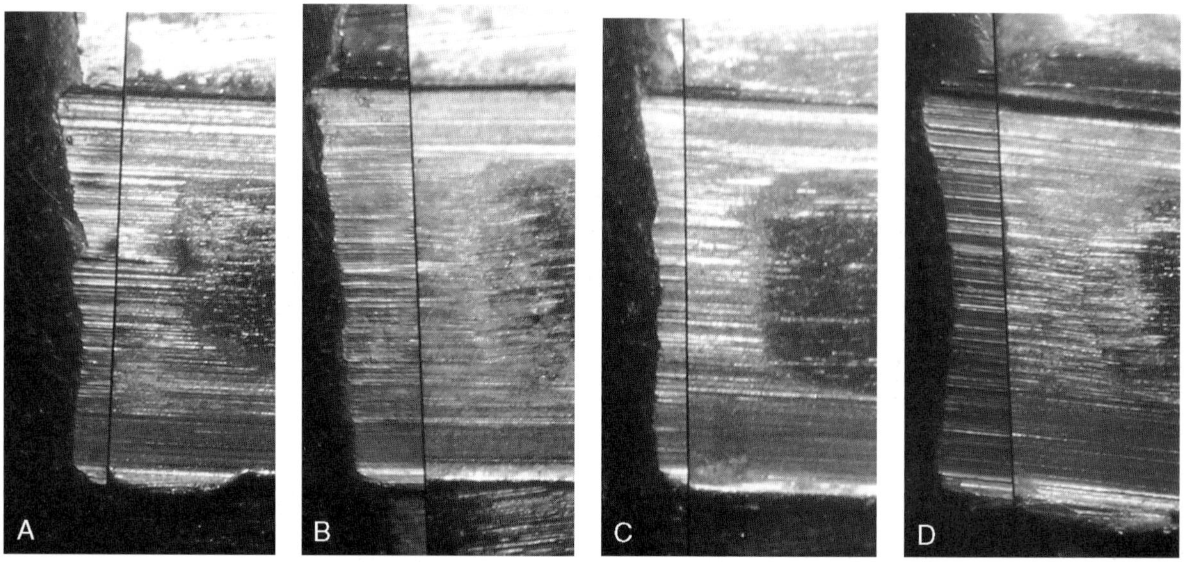

FIGURE 8-24
(a)–(d) Striae patterns in land impressions of two bullets fired from the same gun. These bullets are rotated in sync in (b)–(d). It is not necessary to rely on just one set of land impressions for the examination.

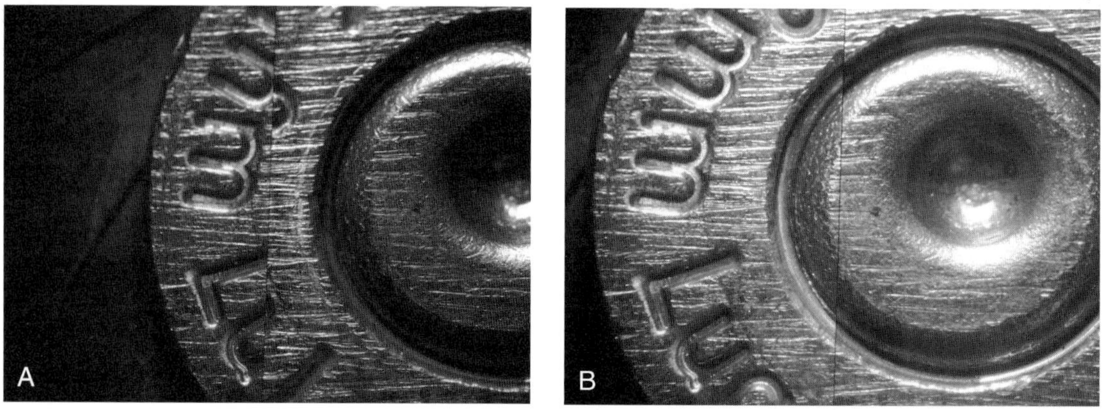

FIGURE 8-25
(a)–(d) Microscope images of breech markings on the heads and primer caps of two cartridge cases that had been fired in the same gun. Different areas of the examination are depicted by changing the location of the line for viewing both images.

(*Continued*)

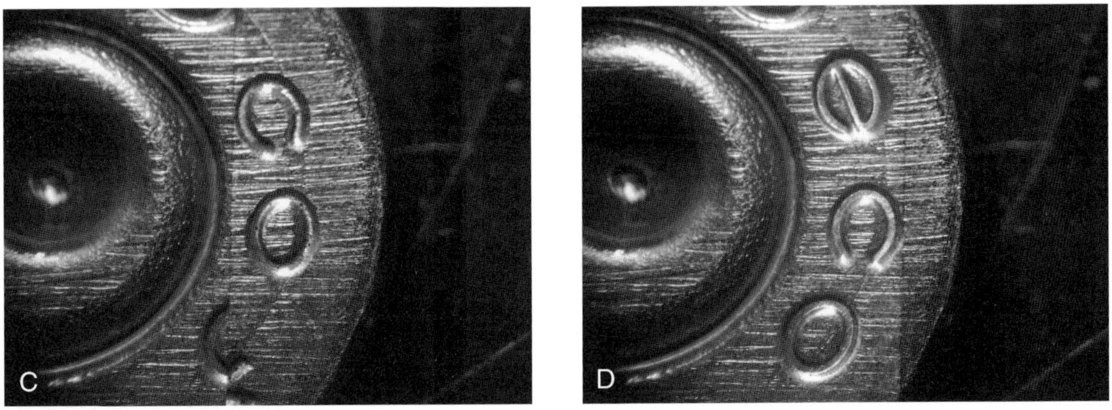

FIGURE 8-25—CONT'D

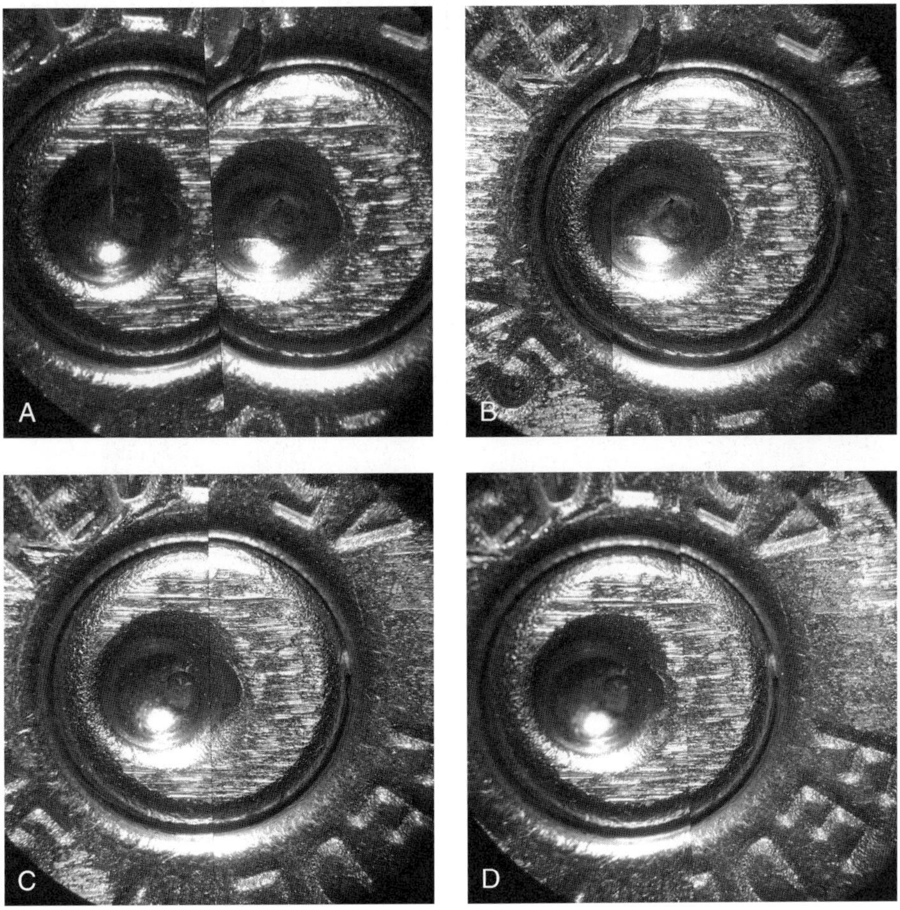

FIGURE 8-26
(a)–(d) Microscope images of breech markings on the primer caps of two cartridge cases that had been fired in the same gun. Different areas of the examination are depicted by changing the location of the line for viewing both images.

Impressed firing pin marks are found in the primer cap of center-fire cartridge cases or in the rim of rim-fire cartridge cases. As the hard metal firing pin strikes the softer metal, its markings can be recorded. Sometimes, there are combinations of impressed and striated marks from this action. Figures 8-27a–d depict firing pin impressions from two primer caps fired in the same gun.

Striated marks can be found under the rim of fired cartridge cases from the extractor. As the hard metal extractor strikes and slides across the underside to the rim, the softer metal of the cartridge case can receive the marks from the extractor. Sometimes, there are combinations of impressed and striated marks from this action. Figures 8-28a and b depict extractor marks as having

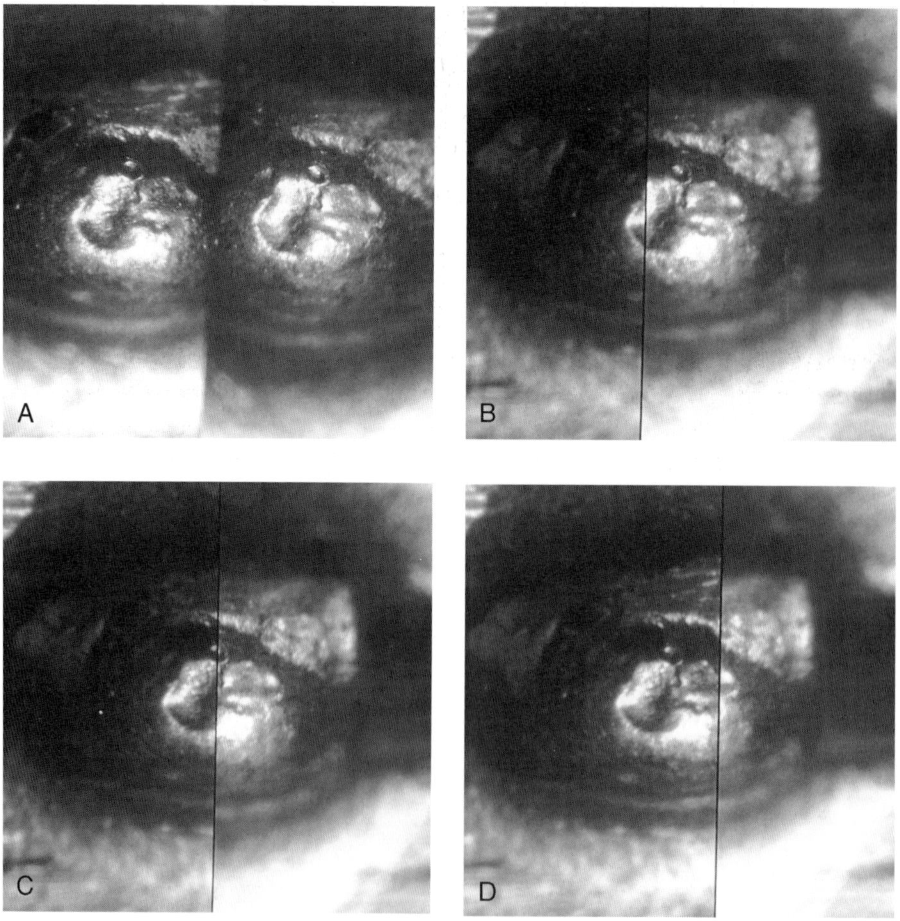

FIGURE 8-27
(a)–(d) Microscope images of firing pin markings in the primer caps of two cartridge cases that had been fired in the same gun.

been through the action of the same gun. The impression could have been made by firing the gun or manually cycling the action of the gun, causing the extractor to remove the cartridge from the chamber.

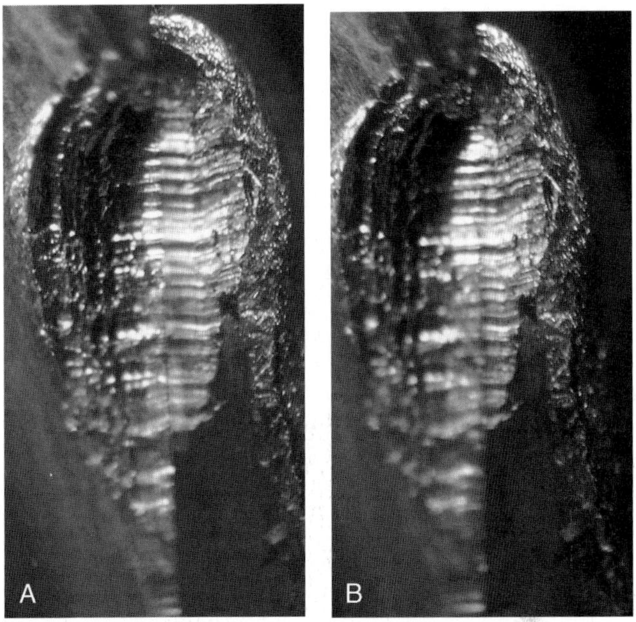

FIGURE 8-28
(a) and (b) Microscope images of extractor marks under the rim of two cartridges cases that had been through the action of the same gun.

CONCLUSIONS

The various tool mark images in this chapter emphasize the variations of appearances that occur when examining tool marks generated from tools or guns. There will always be variation of appearances. There is no such thing as a perfect match between impressions, marks, or images from the same source. It does not matter what the tool, gun, or substrate are. If it leaves a mark or impression in a receiving substrate, it can be examined. Tool marks are tool marks whether they are generated by a screwdriver, wire cutter, rifled bore, extractor, ejector, firing pin, hammer nose, or hammer. Some marks are striated, some are impressed, and some are a combination of striated and impressed.

For conclusions of examinations, refer to Chapter 6. The sufficiency and persistency of the repeatable and unique features must be considered when determining the judgment of conclusion. The determinations of agreement and disagreement rest upon the quality and quantity of three levels of details of the persistent repeatable features and the quality and quantity of three levels of details of the persistent unique features of the source(s) as recorded in the substrates.

BIBLIOGRAPHY

Association of Firearm and Tool Mark Examiners Glossary, 2007, Fifth Edition, Version 5.070207.

Association of Firearm and Tool Mark Examiners Glossary, 'Theory of Identification as it Relates to Toolmarks' 2007, Fifth Edition, Version 5.070207, 157.

Ball, Patrick. D. 'Toolmarks Which May Lead to False Conclusions,' *AFTE Journal*, 2000, 32 (3), 292–293.

Biasotti, A. A. 'Rifling Methods: A Review and Assessment of the Individual Characteristics Produced,' *AFTE Journal*, 1981, 13 (3), 34–39.

Biasotti, A. A. and J. Murdock. 'Criteria for Identification or State of the Art of Firearm and Toolmark Identification,' *AFTE Journal*, 1984, 16 (4), 16–34.

Bishop, Eugene E. 'Tool Mark Identification on Nails,' *AFTE Journal*, 1995, 27 (4), 306–309.

Bonfanti, Monica S. and Jan De Kinder, 'The Influence of the Use of Firearms on their Characteristic Marks,' *AFTE Journal*, 1999, 31 (3), 318–423.

Bonte, Wolfgang.'Tool Marks in Bone and Cartilage,' *Journal of Forensic Sciences*, 1975, 20 (2), 315–325.

Bridgemon, Rondal R. 'The Examination of Cut Tires,' *AFTE Journal*, 1984, 16 (3), 102–103.

Brundage, David. 'The Identification of Consecutively Rifled Barrels,' *AFTE Journal*, 1998, 30 (3), 438–544.

Bunch, S. G. 'Consecutive Matching Striation Criteria: A General Critique,' *Journal of Forensic Sciences*, 2000, 45 (5), 955–962.

Burrard, G. *The Identification of Firearms and Forensic Ballistics*, 1st edition, Charles Scribner Sons, NY, 1934, revised edition, A.S. Barnes & Co., NY,1964.

Cassidy, F. H. 'Examination of Toolmarks from Sequentially Manufactured Tongue-and-Groove Pliers' *Journal of Forensic Sciences*, 1980, 25 (8), 796–809.

Cassidy, Frank H. 'Replication of Identifying Marks when using "Mikrosil" Castings,' *AFTE Journal*, 1993, 25 (2), 130–131.

Chenow, Richard W. and John T. Lemmer. 'The Use of Investment Castings in the Manufacture of Firearm Components,' *AFTE Journal*, 1994, 26 (1), 64–76.

Clow, Charles M. 'Cartilage Stabbing with Consecutively Manufactured Knives: A Response to Ramirez v. State of Florida,' *AFTE Journal*, 2005, 37 (2), 86–116.

Coody, Amy C. 'Consecutively Manufactured Ruger P-89 Slides,' *AFTE Journal*, 2003, 35(2), 157–160.

Cunningham, Jordan. 'Electrical Discharge Machining and its Application to Bunter Manufacturing,' *AFTE Journal*, 2000, 32 (1), 16–18.

Cunningham, Jordan. 'Bunter Information for Major Ammunition Makers,' *AFTE Journal*, 2000, 32 (1), 56.

De Kinder, J., P. Prevot, M. Pirlot, and B. Nys. 'Surface Topology of Bullet Striations: An Innovating Technique,' *AFTE Journal*, 1998, 30 (2), 294–299.

Dodson, Ronald V. and Joseph J. Masson. 'Bunter Marks, What Do They Mean?' *AFTE Journal*, 1997, 29 (1), 33–36.

Dodson, Ronald V. 'Bunter Toolmarks—Differences in Production Methods,' *AFTE Journal*, 1998, 30 (2), 334–335.

Dutton, Gerard. 'Manufacturing Marks on 12 Gauge Battery Cups,' *AFTE Journal*, 1999, 31 (1), 31–35.

Dutton, Gerard. 'Identification of Bullets to a Portion of a Sawn Off Barrel,' *AFTE Journal*, 2000, 32 (3), 294–296.

Dyvesveen, Goran. 'Identification of Toolmarks From a Priming Tool in Reloaded Ammunition,' *AFTE Journal*, 2000, 32 (1), 54–55.

Eckerman, Stephanie J. 'A Study of Consecutively Manufactured Chisels,' *AFTE Journal*, 2002, 34 (4), 379–390.

Ernest, Richard N. 'Toolmarks in Cartilage Revisited,' *AFTE Journal*, 1991, 23 (4), 958–1059.

Featherson, Sam. 'Unique Rifling Structure of a Hi-Point 9mm Pistol,' *AFTE Journal*, 1998, 30 (4), 639.

Flater, Jason A. 'Manufacturing Marks on Winchester USA Brand 9mm Luger Primers,' *AFTE Journal*, 2002, 34 (3), 315.

Fowler, John, and Dave Brundage. 'The Effects of Velocity on Striations,' *AFTE Journal*, 1983, 15 (1), 56–58.

Freels, Ronnie H. 'Mikrosil Casting Material Information,' *AFTE Journal*, 1983, 15 (2), 79.

Freels, Ronnie. H. 'Rifling for the Hi-Point Model 995, 9mm Carbine,' *AFTE Journal*, 2000, 32 (2), 166.

Freeman, Ray. 'Consecutively Rifled Polygon Barrels,' *AFTE Journal*, 1978, 10 (2), 40–42.

Galan, J. I. 'Identification of a Knife Wound in Bone,' *AFTE Journal*, 1986, 18 (4), 72–75.

Garcia, Carol Henderson. 'Are Knife-Prints Reliable Evidence: An Analysis of Tool Mark Evidence and Ramirez v. State,' *AFTE Journal*, 1993, 25 (4), 226–280.

Goddard, C.H. 'History of Firearms Identification,' *AFTE Journal*, 1985, 17 (1), 55–68.

Goddard, C.H. 'History of Firearms Identification,' *AFTE Journal*, 1989, 21 (2), 263–278.

Goddard, C.H. 'History of Firearms Identification to 1930,' *AFTE Journal*, 1993, 25 (3), 214–228.

Grzybowski, Richard A. 'Unique Markings on Cartridge Cases from the Ejection Port of Type 14 Nambu Pistol,' *AFTE Journal*, 1998, 30 (2), 356–359.

Gunther, J.D. and C.O. Gunther. *The Identification of Firearms*. John Wiley and Sons, Inc., New York, 1935.

Haag, L.C. 'Heckler & Koch Polygonal Rifling,' *AFTE Journal*, 1977, 9 (2), 45–47.

Hal, Earl E. 'Bullet Markings From Consecutively Rifled Shilen DGA Barrels,' *AFTE Journal*, 1983, 15 (1), 33–48.

Hall, James. M. 'Consecutive Cuts by Bolt Cutters and Their Effect on Identification,' *AFTE Journal*, 1992, 24 (3), 260–272.

Hamby, James E. and James W. Thorpe. 'The History of Firearms Identification,' *AFTE Journal*, 1999, 31 (3), 266–284.

Hatcher, J.S. *Hatcher's Notebook*. Military Service Publishing Company, Harrisburg, PA, 1947.

Hatcher, J.S., F.J. Jury and J. Weller. *Firearms Investigation, Identification and Evidence*. 2nd edition, Stackpole Books, Harrisburg, PA, 1957.

Heard, B.E. *Handbook of Firearms and Ballistics: Examining and Interpreting Forensic Evidence*. John Wiley & Sons, New York, 1997.

Hocherman, Gil, Pavel Giverts, and Ezra Shosani. 'Identification of Polygonal Barrel Sub-Family Characteristics,' *AFTE Journal*, 2003, 35 (2), 197–200.

Hornsby, Billy. 'MCC Bolt Cutters,' *AFTE Journal*, 1989, 21 (3), 508.

Hornsby, Billy J. 'Pushed Bullet Comparison,' *AFTE Journal*, 1999, 31 (4), 486–488.

http://www.afte.org/.

http://www.swggun.org/.

Jordan, Tom. 'Individual Characteristics on Copper Insulated Wire,' *AFTE Journal*, 1982, 14 (1), 53–56.

Kennington, Robert H. 'Identification of Cartridge Cases Fired in Different Firearms: 'Pre-Identified Cartridges,' *AFTE Journal*, 1999, 31 (1), 15–19.

Kirk, Paul L. *Crime Investigation – Physical Evidence and the Police Laboratory.* Interscience Publishers, Inc. a division of John Wiley & Sons, Inc. New York 1953; 311–359.

Kirk, Paul L. edited by John I. Thornton. *Crime Investigation: Second Edition.* John Wiley & Sons, New York 1974, 360–409.

Komar, Susan M., and Gregory E. Scala. 'Examiner Beware New Bolt Cutter Blades Class or Individual,' *AFTE Journal,* 1993, 25 (4), 298–300.

Lee, Susan E. 'Examination of Consecutively Manufactured Slotted Screwdrivers,' *AFTE Journal,* 2003, 35 (1), 66–70.

Lindsay, David C. 'The Effect of Powder Load and Bullet Material on an Identification' *AFTE Journal,* 2000, 32 (3), 271–276.

Lopez, Laura L. 'Striae Matching and Angle of Incident: A Study of the Foreshortening Effect,' *AFTE Journal,* 1998, 30 (2), 271–275.

Lopez, Laura L. and Sally Grew. 'Consecutively Machined Ruger Bolt Faces,' *AFTE Journal,* 2000, 32 (1), 19–24.

Maruoka, Richard K. 'Guilty before the Crime? The Potential for a Possible Misidentification or Elimination,' *AFTE Journal,* 1994, 26 (3), 206–213.

Maruoka, Richard K. and Patrick Ball. 'Title: Guilty before the Crime II?' *AFTE Journal,* 1995, 27 (1), 20–21.

Mathews, J.H. *Firearms Identification Volumes I–III.* Charles C. Thomas, Springfield, IL, 1962.

Matty, Bill. 'Lorcin L9MM and L380 Pistol Breechface Toolmark Patterns,' *AFTE Journal,* 1999, 31 (2), 134–137.

Matty, W. 'The Formation and Persistence of Toolmarks in the Cartridge Case Head Forming Process,' *AFTE Journal,* 1983, 15 (1), 108–122.

Matty, William, and Torrey Johnson. 'A Comparison of Manufacturing Marks on Smith & Wesson Firing Pins,' *AFTE Journal,* 1984, 16 (3), 51–56.

Matty, William. 'Raven 25 Automatic Pistol Breech Face Tool Marks,' *AFTE Journal,* 1984, 16 (3), 57–60.

Matty, William. 'A Comparison of Three Individual Barrels Produced From One Button Rifled Barrel Blank,' *AFTE Journal,* 1985, 17 (3), 64–66.

Meyers, Charles R. 'Firearms and Toolmark Identification: An Introduction,' *AFTE Journal,* 1993, 25 (4), 281–285.

Meyers, Charles. 'Some Bullet Striae Considerations,' *AFTE Journal,* 2002, 34 (2), 158–160.

Mikko, Don and Billy J. Hornsby. 'On the Cutting Edge II – An Identification Involving a Knife,' *AFTE Journal,* 1995, 27 (4), 293.

Miller, Jerry and Mike McLean. 'Criteria for Identification of Toolmarks,' *AFTE Journal,* 1998, 30 (1), 15–61.

Miller, Jerry. 'Reproducibility of Impressed and Striated Toolmarks: 4d Cut Flooring Nails,' *AFTE Journal,* 1998, 30 (4), 631–638.

Miller, Jerry. 'Criteria For Identification Of Toolmarks Part II* Single Land Impression Comparisons,' *AFTE Journal,* 2000, 32 (2), 116–131.

Miller, Jerry. 'An Examination of Two Consecutively Rifled Barrels and a Review of the Literature,' *AFTE Journal,* 2000, 32 (3), 259–270.

Miller, Jerry. 'An Examination of the Application of the Consecutive Criteria for Identification of Striated Toolmarks Using Bullets From Ten Consecutively Rifled Barrels,' *AFTE Journal,* 2001, 33 (2), 125–132.

Miller, Jerry. 'An Introduction to the Forensic Examination of Toolmarks,' *AFTE Journal,* 2001, 33 (3), 233–248.

Miller, Jerry. 'Criteria For Identification Of Toolmarks Part III* Supporting The Conclusion,' *AFTE Journal,* 2004, 36 (1), 7–38.

Miller, Jerry and Glen Beach. 'Toolmarks: Examining The Possibility of Subclass Characteristics,' *AFTE Journal,* 2005, 37 (4), 296–345.

Moenssens, Andre A., Carol E. Henderson and Sharon G. Portwood. *Scientific Evidence in Civil and Criminal Cases—Fifth Edition,* Foundation Press, New York 2007; 425–517.

Monturo, Chris. 'Breech Face Marks of the Bryco Arms Model Jennings Nine,' *AFTE Journal,* 1998, 30 (4), 652–654 and 1999, 31 (1), 67–69.

Moran, Bruce. 'The Application of Numerical Criteria for Identification in Casework Involving Magazine Marks and Land Impressions,' *AFTE Journal,* 2001, 33 (1), 41–46.

Moran, Bruce and John Murdock. 'Joseph Ramirez vs. State of Florida—Supreme Court Decision December 20, 2001,' *AFTE Journal,* 2002, 34 (2), 215–226.

Moran, Bruce. 'A Report on the AFTE Theory of Identification and Range of Conclusions for Tool Mark Identification and Resulting Approaches to Casework,' *AFTE Journal,* 2002, 34 (2), 227–235.

Moran, Bruce. 'Comments and Clarification of Responses from a Member of the AFTE 2001 Criteria for Identification of Toolmarks Discussion Panel,' *AFTE Journal,* 2003, 35 (1), 55–65.

Moran, Bruce. 'Toolmark Criteria for Identification: Pattern Match, CMS, or Bayesian?' *AFTE Journal,* 2003, 35 (4), 359–360.

Murdock, John. 'A General Discussion of Gun Barrel Individuality and an Empirical Assessment of the Individuality of Consecutively Button Rifled .22 Caliber Rifle Barrels,' *AFTE Journal,* 1981, 13 (3), 84–111.

Murry, Kurt. 'Toolmark Identifications on Unfired Primers: More Fiocchi Manufacturing Marks,' *AFTE Journal,* 2004, 36 (4), 313–314.

Nichols, Ronald G. 'Firearm and Toolmark Identification Criteria: A Review of the Literature,' *Journal of Forensic Sciences,* 1997, 48 (2), 466–474.

Nichols, Ronald G. 'Consecutive Matching Striations (CMS): Its Definition, Study and Application in the Discipline of Firearms and Tool Mark Identification,' *AFTE Journal,* 2003, 35 (3), 298–406.

Nichols, Ronald G. 'Firearm and Toolmark Identification Criteria: A Review of the Literature, Part II,' *Journal of Forensic Sciences,* 2003, 48 (2), 318–327.

Nichols, Ronald G. 'Firearm and Tool Mark Identification: The Scientific Reliability and Validity of the AFTE Theory of Identification Discussed Within the Framework of a Study of Ten Consecutively Manufactured Extractors,' *AFTE Journal,* 2004, 36 (1), 67–88.

Nichols, Ronald G. 'Defending the Scientific Foundations of the Firearms and Tool Mark Identification Discipline: Responding to Recent Challlenges,' *Journal of Forensic Sciences,* 2007, 52 (3), 586–594.

O'Hara, Charles E. and James W. Osterburg. *An Introduction to Criminalistics – The Application of the Physical Sciences to the Detection of Crime.* The Macmillan Company, New York 1949 fourth printing 1960, 121–130.

Osterburg, James W. *The Crime Laboratory – Case Studies of Scientific Criminal Investigation,* Clark Boardman Company, Ltd. New York 1982, 62–113.

Papke, Roger E. 'Electrochemical Machining: A New Barrel Making Process,' *AFTE Journal,* 1988, 20 (1), 48–52.

Patty, Beth A. 'Manufacturing Marks on Primers,' *AFTE Journal,* 2000, 32 (3), 300–301.

Rao, Valerie J. and Robert Hart. 'Tool Mark Determination in Cartilage of Stabbing Victim,' *Journal of Forensic Sciences,* 1983, 28 (3), 794–799.

Rathman, Garry A. 'Tires and Toolmarks,' *AFTE Journal,* 1992, 24 (2), 146–150.

Rathman, Garry A. 'Part II: Bladed Toolmarks – One Mark or Two?' *AFTE Journal,* 1992, 24 (2), 151–159.

Rawls, Donald D. 'Identification of Hatchet Toolmarks in Human Skull Bone,' *AFTE Journal,* 1998, 30 (2), 349–351.

Robinson, Marshall K. 'Another Manufactured Toolmark,' *AFTE Journal,* 1996, 28 (3), 164–165.

Rosati, Carlo J. 'Examination of Four Consecutively Manufactured Bunter Tools,' *AFTE Journal,* 2000, 32 (1), 49–50.

Rosati, Carlo J. 'The Bunter Controversy,' *AFTE Journal,* 2000, 32 (2), 164–165.

Silverwater, Howard and Avi Koffman, 'Firing Pin Hole Drag,' *AFTE Journal,* 1998, 30 (4), 658–660.

Smith, Erich D. 'Cartridge Case and Bullet Comparison Validation Study with Firearms Submitted in Casework,' *AFTE Journal,* 2004, 36 (4), 130–135.

Stone, Rocky S. 'How Unique are Impressed Toolmarks?' *AFTE Journal,* 2003, 35 (4), 376–383.

Tam, Chi King. 'Overview of Manufacturing Marks on Center Fire Cartridges,' *AFTE Journal,* 2001, 33 (2), 112–115.

Thompson, Evan. 'False Breechface IDs,' *AFTE Journal,* 1996, 28 (2), 95–96.

Thompson, Evan. 'Phoenix Arms (Raven) Breech Face Toolmarks,' *AFTE Journal,* 1994, 26 (2), 134–135.

Thompson, Evan. 'Individual Characteristics Criteria,' *AFTE Journal,* 1998, 30 (2), 276–279.

Thompson, Evan. 'False Impressed Land Impressions on Bullet Cores,' *AFTE Journal,* 1999, 31 (1), 55–56.

Thompson, Evan and Rick Wyant. '9mm Smith & Wesson Ejectors,' *AFTE Journal,* 2002, 34 (4), 406–407.

Thompson, Evan and Rick Wyant. 'Consecutively Made Cartridge Cases,' *AFTE Journal,* 2002, 34 (4), 407–408.

Thornton, John I. 'The Validity of Firearms Evidence,' reprinted *AFTE Journal,* 1979, 11(2), 16–19.

Tomasetti, Kristin A. 'Analysis of the Essential Aspects of Striated Tool Mark Examinations and the Methods for Identification,' *AFTE Journal,* 2002, 34 (3), 289–301.

Tuira, Y. J. 'Tire Stabbing with Consecutively Manufactured Knives,' *AFTE Journal,* 1982, 14 (1), 50–52.

Tulleners, Fred, and Mike Giusto. 'Striae Reproducibility on Sectional Cuts of One Thompson Contender Barrel,' *AFTE Journal*, 1998, 30 (1), 62–81.

Tulleners, Fred, and James S.Hamiel. 'Sub Class Characteristics of Sequentially Rifled 38 Special S&W Revolver Barrels,' *AFTE Journal*, 1999, 31 (2), 117–122.

Uchiyama, Tsuneo. 'Similarity among Breech Face Marks Fired from Guns with Close Serial Numbers,' *AFTE Journal*, 1986, 18 (3), 15–52.

Uchiyama, Tsuneo. 'A Criterion for Land Mark Identification,' *AFTE Journal*, 1988, 20 (3), 236–251.

Uchiyama, Tsuneo. 'The Probability of Corresponding Striae in Toolmarks,' *AFTE Journal*, 1992, 24 (3), 273–290.

Vandiver, J. 'New Screwdrivers, Production and Identification' *AFTE Journal*, 1976, 8 (1), 29–52.

Vinci, Francesco. 'Morphological Study of Class and Individual Characteristics Produced by Firing 2500 Cartridges in a .45 Caliber Semi-Automatic Pistol,' *AFTE Journal*, 2005, 37 (4), 368–473.

Walsh, Kevan and Gerhard Wevers. 'Toolmark Identification: Can We Determine a Criterion?' *AFTE Journal*, 35 (4), 361–363.

Watson, Donald J. 'The Identification of Consecutively Manufactured Crimping Dies,' *AFTE Journal*, 1978, 10 (2), 19–20.

Watson, Donald J. 'The Identification of Tool Marks Produced from Consecutively Manufactured Knife Blades in Soft Plastic,' *AFTE Journal*, 1978, 10 (3), 43–45.

Williams, D.L. 'Comparison of Cut Telephone Cables,' *AFTE Journal*, 1979, 11(2), 39–41.

Wyant, R. T. 'Variation in Bolt Face Marking Characteristics on the Sig Sauer P226, .357 Sig Pistol,' *AFTE Journal*, 1998, 30 (4), 629–630.

CHAPTER 9

Shoes and Tires

CONTENTS

Shoes and tires are similar in that they are both designed to make contact with a surface. This contact can leave prints, impressions, or images on or in that surface. The prints they leave can be two- or three-dimensional. Two-dimensional prints involve a transfer of a matrix or residue between the sole or tread and the surface. Three-dimensional prints result from the shoe or tire displacing a substrate such as soil or snow.

Shoes and tires bear the repeatable features resulting from design specifications or molds that put them into certain categories. Unique features will be detectable on the newly finished tread if they are examined closely enough. As more human involvement occurs in finishing the tread, the greater the chance for variability to be present and to be found. As tread wears, fractures, or acquires natural imperfections, uniqueness gets easier to detect because wear and damage typically leave larger marks than the features on a newly manufactured item.

SHOES

Figures 9-1a–h depict the surfaces of shoe soles, many of which appear to have similarities. Soles that come from the same mold should have indistinguishable repeatable features of make, model, and size, although wear and damage that change a mold do occur through time. Soles that come from different molds often have similar repeatable features, although some different features may be present. The specific designed elements of the mold will impart its intended features as repeatable features into the sole. Since molds are unique like everything else, they will impart that mold uniqueness as repeatable features into the tread of many soles made from them. Occasionally, unintended mold defects are seen on soles.

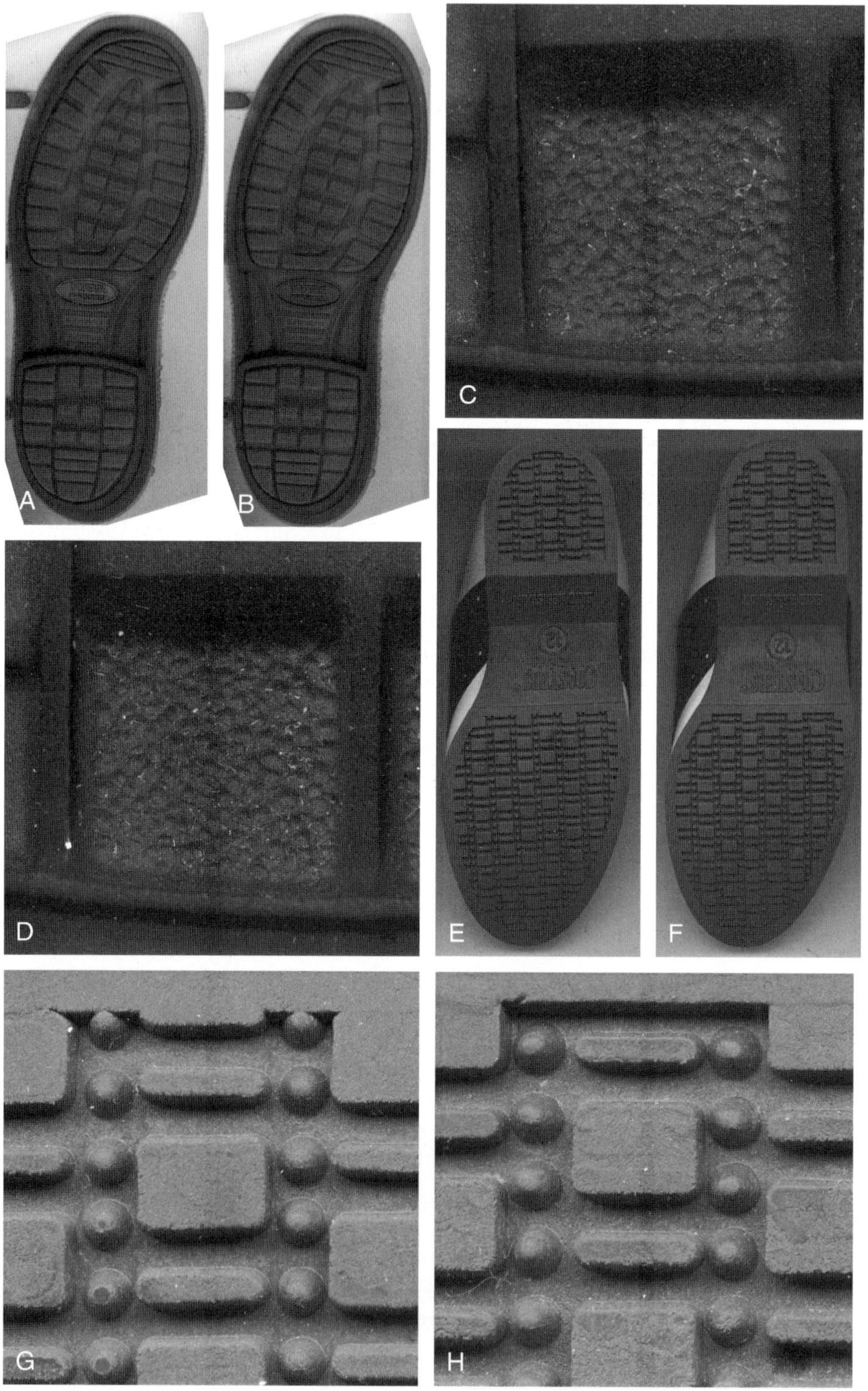

FIGURE 9-1
(a) and (b) soles with tread from the same mold. (c) and (d) Enlarged areas from a tread element of two soles from the same mold. (e) and (f) Shoe tread from different molds. (g) and (h) Enlarged areas from a similar location of tread elements of two soles from different molds.

Not all soles come from molds. Another design process of cutting shoe soles from a sheet of treaded material could produce similar yet different tread on the same size, make, and model of shoes. Figures 9-2a–e show this process. The variations of tread from cut sheets of sole material are shown in Figures 9-2d and e. Photographs of actual tread are shown in Figures 9-3a and b.

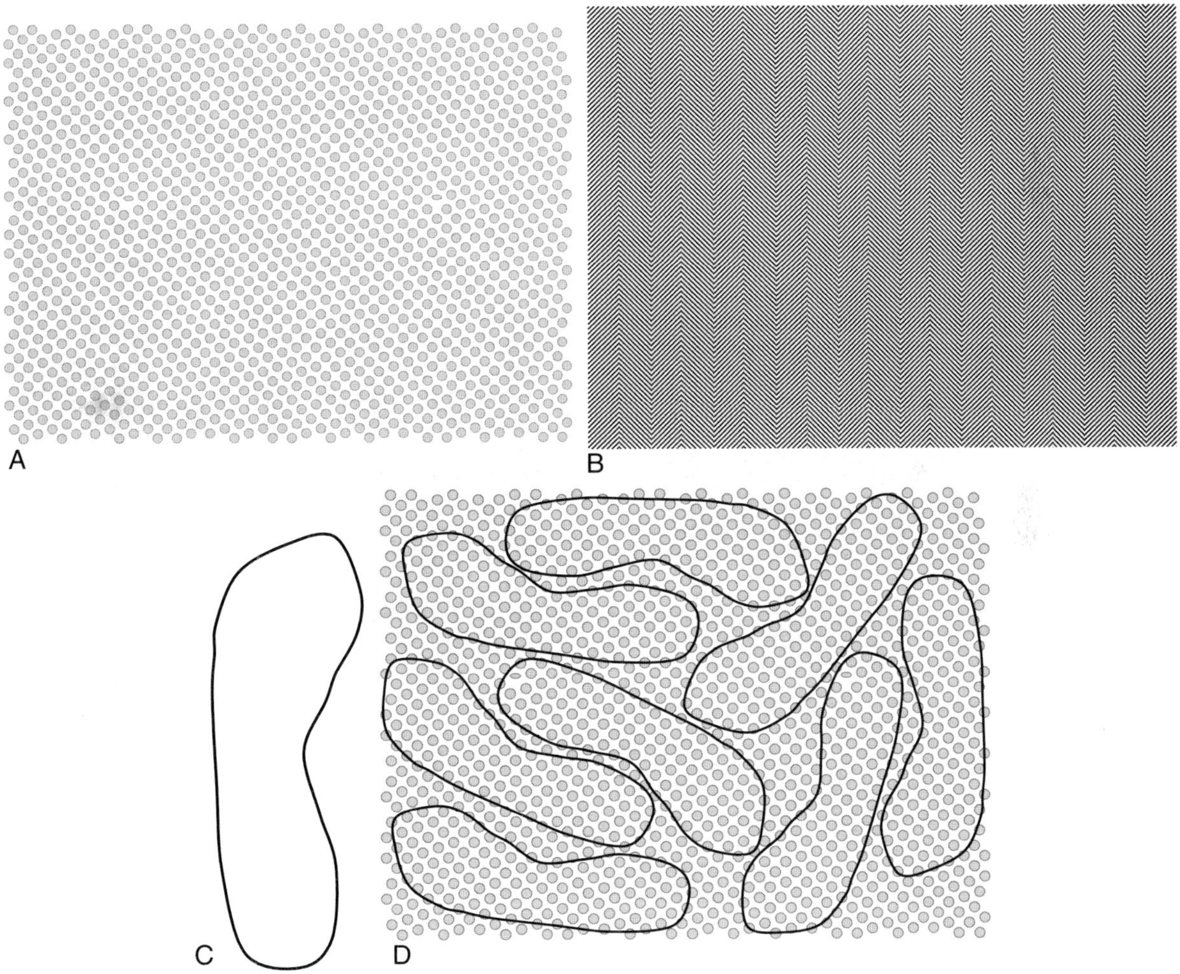

FIGURE 9-2

(a) A representation of a sheet of material to be cut into outsoles. The intended shape of the tread elements is round. Note the two defects resulting in oval elements. (b) A representation of a different sheet of material to be cut into outsoles. (c) An outline of a cutting tool. (d) The same cutting tool applied in different areas of the sheet of outsole material in Figure 9-2a, resulting in different arrangements of elements in relation to the edges of the sole and the two defects.

(Continued)

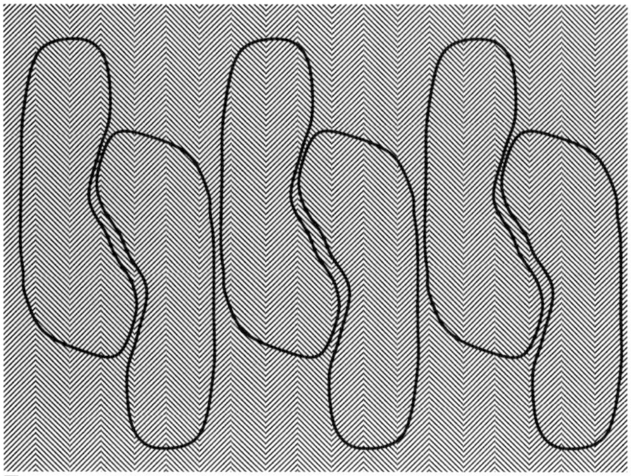

FIGURE 9-2—CONT'D
(e) The same cutting tool applied in different areas of the sheet of outsole material in Figure 9-2b, resulting in different arrangements of elements in relation to the edges of the sole.

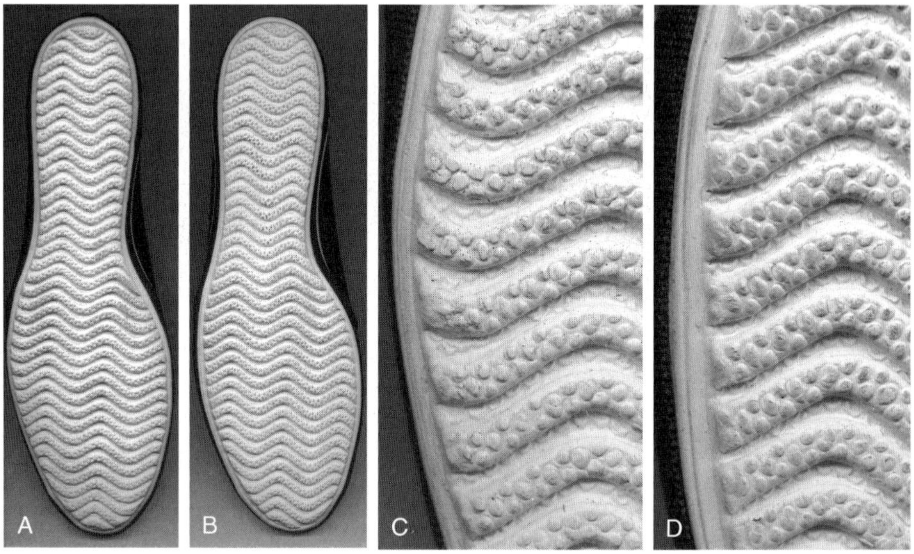

FIGURE 9-3
(a) and (b) Two soles cut from different locations on a sheet of treaded material. Note the arrangement of tread at the edges of the sole and the textures along the surfaces of the individual tread elements. (c) and (d) Enlarged areas from the tread of a sole from different areas of a sheet of material.

Tires

Like the shoe treads, Figures 9-4a–d show the surfaces of tire treads. Many tires are designed with varying sizes, shapes, and sequences of individual elements around the circumference of tires. This is called "noise treatment" and is a design factor intended to reduce the noise generated by the motion of the rolling tires. Figures 9-4a–d demonstrate the variations in elements throughout the circumference of one passenger car tire.

FIGURE 9-4
(a)–(d) Sections of one tire depicting sequences and configurations of various sizes and shapes of tread elements for noise treatment.

Among the elements of the tire tread are tie bars, sipes, and wear bars. Tie bars hold the elements together below the original surface of the elements. Sipes are small slots or voids in elements. Wear bars become flush with the tread elements as the tread wears significantly. These features are constructed between and below the summits of the primary elements and above the grooves within the tread. As the tread wears, the elements become flush with the tie bars and then the wear bar indicators. Sipes, or intentionally manufactured small openings within an element, will become less apparent as the element wears. These manufactured features are shown in Figures 9-5a–c.

Figures 9-6a–d show changes in the appearance of the repeatable manufactured tread as it wears. Black depicts where the tread would make contact with a surface. At first, the elements appear separated, and the sipes are apparent. With wear, the elements become joined at the surface, and the sipes are less pronounced. Eventually, the tread changes its surface appearance from independent elements into continuous ribs around the circumference of the tire. The sipes

FIGURE 9-5

(a) The tie bar between two elements can be seen with the help of the lines between the elements. (b) The sipe, or slot in an element. Note the depth of the sipe. As the tread wears, the sipe will wear away, and the element will appear solid in this area. (c) A wear indicator bar is in the groove of the tread between elements. When the tread elements become flush with the wear indicator bar, it is time to replace the tire.

can disappear, depending on their design and degree of wear. Figures 9-6a–d show this type of tread wear, although not necessarily in the sequence it occurs. This demonstrates the change in the designed repeatable features of a tire. The worn tread changes its designed appearance at its surface.

Figures 9-7a and b show the surfaces of two tire treads from the same mold. If a mold is damaged—in this case a missing sipe—that damage is imparted into the subsequent treads for as long as the defect remains in the mold. This unintentional damage produces repeatable features for tread coming from this mold as long as this feature of the mold is not repaired.

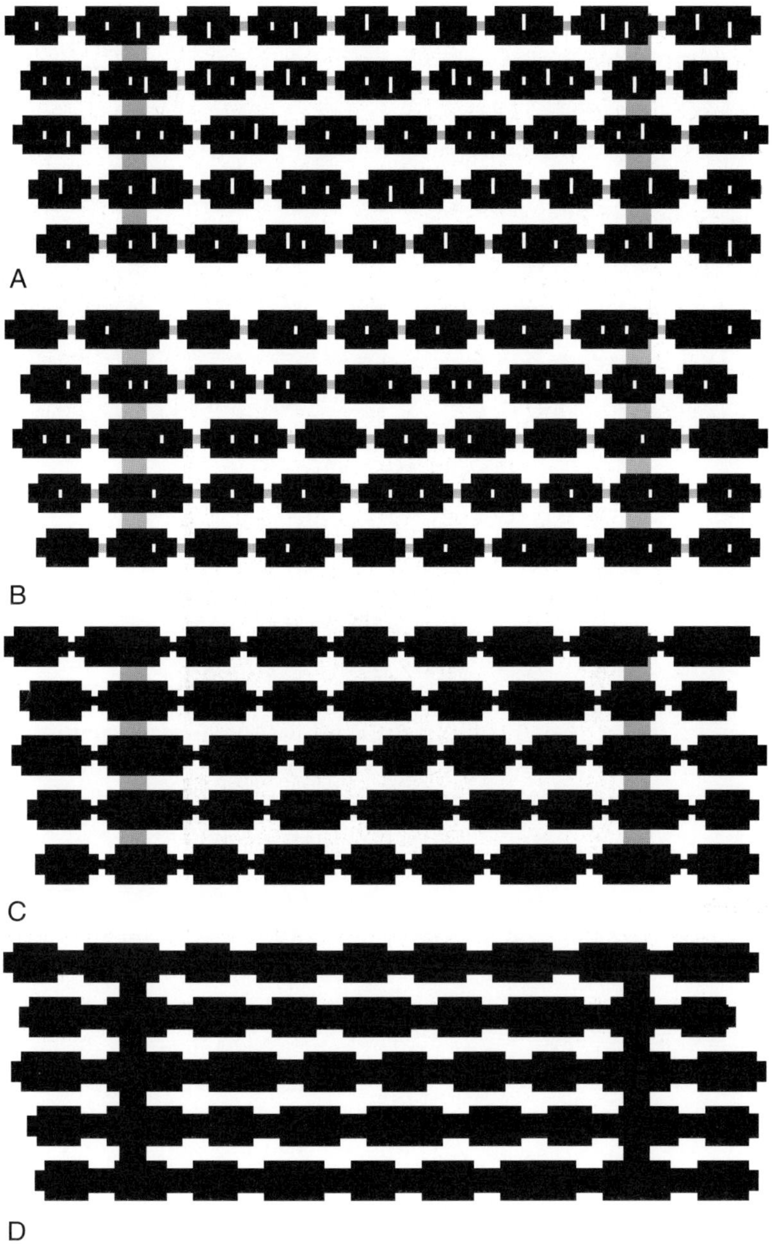

FIGURE 9-6

(a) Depiction of tire tread. The elements are black shapes. Sipes are represented by the white short lines within an element of tread. Tie bars are represented as gray connections between individual elements around the circumference of a tire. Wear bars are represented as the two wider gray bars across the ribs of tread. (b) As the tread elements wear, sipes become less prominent. (c) As the tread elements wear more, sipes become less prominent and could disappear, while tie bars that connect the elements become flush with the surface of the elements. (d) Much wear; sipes are worn away, and tie bars and wear bars are flush with the elements.

FIGURE 9-7
(a) and (b) Tires. Note the corresponding manufactured repeatable dimensions of the tread elements and the missing sipe in the upper right element.

SHOE OR TIRE PRINTS

Several different shoe prints are shown in the figures in this chapter. Athletic shoes with varying tread patterns were used to create the images. No matter the shoe used to generate tread patterns on or in a particular substrate, the concept of shoe prints on a particular surface carries over to any other shoe print on any other substrate. If the features of the shoe had been sufficiently recorded in a substrate at a scene, and the features of a shoe are sufficiently recorded in a standard substrate, a shoe print examination can be conducted. The significance of the conclusion relies on the sufficiency of details of the persistent unique and persistent repeatable features of the sole and the ability of the substrates to capture sufficient details of the sole. Persistency of features on the sole ranges from very persistent cuts or gouges to fragile mud, dirt, sand, or pebbles that could be stuck to the sole. The clarity of the details of the features that persist is also influenced by the substrate that receives the image.

The features of the shoe can be recorded as first-, second-, and third-level details. For repeatable features of a sole, the first-level details indicate the general manufactured design of the tread. Second-level details are the recorded dimensions and paths, sequences, and configurations of the tread elements, and third-level details indicate the designed contours and textures within the individual elements. Figures 9-8a–c depict variations in the levels of clarity of the repeatable manufactured design of tread elements.

The unique features of the sole can be recorded as first-, second-, and third-level details. For the unique features of a sole, the first-level details indicate the general appearance and locations of the unique imperfections. Second-level details record the paths and outlines of the uniqueness, and third-level details are the contours and textures within or along the unique paths. Variations in the recordings of details of unique features of the tread are shown in Figures 9-9a–c.

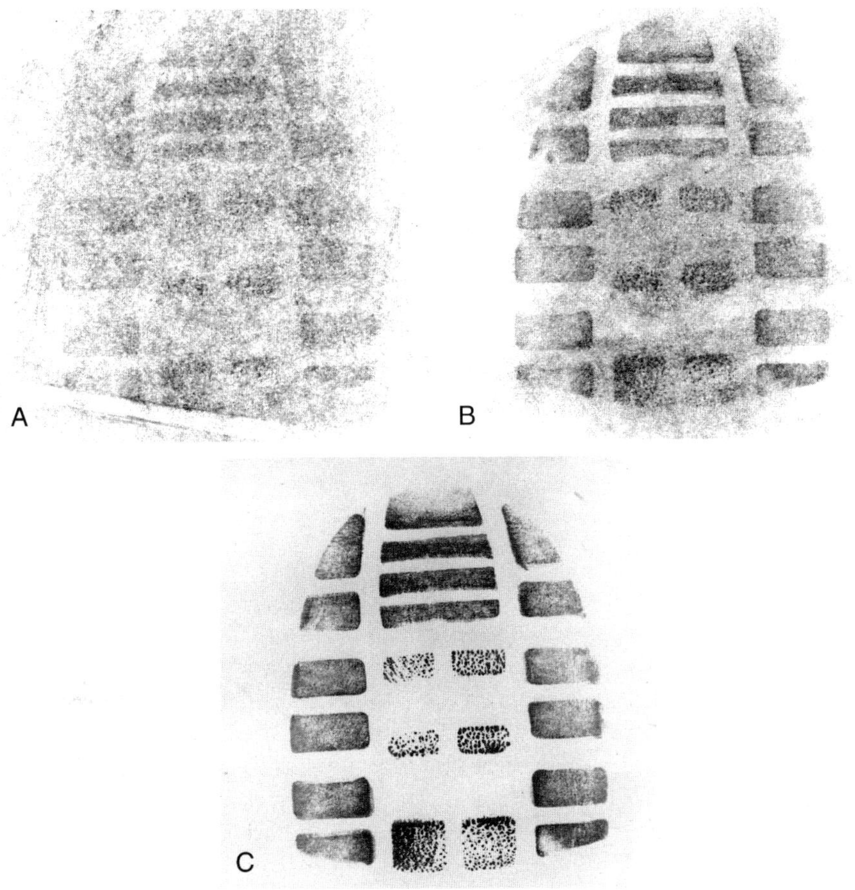

FIGURE 9-8
(a) A shoe print demonstrating details of repeatable features as first-level general tread paths and some second-level details of specific tread paths. (b) A shoe print demonstrating details of repeatable features as first-level general tread paths, second-level details of specific tread paths, and maybe some third-level details of textures. (c) A shoe print demonstrating details of repeatable features as first-level general tread paths, second-level details of specific tread paths, and third-level details of textures. Some details of unique features might be visible.

Beyond damage, unique shapes can be added to soles by the wearer stepping on debris such as tacks, mud, or gum. The value of these additional features depends on the clarity and amount of the recordings and the persistency of the object that remains attached to the tread between the time of the deposition at the scene and when it is recording as a standard. Any impressed mark is similar to tool marks as discussed in Chapter 8. It does not matter what the object is that created an impression. When examining these prints, the quality and quantity (QQ) of the details' levels of clarity are considered for the debris beyond the tread on the sole. The patterns of the debris and their persistencies

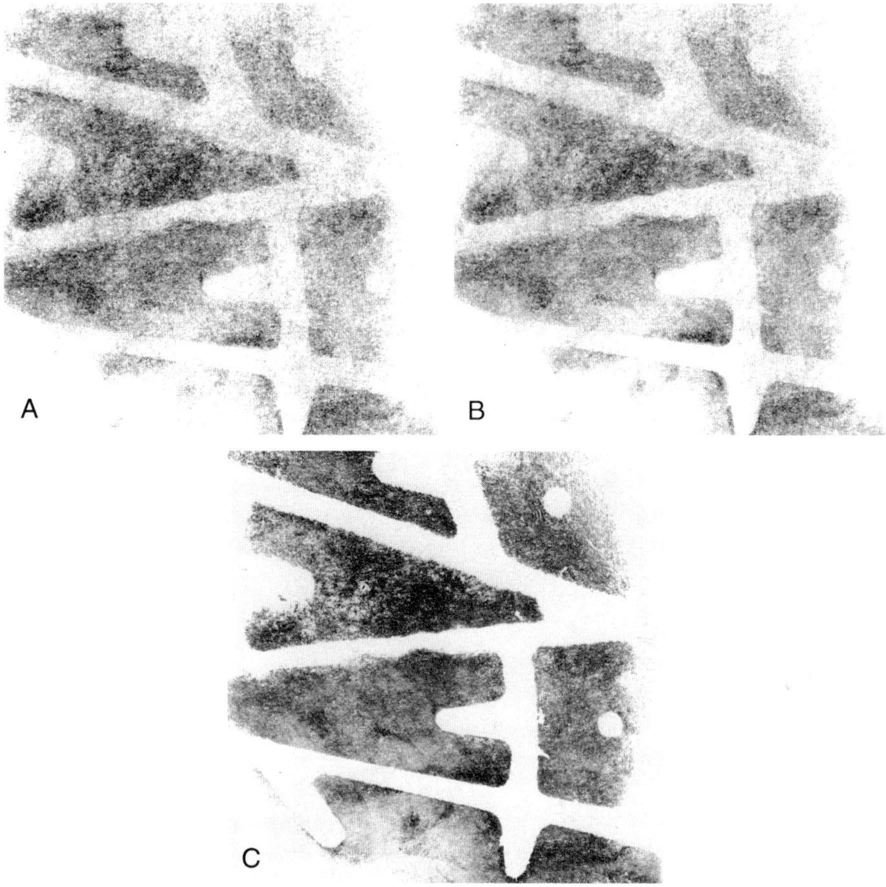

FIGURE 9-9

(a) A shoe print demonstrating details of unique features as first-level general paths and some second-level details of specific paths. (b) A shoe print demonstrating details of unique features as first-level general paths, second-level details of specific paths, and some third-level details of textures. (c) A shoe print demonstrating details of unique features as first-level general paths, second-level details of specific paths, and third-level details of textures. The details of unique features are within the details of repeatable features.

are being significantly considered in these examinations. The manufactured tread patterns are used to locate the unique patterns of the tread and debris. Figures 9-10a–f show sets of impressions of soles with a tack, mud, or clay affixed to the tread of the shoe. There are first, second, and third levels of details of repeatable features and first, second, and third levels of details of unique features of the shoe recorded in some of these shoe prints. Do not confuse details of repeatable features for details of unique features. It is important for the examiner to study the shoe in conjunction with studying the impressions.

FIGURE 9-10
(a) and (b) Shoe prints with a tack attached to an element of the tread. Note the round void from the tack in the lower left corner of the image in relation to the other details. (c) and (d) Shoe prints with mud attached to the tread. The fragile nature of mud influences the quality of the recordings. (e) and (f) Shoe prints with clay attached to the tread. The clay fills the voids or grooves between the tread elements.

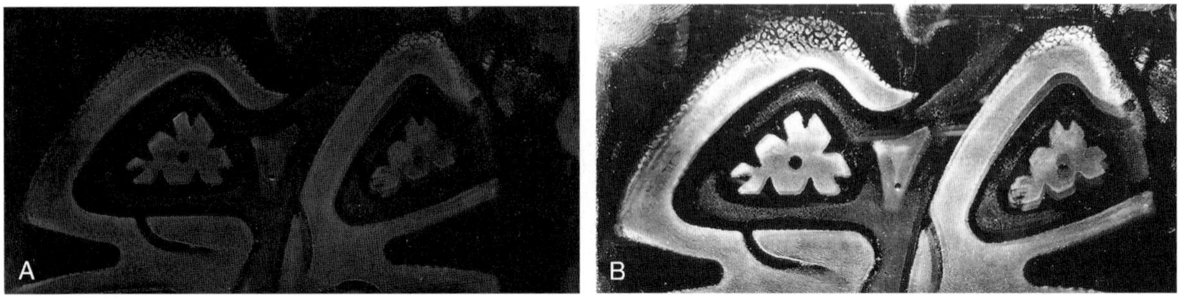

FIGURE 9-11
(a) and (b) Dusty shoe prints lifted with a black gelatin lifter. Notice the tread appears light and the furrows dark.

A black gelatin lift of a dusty shoe print is shown in Figure 9-11a and b. These are the same shoe print but viewed using different lighting angles. Changing the applications of light makes the print appear differently. This emphasizes the advantage of using similar lighting for the examination of the questioned and standard shoe prints. Application of different lighting will result in varying images of shoe prints from the same source.

Applying the same sole but using different matrices or residues will generate variations of appearances because the receiving substrate will not accept the residues the same way. Figures 9-12a and b represent these variations. Even though the residues vary, sufficiency might still exist between the two prints to determine the prints had been produced by the same shoe.

Applying the same shoe but using different applications of matrices or residues will generate variations of appearances such as color reversals. In the examples in Figures 9-13a and b, more residues were in the furrows of tread than on their

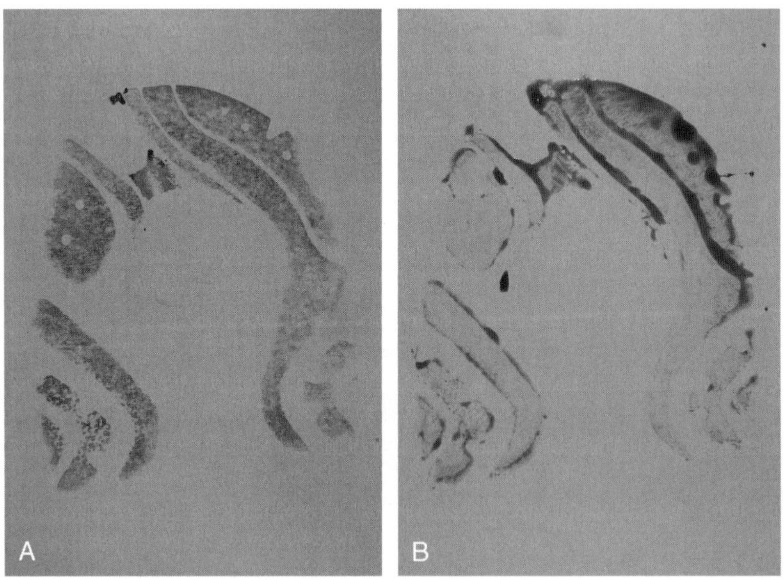

FIGURE 9-12
(a) and (b) Prints deposited with the same sole using different matrices.

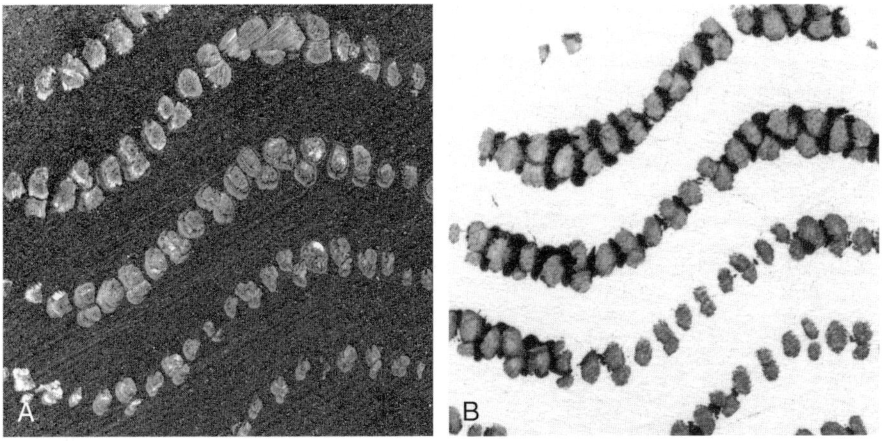

FIGURE 9-13
(a) Color reversal in which the tread appears lighter than the grooves or furrows. The tread elements removed residues from the substrate. (b) Color reversals between some tread elements. Extra matrices were between some of the tread elements, appearing darker than the gray elements and white furrows.

summits or dry tread to remove residues from the moist substrate. Even though the applications of residues vary, sufficiency might still exist between the two prints to determine the prints had been produced by the same shoe.

Figures 9-14a and b show two shoe prints made by the same sole. However, in this case, I rubbed the sole over textured concrete between printings, simulating the use and abuse that might occur to a shoe over time. The wear on the surface of the sole produced different uniqueness—in this case, at the third level. The sources of the prints changed through use or abuse of the shoe, even though the same sole made the prints.

Figures 9-15a and b depict the prints generated from different shoes with similar repeatable manufactured tread patterns. Although the details of the manufactured tread element dimensions are similar, the unique patterns generated within the repeated dimensions are specific to only one source.

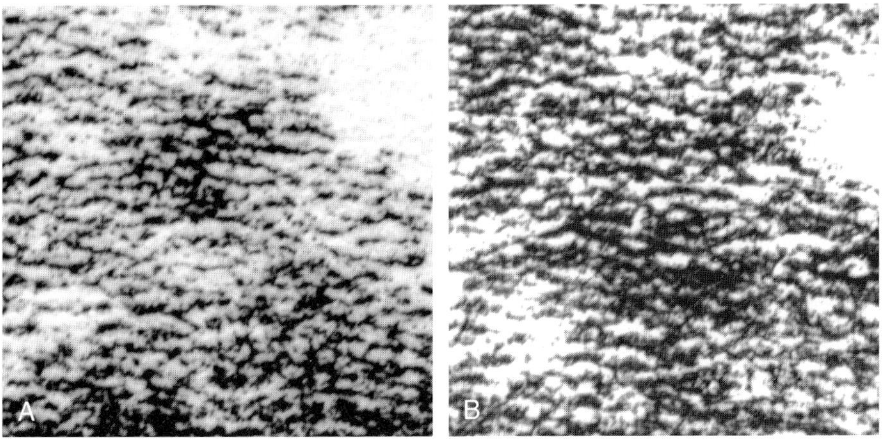

FIGURE 9-14
(a) and (b) Shoe prints made by the same sole. Between applications, the sole was rubbed over concrete, destroying the old textures within the wear and generating new textures and depositing third-level details.

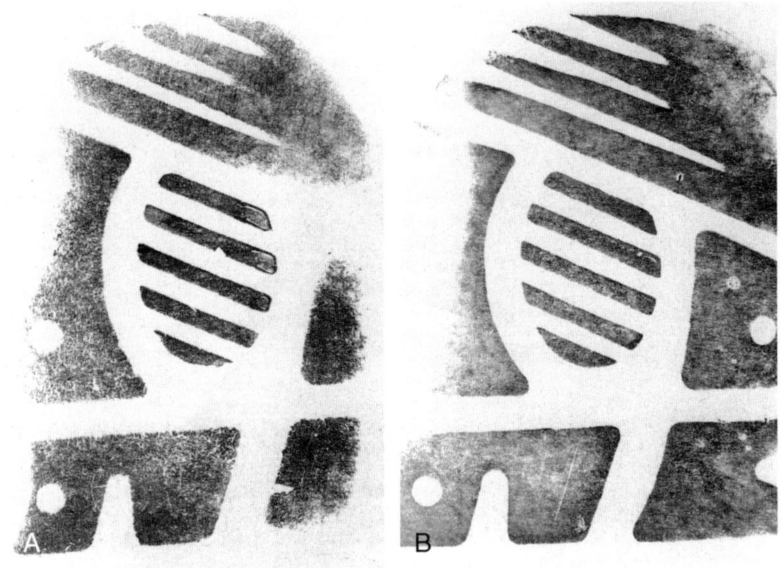

FIGURE 9-15
(a) and (b) Shoe prints with details made by different soles with similar repeatable features and different unique features.

Applying the same sole to a similar substrate but in different manner could result in a variation of appearance. Figures 9-16a and b denote a sole applied to a flat piece of paper with light pressure and the same sole applied to paper while rolling the paper over a tube. This variation of appearance emphasizes the need to submit shoes to the examiner for making standards so sufficient standards can be obtained.

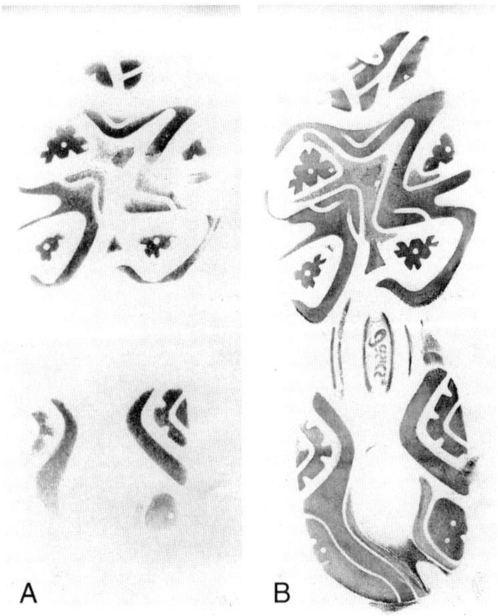

FIGURE 9-16
(a) The same tread as Figure 9-16b deposited a print in a flat motion with light pressure. (b) The same tread as Figure 9-16a deposited a print in a rolling motion and more pressure. Details of more features are captured in this manner.

SMOOTH SOLES

Smooth leather soles and heels quickly acquire wear marks. The application of the sole to a variety of surfaces cannot be controlled, and the resulting patterns of nicks and cuts generated will be unique. Figure 9-17 shows a smooth heel that acquired many imperfections in its surface. Lack of tread in the leather sole should not discourage the attempt of comparison of these types of prints as depicted in Figures 9-18a and 9-18b. Prints from smooth heels with wear imperfections are shown in Figures 9-19a and 9-19b. Remember to examine for the three levels of details of repeatable features then three levels of details of unique features.

FIGURE 9-17
A smooth heel that acquired many imperfections.

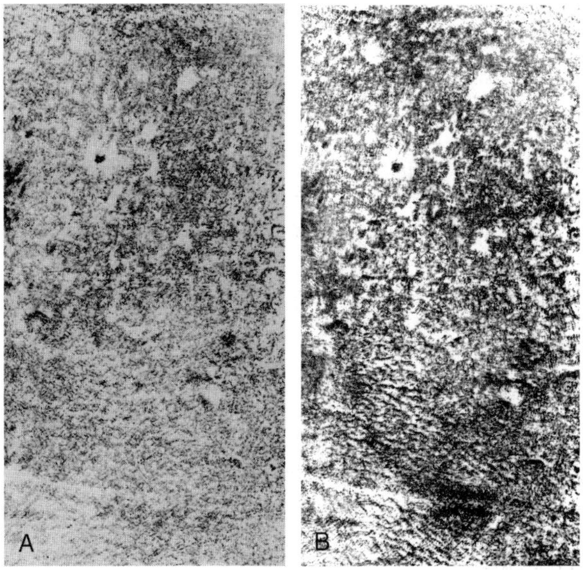

FIGURE 9-18
(a) and (b) Prints from the same area of soles. Lack of tread should not discourage an examination of first-, second-, and third-level details of unique features.

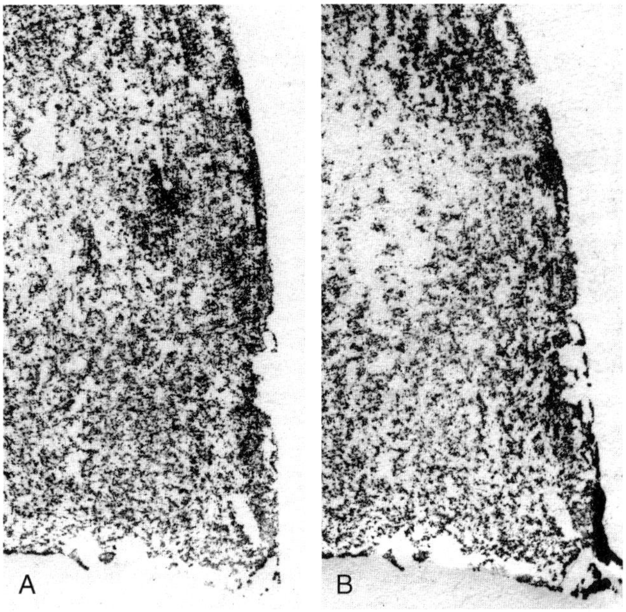

FIGURE 9-19
(a) and (b) Prints from same area of a heel with unique wear marks.

TIRE PRINTS

The remaining figures show several tire prints made with tires that have different tread patterns. No matter which type of tire is used to generate tread patterns on or in a particular substrate, the concept of tire prints on a particular surface carries over to any other print on any other substrate. If the features of the tire had been sufficiently recorded in a substrate at a scene and the features of a tire are sufficiently recorded in a standard substrate, a tire print examination can be conducted. The significance of the conclusion relies on the sufficiency of details of the persistent unique and persistent repeatable features of the tread, the ability of the substrates to capture sufficient details of the tread, and the skill of the examiner.

As with shoe prints, or any type of prints, the features of the tire can be recorded as first-, second-, and third-level details. For repeatable features of a tread, the first-level details indicate the general manufactured design of the tread. Second-level details are recorded dimensions and paths of the tread elements, and third-level details indicate the designed contours and textures within the individual elements. The unique features of the tread can be recorded as first-, second-, and third-level details as well. For the unique features of a tread, the first-level details indicate the general appearance and locations of the unique imperfections. Second-level details record the paths and outlines of the uniqueness, and third-level details are the contours and textures within or along the paths.

Unique shapes can be added to treads by driving over stones, tacks, or dirt. The value of stones, tacks, or dirt depends on the clarity and amount of the recordings and the persistency of the object that remains attached to the tread between the time of the deposition at the scene and the recording as a standard. The mark from the flat head of a tack attached to the tread is similar to the tool mark discussed in Chapter 8. Any impressed tire mark is similar to tool marks or shoe prints. It does not matter what the object is that created an impression.

Figures 9-20a–d show a tire print cast from a three-dimensional impression. Figures 9-21a–d show a standard tire. The directions and angles of oblique lighting vary within each set, making different details visible. This tire made the print that was cast.

FIGURE 9-20
(a)–(d) A tire print cast using different directions of oblique lighting, causing shadows. Different directions of oblique lighting assist in seeing the details in the cast.

FIGURE 9-21
(a)–(d) A tire tread that made the impression that was cast in Figures 9-20a–d. Different directions of oblique lighting assist in seeing the details in the tire.

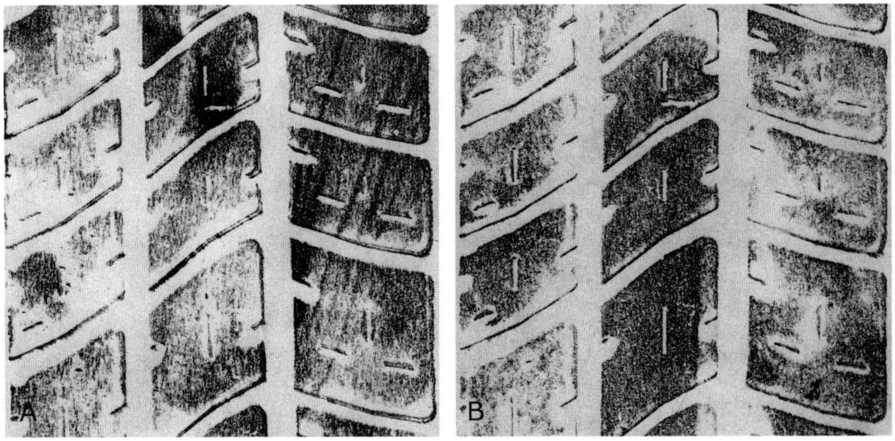

FIGURE 9-22
(a) and (b) The same tire produced both prints. Detail of one unique feature can be found in the top center element.

Like shoes and their prints, applying the same tread but using similar or different matrices or residues will generate variations of appearances because the receiving substrate will not accept the residues the same way. Even though the residues vary, sufficiency might still exist between the two prints to determine the prints had been produced by the same tire. Applying the same tire but using different applications of matrices or residues will generate variations of appearances as color reversals. More residues could be in the furrows of tread than on the summits of the elements. Another method for color reversal to occur is for dry tread to remove moist residues from the substrate. Even though the applications of residues vary, sufficiency might still exist between the two prints to determine that the prints had been produced by the same tire.

Even if matrices, substrates, and development techniques are similar, sufficiency might not exist. Figures 9-22a and b show tire prints made by the same tread. The examination would continue beyond this limited section of the impressions. As all other examinations, the amount of details needed for sufficiency depends on their clarity.

CONCLUSIONS

The figures in this chapter emphasize just some of the variations of appearances that occur when examining prints. No two applications of the same shoe or tire to a similar substrate will result in an identical print. There will always be variation of appearances in the application of a tread to a substrate. There is no such thing as a perfect match between impressions, prints, or images from the same source. It does not matter what the tread and substrate are. If it leaves a mark or impression in a receiving substrate, it can be examined.

For conclusions of examinations, refer to Chapter 6. The sufficiency and persistency of the repeatable and unique features must be considered when determining judgment. The determinations of agreement and disagreement rest upon the quality and quantity of three levels of details of the persistent repeatable features and the quality and quantity of three levels of details of the persistent unique features of the source(s) as recorded in the substrates.

BIBLIOGRAPHY

Abbott, John R. *Footwear Evidence—The examination, identification, and comparison of footwear impressions,* Charles C. Thomas, Publisher, Springfield, Illinois, 1964.

Bodziak, William J. 'Shoe and Tire Impression Evidence,' *FBI Law Enforcement Bulletin,* July 1984, 2–12.

Bodziak, William J. 'Manufacturing Processes for Athletic Show Outsoles and Their Significance in the Examination of Footwear Impression Evidence,' *Journal of Forensic Sciences,* 31 (1), 1986, 153–176.

Bodziak, William J. *Footwear Impression Evidence,* CRC Press, Boca Raton, Florida, 1995.

Bodziak, William J. 'Some Methods for Taking Two-Dimensional Comparison Standards of Tires,' *Journal of Forensic Identification,* 1996, 46 (6), 689–701.

Bodziak, William J. *Footwear Impression Evidence: Detection, Recovery, and Examination,* second edition, CRC Press, Boca Raton, Florida, 2000.

Cassidy, Michael J. *Footwear Identification,* Public Relations Branch of the Royal Canadian Mounted Police, Ottawa, Ontario, Canada, 1980.

Cook, Claude W. 'Comparative Analysis (Foot and Tire Track Impressions),' *Identification News,* 1979, 29 (4), 3–6.

Cook, Claude W. 'Footprints and Tire Tracks (Class or Individual Characteristics?),' *Identification News,* 1981, 31 (7), 7–10.

Grogan, R. J. and T. R. Watson. 'Tyres and Crime,' *Journal of the Forensic Science Society,* 1971, 11 (1), 3–14.

Hamm, Ernest D. 'Tire Tracks and Footwear Identification,' *Identification News,* 1975, 25 (1), 3–6.

Hamm, Ernest D. 'Locating an Area on a Suspect Tire for Comparative Examination to a Questioned Track,' *Journal of Forensic Identification,* 1988, 38 (4), 143–151.

Hamm, Ernest D. 'The Individuality of Class Characteristics in Converse All-Star Footwear,' *Journal of Forensic Identification,* 1989, 39 (5), 277–292.

Hamm, Ernest D. 'Track Identification: An Historical Overview,' *Journal of Forensic Identification,* 1989, 39 (6), 333–338.

Keijzer, J. 'Identification Value of Imperfections in Shoes with Polyurethane Soles in Comarative Shoeprint Examination,' *Journal of Forensic Identification,* 1990, 40 (4), 217–223.

Kirk, Paul L. *Crime Investigation—Physical Evidence and the Police Laboratory,* Interscience Publishers, Inc. a division of John Wiley & Sons, Inc. New York 1953, 301–310.

Kirk, Paul L. edited by John I. Thornton. *Crime Investigation:* Second Edition, John Wiley & Sons, New York 1974, 74–83.

McDonald, Peter. *Tire Imprint Evidence,* Elsevier, New York, 1989.

Moenssens, Andre A., Carol E. Henderson and Sharon G. Portwood. *Scientific Evidence in Civil and Criminal Cases* – Fifth Edition, Foundation Press, New York 2007, 775–776.

Music, Doreen K. and William J. Bodziak. 'Evaluation of the Air Bubbles Present in Polyurethane Shoe Outsoles as Applicable in Footwear Impression Comparisons,' *Journal of Forensic Sciences,* 1988, 33 (5), 1185–1197.

Nause, Lawren A. 'Tire Impressions as Evidence,' *Identification Canada,* 1985, 8 (3) and 8(4).

Nause, Lawren A. 'The Science of Tire Impression Identification,' *Royal Canadian Mounted Police Gazette,* 1987, 49 (1), 1–25.

O'Hara Charles E. and James W. Osterburg. *An Introduction to Criminalistics—The Application of the Physical Sciences to the Detection of Crime,* The Macmillan Company, New York 1949 fourth printing 1960, 103–120.

Osterburg, James W. *The Crime Laboratory—Case Studies of Scientific Criminal Investigation,* Clark Boardman Company, Ltd. New York 1982, 41–51, 241–269.

Zeldes, Ilya. 'Footwear and Tire Track Examination in the Soviet Union,' *Journal of Forensic Identification,* 1989, 39 (6), 367–374.

Zugibe, Frederick and James T. Costello. 'Identification of the Murder Weapon by Intricate Patterned Injury Measurements,' *Journal of Forensic Sciences,* 1986, 31(1), 329–332.

CHAPTER 10

Surface Structures on a Body

CONTENTS

SKIN

Studying the surfaces of skin and the receiving substrates helps the examiner to determine whether the known skin made the questioned print from a scene. As skin is part of nature, all parts of skin are unique. The embryological and fetal development and then the later regeneration of skin produce surfaces that bear the unique natural patterns of textures, creases, wrinkles, ridges, and imperfections. As skin ages or heals, the regeneration process strives for but cannot reach perfect replication, as each skin cell is part of nature's unique tapestries. Skin has unique persistent natural patterns but not permanent patterns.

A print from a crime scene needs to be collected, and a candidate must be found before the surface of its source is altered through significant damage, disease, scarring, or aging and healing. The correct object can be found and examined, but if the surface that had been the source of the print is sufficiently damaged through trauma or disease, the new prints will not correspond to the uniqueness that is visible in the questioned print. Even though it is the same object, it is now a different surface of the source for the details that had been recorded in the first image.

The patterns of features found in skin do not share commonality with any other source. Figures 10-1a–d depict a few of the various surfaces of patterned skin found on a body. These pictures show skin from the palm, wrist, elbow, and lips. As can be seen, many areas of skin have textured patterns. As found in all natural patterns, skin is unique.

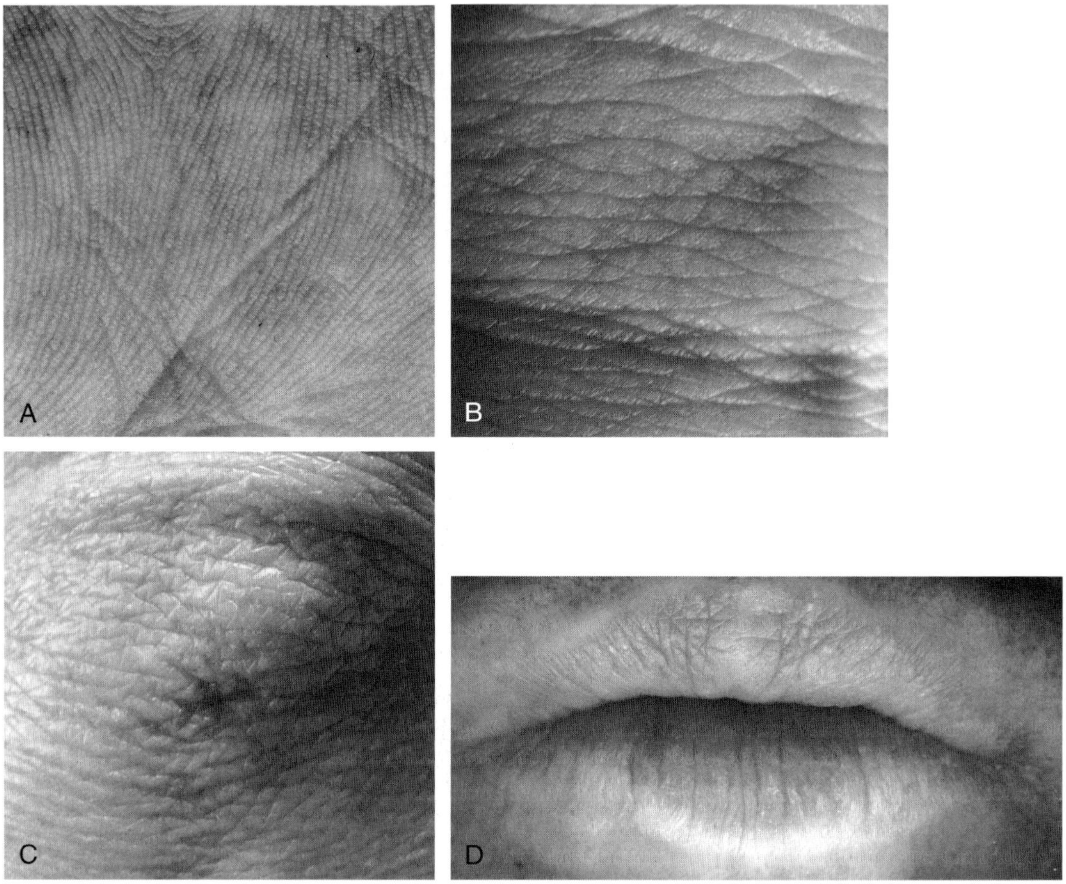

FIGURE 10-1
(a) Palm skin. (b) Wrist skin. (c) Elbow skin. (d) Lip skin.

Volar Skin

The palm side of a hand or finger (palmar) and the sole of a foot or toe (plantar) are volar surfaces. An impression from a section of palmar surface is often referred to as a finger- or palmprint or from the plantar surface as a sole- or toeprint, as these are all subsets of overall volar prints.

Examiners have labeled the ridges in volar as both permanent and unique. The overall ridge paths and their sequences and configurations are extremely persistent. This enables the classification, filing, and record keeping of fingerprint cards. Classification does not use all the features found in friction skin as it uses just the friction ridge paths and their configurations. It does not use the edges and textures of the ridges. For its purposes with the rules of classifying prints, these ridge path configurations had been deemed permanent. However, the skin cells regenerate but do not perfectly replicate themselves, as the cells result from the template of the generating layer of skin. Skin ages, is traumatized, and heals at the cellular level. All skin does this. When skin is significantly traumatized, the generating layer is damaged, heals, and forms scars. Permanency at the cellular level is found to be lacking. The resulting scar is unique and remains persistent unless additional significant trauma occurs. Forensic comparative science uses persistency between the times of contact between the source and substrate. Permanency is not needed.

There are more features within this type of skin than just friction ridges. Friction ridges, furrows, and creases, and possibly scars, cuts, warts, blisters, wrinkles, healing skin, or other imperfections are all parts of the volar skin. This is why the term *persistent* is much more appropriate than *permanent.* Scientists should not intentionally ignore details of features of the source when examining images but rather understand and use all the available features of the source and their image details when examining natural patterns of any prints, including volar prints. Persistency is used in fracture examinations, tool marks, shoe and tire prints, and any comparative science. When details of these features are present in images, scientists should not consciously ignore them as the rules of classifying fingerprint ridge flow and paths are expanded to include the examination of unique patterns beyond ridges. The strict rules of classifying fingerprints are not needed for determining the origin of an image. The images of all the features of volar skin result in different clarity of the levels of details that can exist as general appearances, paths, and textures of creases, scars, cuts, warts, blisters, and regenerating skin. Figures 10-2a–f show various surfaces of patterned volar skin. As can be seen, many areas of volar skin have patterns beyond ridges.

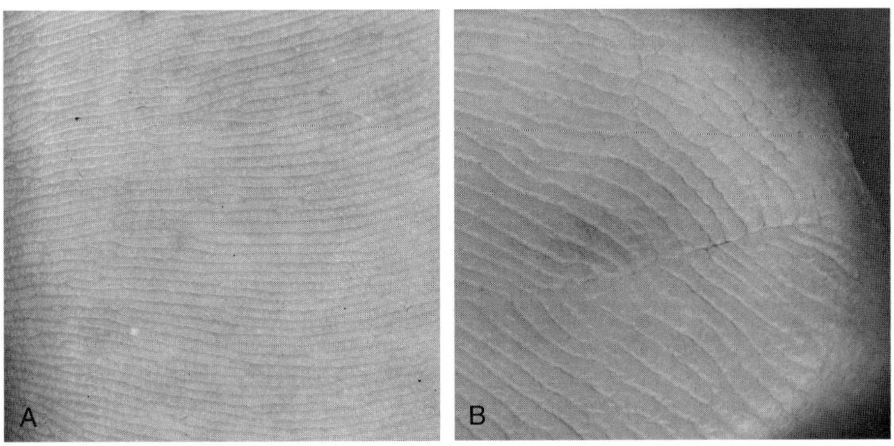

FIGURE 10-2
(a) Volar skin with friction ridges. (b) Volar skin with friction ridges and a scar.

(Continued)

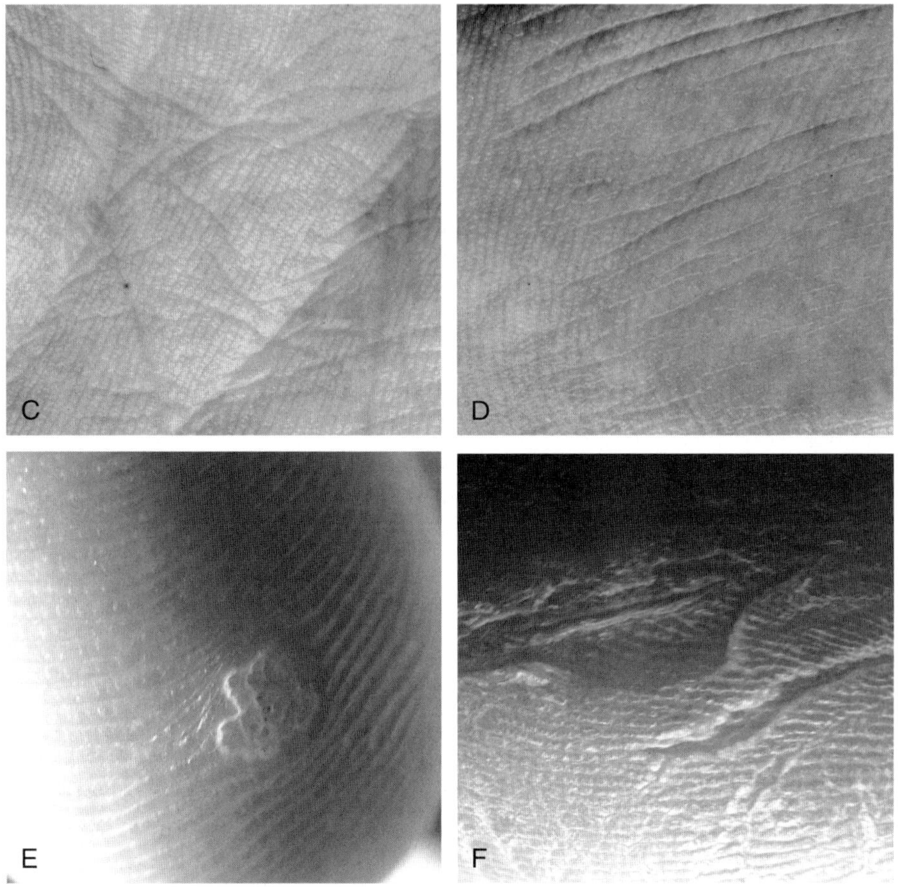

FIGURE 10-2—CONT'D

(c) Volar skin with friction ridges and many creases. (d) Volar skin with less-prominent ridges and many creases. (e) Volar skin with a wart. (f) Cracked, dry volar skin.

Pictures of volar skin, before and after significant trauma, are presented in Figures 10-3a and b. Notice that the volar skin has been damaged in its generating layer as a result of injury from a high-speed drill, producing a scar in the delta or triangular ridge path area in the upper-right side of this image and realignment of some ridge to crease configurations in the lower-left area of the image, away from the site of the direct injury. This demonstrates a dramatic change in the generating layer of the features of the skin. Persistency of the source must be considered when examining images from this skin.

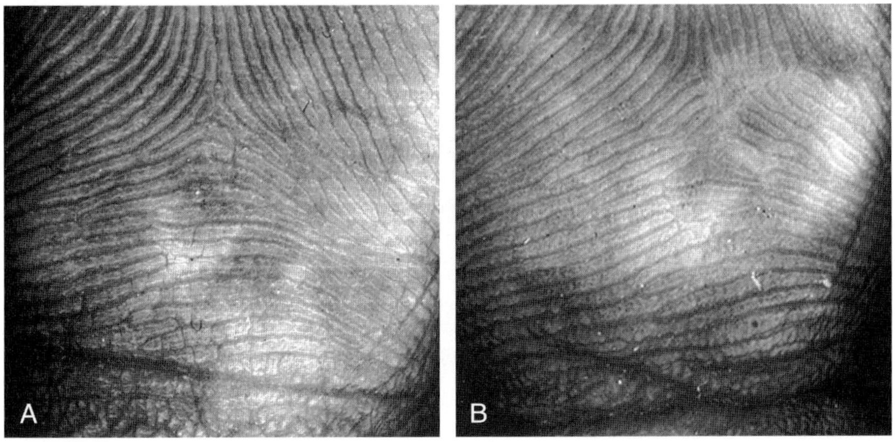

FIGURE 10-3
(a) Image of volar skin before trauma. (b) Image of volar skin after significant trauma. This trauma is found as a scar in the upper-right area in this image. Significant trauma to the generating layer of skin affected the generation of ridges and creases away from the scar. Note the crease and ridge arrangements near the lower left area of the image. (Figures 10-3a and b courtesy of Mike Grimm.)

Skin Prints

The scientist studies the details in the questioned skin print for the unique features and then examines the standard skin prints to determine whether the questioned prints were made by the known standard skin. After analyses, comparisons, and evaluations, the examiner makes a determination of whether the prints had been made by this skin based on the quality and quantity of the first, second, and third levels of details of the persistent unique features of the skin.

Many skin prints are presented in this chapter, but no matter what skin is used to generate prints on or in a particular substrate, the concept of skin prints on a particular surface carries over to any other print from a unique natural source on any other substrate. If the features of the skin had been recorded with sufficient quality and quantity of details on a substrate at a scene, and the features of skin are sufficiently recorded on a standard substrate, a skin print examination can be done. The significance of the conclusion relies on the sufficiency of details of the persistent unique features of the skin and the ability of the substrates to capture sufficient details in the impressions.

The unique features of the skin can be recorded as first-, second-, and third-level details. The first-level details indicate the general appearances, directions, and locations of the unique features. Second-level details record the paths and outlines of the uniqueness, and third-level details are the contours and textures within or along the paths. Figures 10-4a–i depict variations in the recorded quality and quantity of levels of details of wrist, elbow, and lip skin.

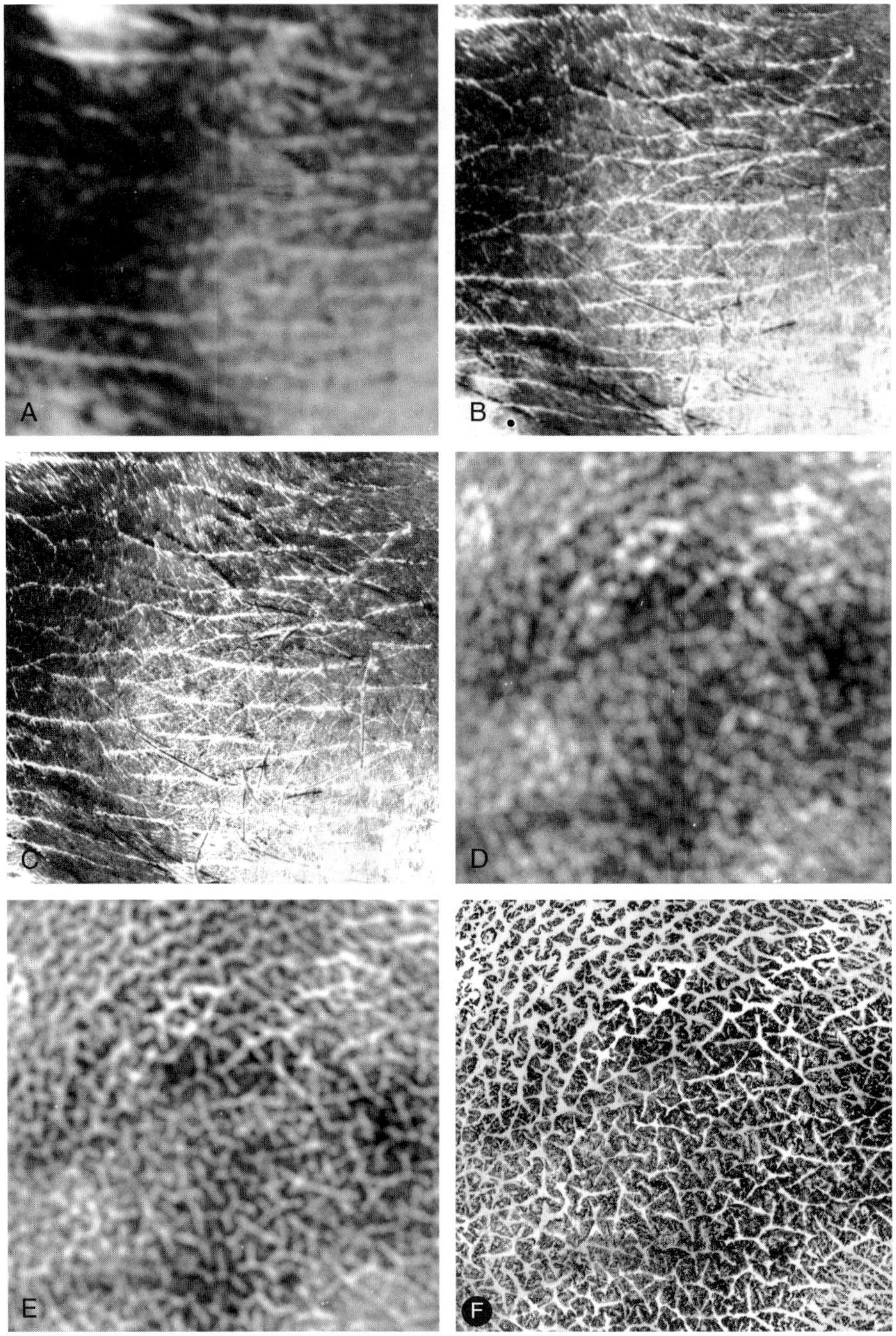

FIGURE 10-4
(a) First-level general appearance and some second-level paths of creases in wrist print. (b) First-level general appearance, second-level specific paths of creases, and some third-level texture within skin elements among the creases in wrist print. (c) First-level general appearance, second-level specific paths of creases, and much third-level texture within wrist print. (d) First-level general appearance and some second-level paths of creases in elbow print. (e) First-level general appearance, second-level specific paths of creases, and maybe some third-level texture within skin elements among the creases in elbow print. (f) First-level general appearance, second-level specific paths of creases, and much third-level texture within elbow print.

(Continued)

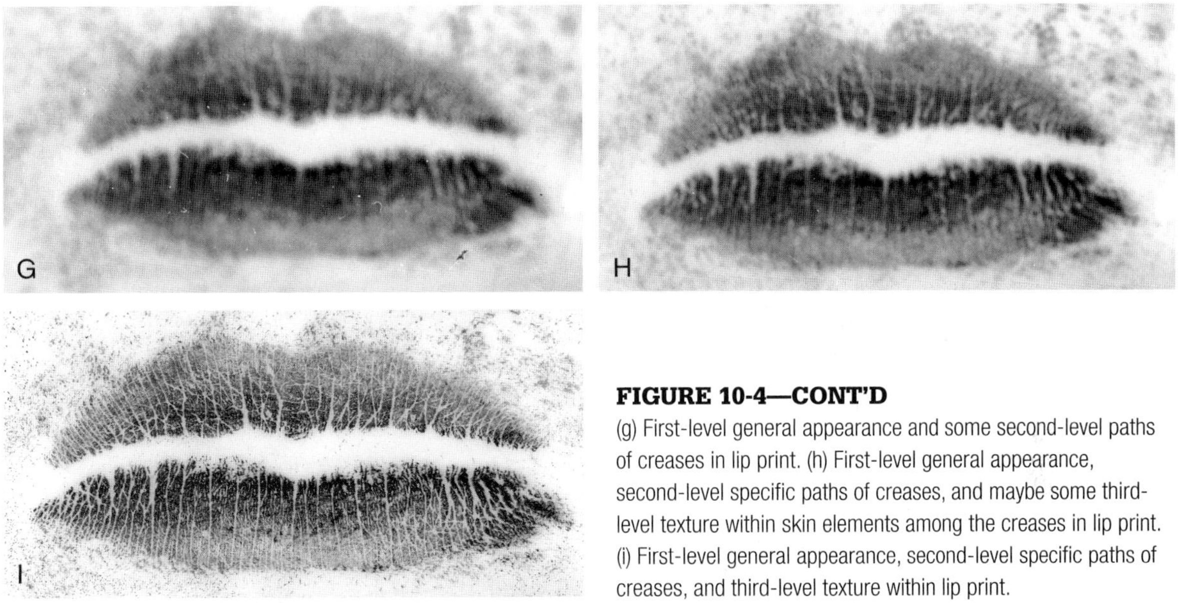

FIGURE 10-4—CONT'D

(g) First-level general appearance and some second-level paths of creases in lip print. (h) First-level general appearance, second-level specific paths of creases, and maybe some third-level texture within skin elements among the creases in lip print. (i) First-level general appearance, second-level specific paths of creases, and third-level texture within lip print.

Figures 10-5a–l show sets of prints from elbow and wrist skin. The sets of impressions are recorded with varying expressions of bending the elbow or wrist as the skin is applied to the substrate. As the expressions of the elbow or wrist vary from bent out, flat, or bent in, the features that are captured as details vary in their appearances. As the quality and quantity of levels of details vary, some images cannot be determined as having originated from the same elbow or wrist. Similar expressions of the source are needed to help determine whether the skin made the impressions.

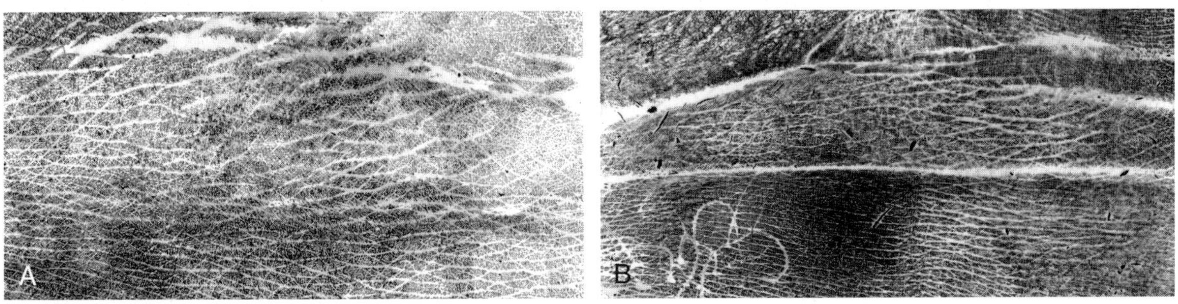

FIGURE 10-5

(a) A print of wrist skin, hand and fingers held up or out. The same wrist made the print in (b). (b) A print of wrist skin, hand and fingers held flat with arm.

(Continued)

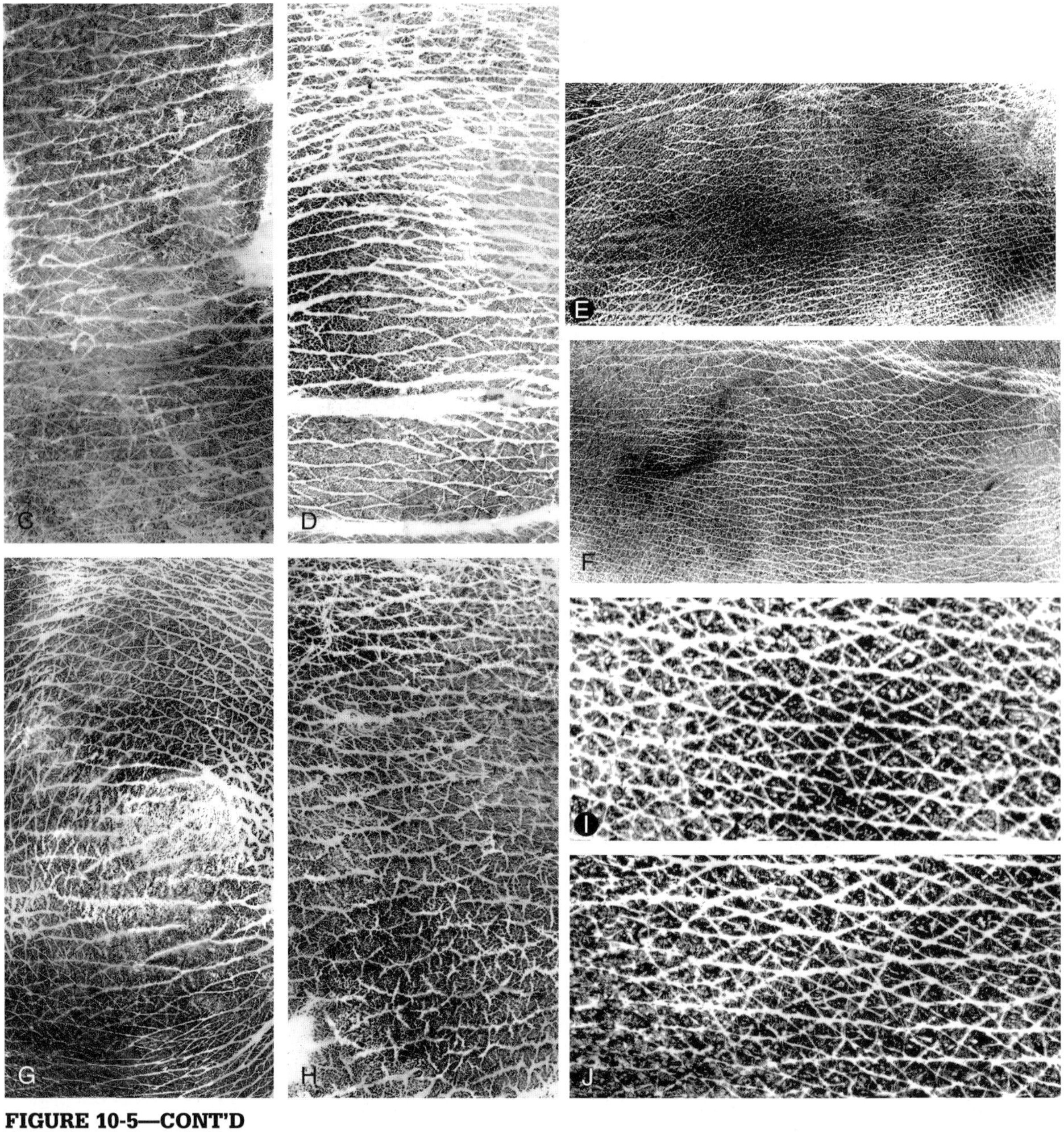

FIGURE 10-5—CONT'D

(c) A print of elbow skin, arm bent. The same elbow made the print in (d). (d) A print of elbow skin, arm straight. (e) and (f) Two impressions of different wrists. (g) and (h) Two impressions of different elbows. (i) and (j) Two impressions of the same wrist.

(Continued)

Lips have creases and textured surfaces and can have a wide variety of expressions. Recorded prints at crime scenes might be found on the sticky side of tape, glass windows, or paper. For examinations, the standards need to be captured in a similar expression as the evidence was recorded. A variety of expressions were used to record the impressions in Figures 10-6a–h. Note the quality and quantity of details with similar or different expressions of the lips. Some of the prints were made by the same person.

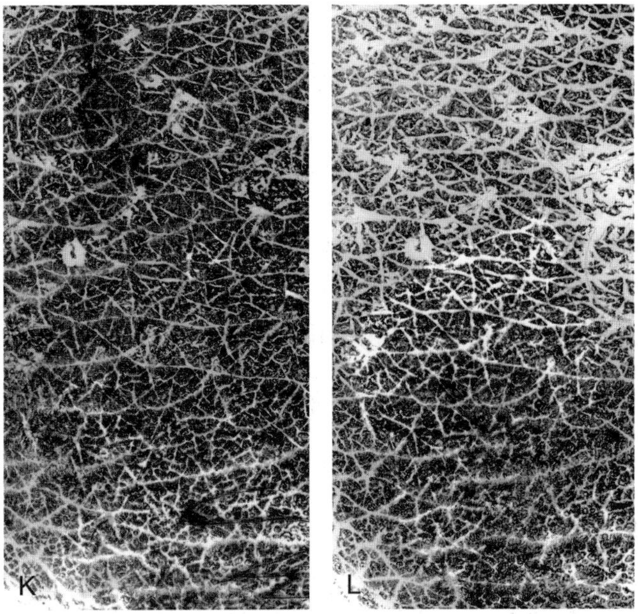

FIGURE 10-5—CONT'D
(k) and (l) Two impressions of the same elbow.

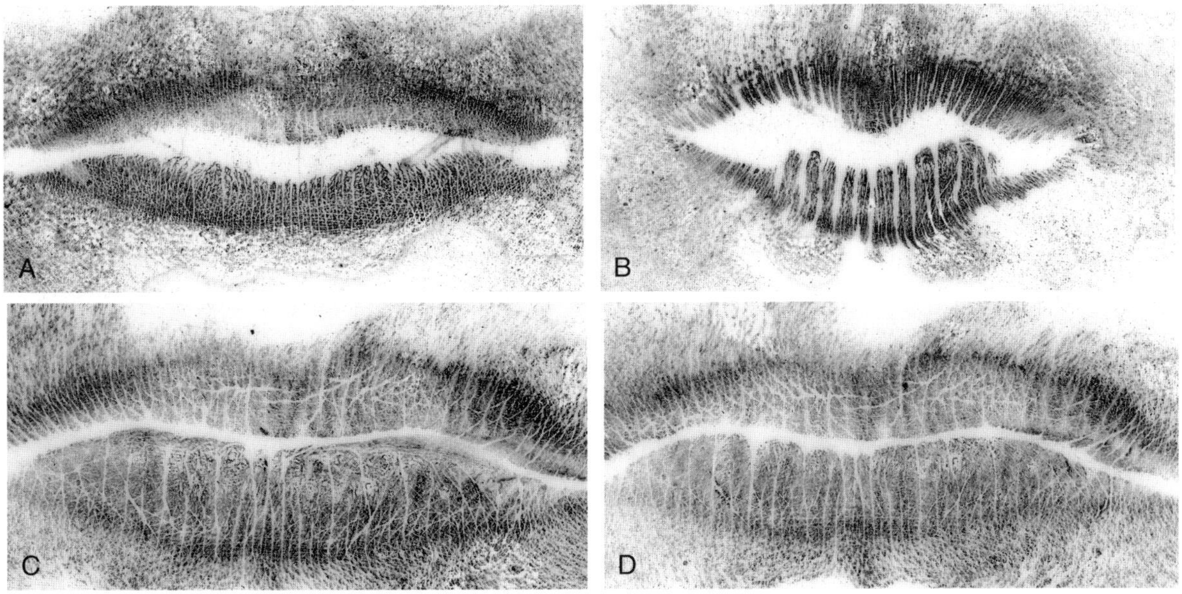

FIGURE 10-6
(a) Lip print of relaxed lips. (b) Lip print of puckered lips of the same person in (a). (c) Lip print of relaxed lips of a second person. (d) Lip print of relaxed lips of the same person in (c).

(Continued)

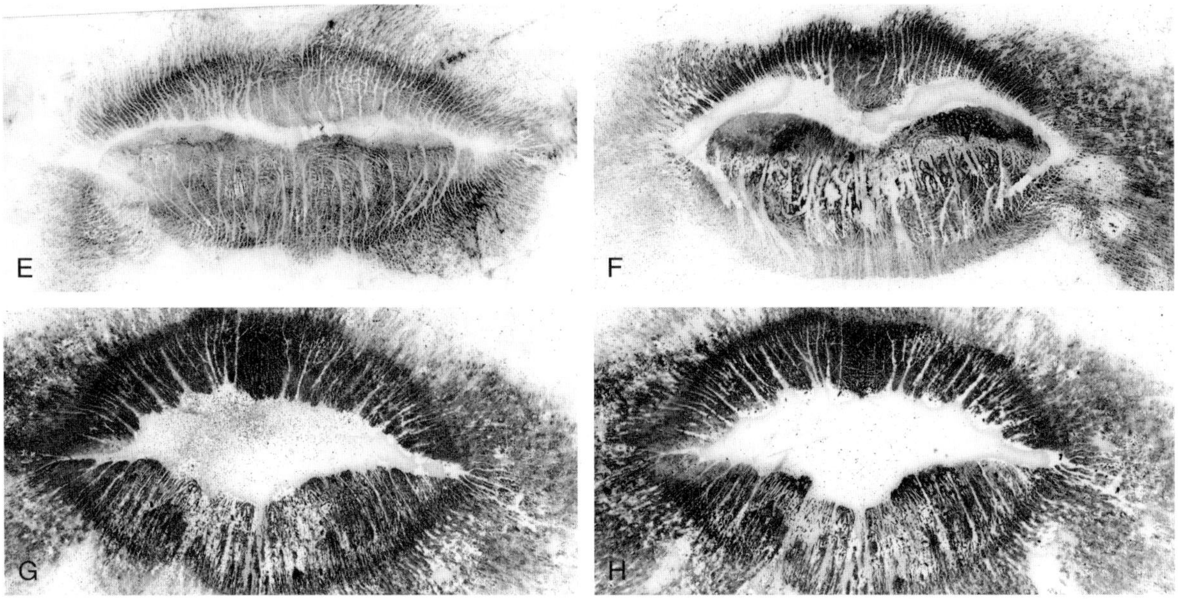

FIGURE 10-6—CONT'D

(e) Lip print of puckered lips of the same person in (c) and (d). (f) Lip print of puckered lips of a third person. (g) Lip print of puckered lips of a fourth person. (h) Lip print of puckered lips of the same person in (g).

Volar Skin Prints

Many volar skin prints are presented in this chapter. No matter which volar skin is used to generate prints on or in a particular substrate, the concept of volar skin prints on a particular surface carries over to any other print from a unique natural source on any other substrate. The variety of unique features of the volar skin can be recorded as various quality and quantity of first-, second-, and third-level details. Creases, scars, warts, and blistered skin can all be recorded as first-, second-, and third-level details, independent of or in conjunction with the ridges. The first-level details indicate the general appearances, directions, and locations of the unique patterns. Second-level details record the paths and outlines of the unique feature, and third-level details are the contours and textures within or along the paths of the feature. Figures 10-7a–o depict variations in the recorded details.

Applying the same volar skin but using different matrices or residues will generate variations of appearances because the receiving substrate will not accept an image the same. Figures 10-8a–d represent some of these variations. Even though the residues vary, sufficiency often exists between the two prints to determine that the prints had been produced by the same skin.

Examiners often expect images of friction ridges to appear dark on a light background, typical of many latent prints and standard ink prints. Applying the same volar skin but using different applications of matrices or residues and different

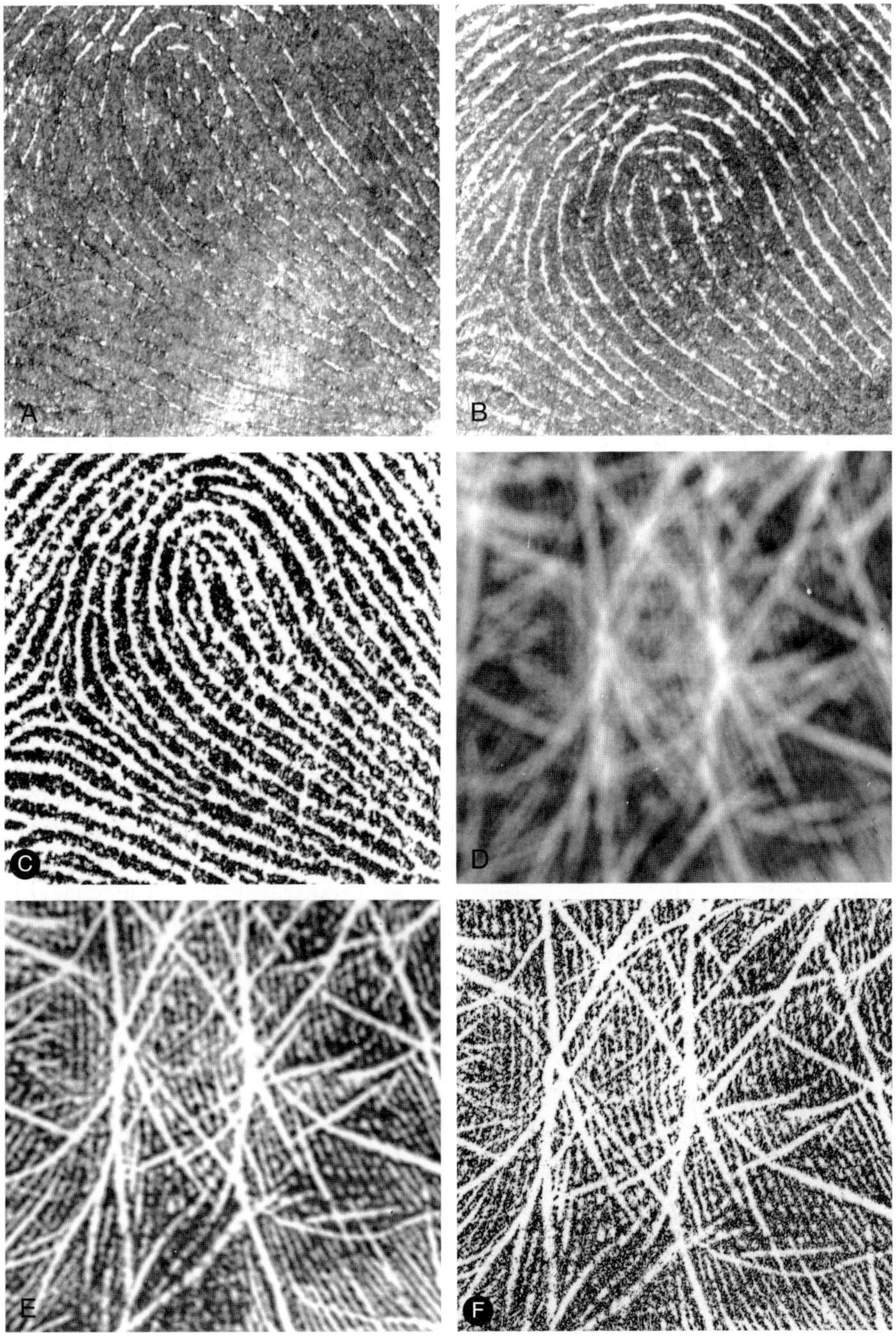

FIGURE 10-7
(a) First- and some second-level details of friction ridges. (b) First-, second-, and some third-level details of friction ridges. (c) First-, second-, and third-level details of friction ridges. (d) First- and some second-level details of creases and friction ridges. (e) First-, second-, and some third-level details of creases and friction ridges. (f) First-, second-, and third-level details of creases and friction ridges.

(Continued)

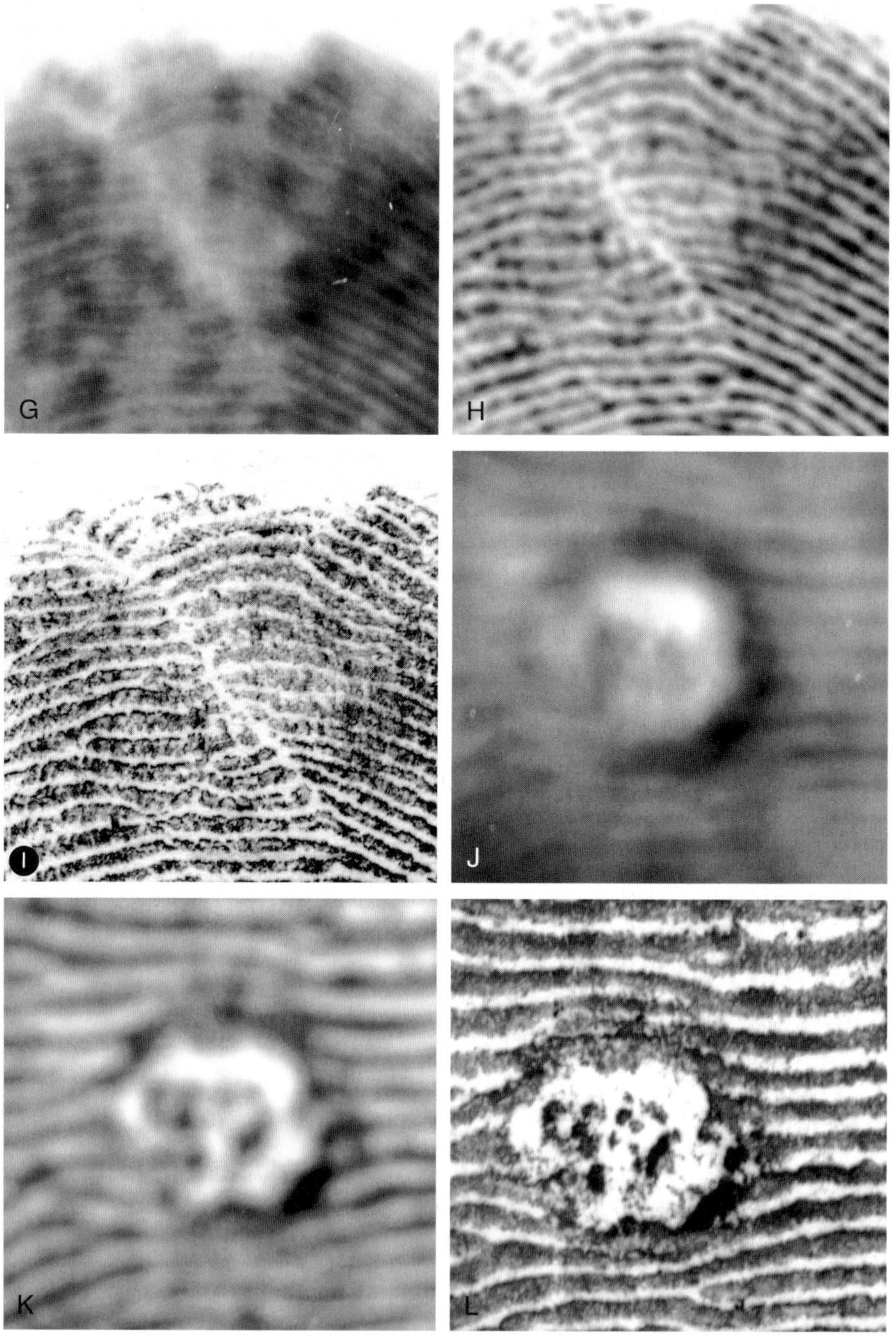

FIGURE 10-7—CONT'D
(g) First- and some second-level details of a scar and friction ridges. (h) First-, second-, and some third-level details of a scar and friction ridges. (i) First-, second-, and third-level details of a scar and friction ridges. (j) First- and some second-level details of a wart and friction ridges. (k) First-, second-, and some third-level details of a wart and friction ridges. (l) First-, second-, and third-level details of a wart and friction ridges.

(Continued)

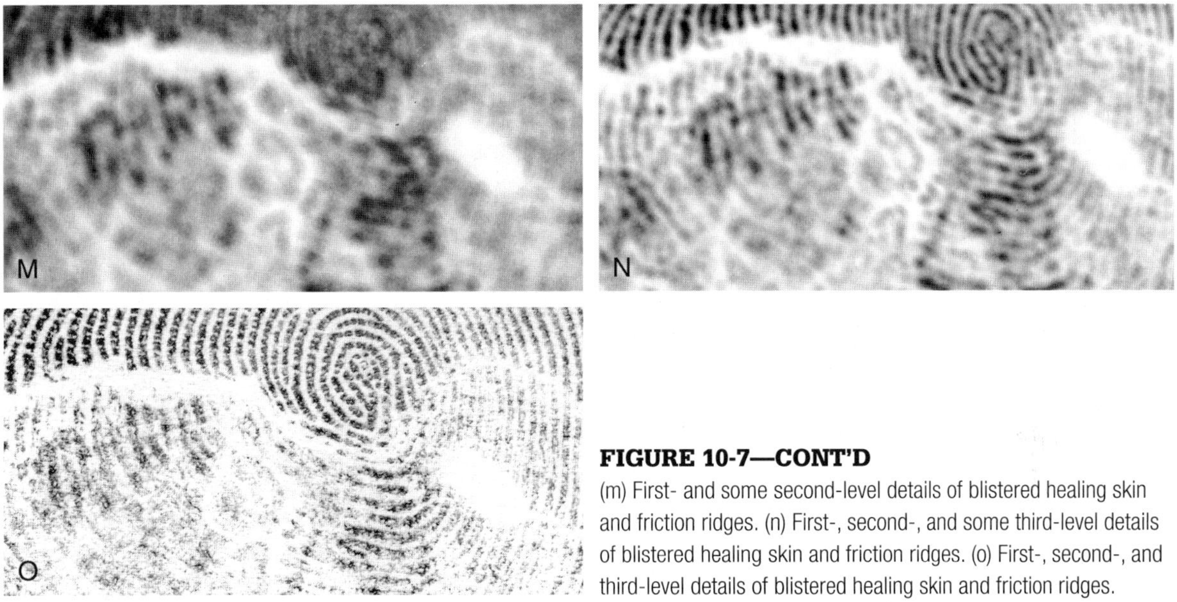

FIGURE 10-7—CONT'D
(m) First- and some second-level details of blistered healing skin and friction ridges. (n) First-, second-, and some third-level details of blistered healing skin and friction ridges. (o) First-, second-, and third-level details of blistered healing skin and friction ridges.

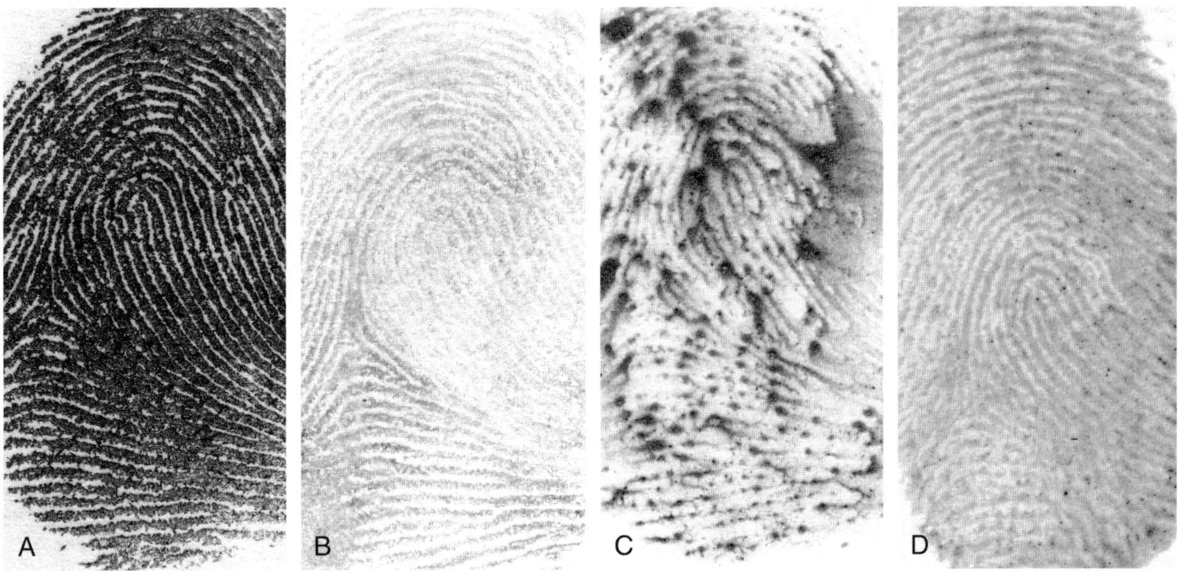

FIGURE 10-8
(a) Volar print with a heavy grease matrix, developed with powder. (b) Volar print with a watery matrix, developed with powder. (c) Volar print with moist dirt matrix, no development. (d) Volar print with dark syrup matrix, no development.

development or processing techniques will generate variations of appearances as color reversals. During application of the skin to the substrate, more residues could be in the furrows of volar skin than on the summits of the ridges. Another way color reversal can occur is if dry volar skin removes residues from a dirty and moist substrate. A processing technique such as white powder or cyanoacrylate glue fuming that develops light ridges on a dark background often results in color reversal. Figures 10-9a–f represent some of the results of these variations.

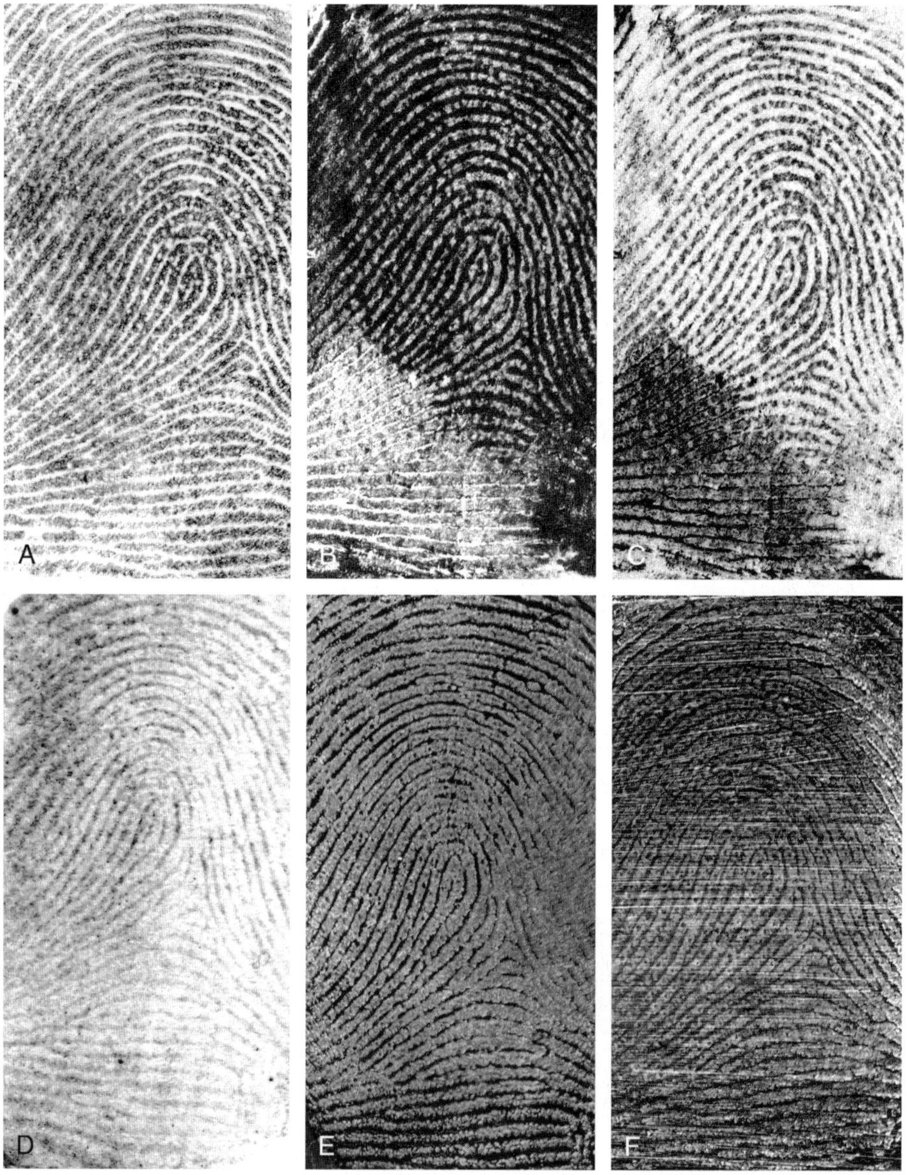

FIGURE 10-9
(a) Volar print with ridges recorded with black ink on white paper. (b) Ink volar print with color reversal in upper and right part of the image. More ink is in the furrows and pores in most areas of the volar skin that made this print. (c) Same volar skin print as in (b), but the color is reversed to demonstrate ink in furrows and ink on summits of the ridges. (d) Volar print with color reversal caused by matrices such as oils or blood in the furrows with less on the summits of ridges. (e) Volar print on black surface developed with light-colored powder. (f) Volar print with color reversal caused by dry ridges removing some dark residues from a light-colored substrate.

Other unique shapes can be part of volar skin by the addition of warts, blisters, scars, or other imperfections from trauma, disease, or aging. The value of these unique patterns also depends on their persistency between the time of the deposition at the scene and recording as a standard. Figures 10-10a–f show sets of impressions of volar skin with a variety of imperfections. Clear details are recorded to demonstrate the value of these imperfections.

Figures 10-11a–f show prints from the same finger on a plastic substrate developed with powder. The variations of appearances in these figures primarily resulted from distorted skin as the directions or motions of applying a finger to a substrate are expressed here. Motions when applying a source to substrate influence the appearances of recorded details in the images. Note the general appearance as first-level details. Also, look for misalignments and color reversals of some ridges and furrows.

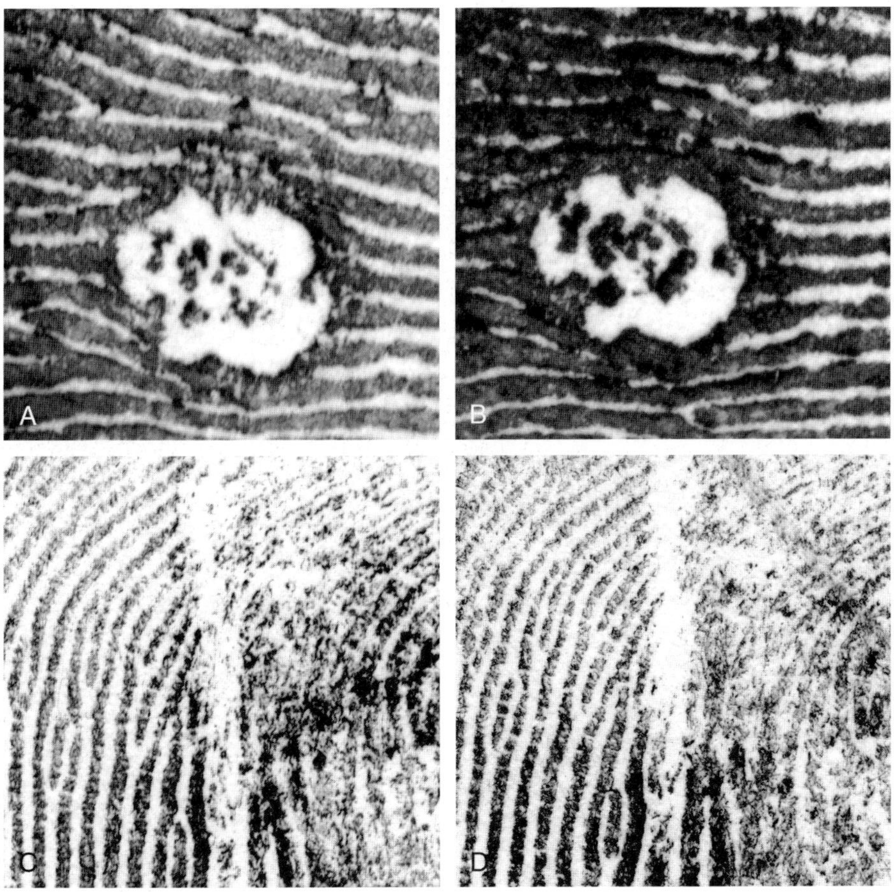

FIGURE 10-10

(a) and (b) Prints from volar skin with a wart. (c) and (d) Prints from volar skin with a healing blister.

(Continued)

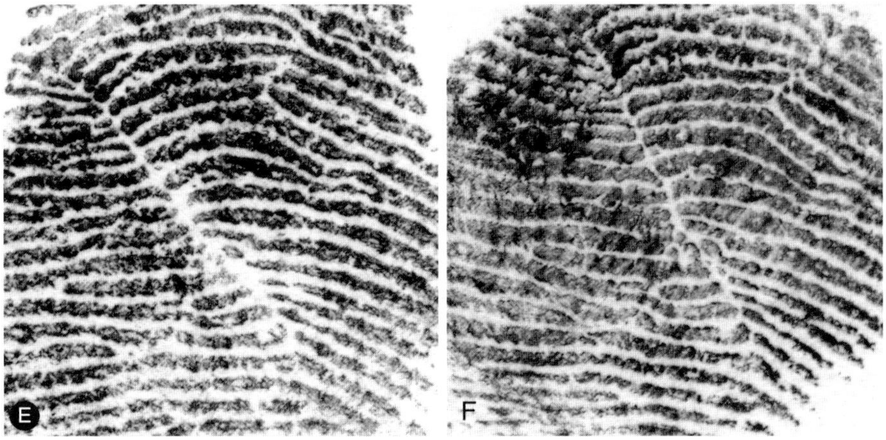

FIGURE 10-10—CONT'D
(e) and (f) Prints from volar skin with a scar.

FIGURE 10-11
(a) Fingerprint applied with slight upward motion distortion. (b) Fingerprint applied with slight downward motion distortion. (c) Fingerprint applied with slight left to right motion distortion. (d) Fingerprint applied with slight right to left motion distortion.

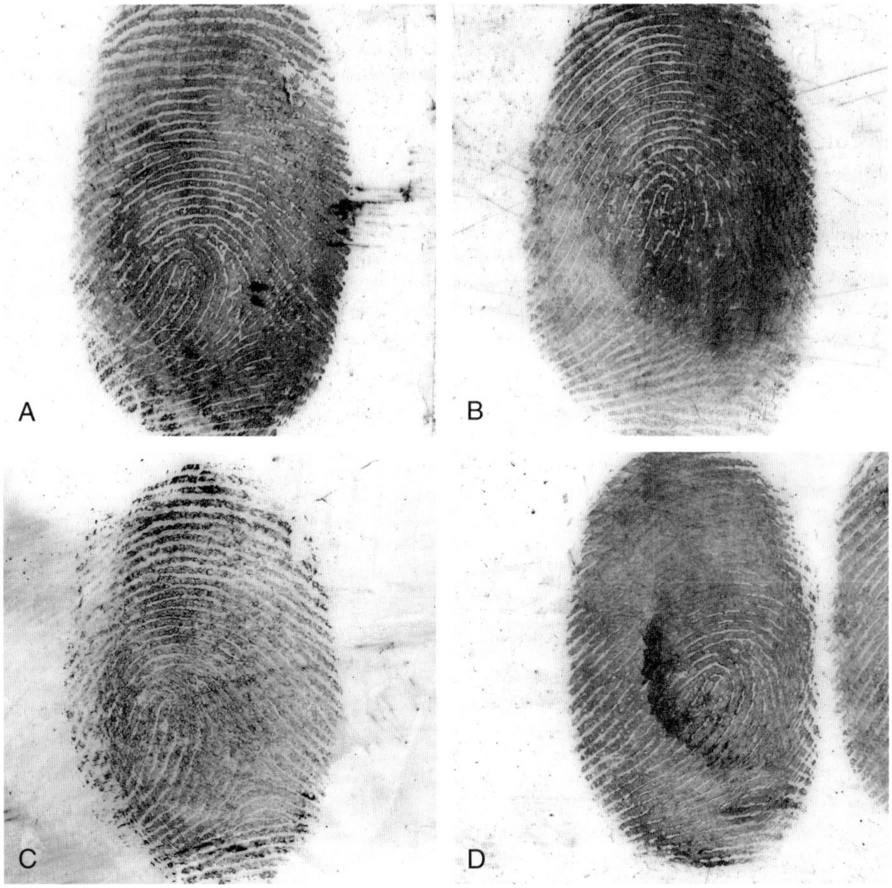

(Continued)

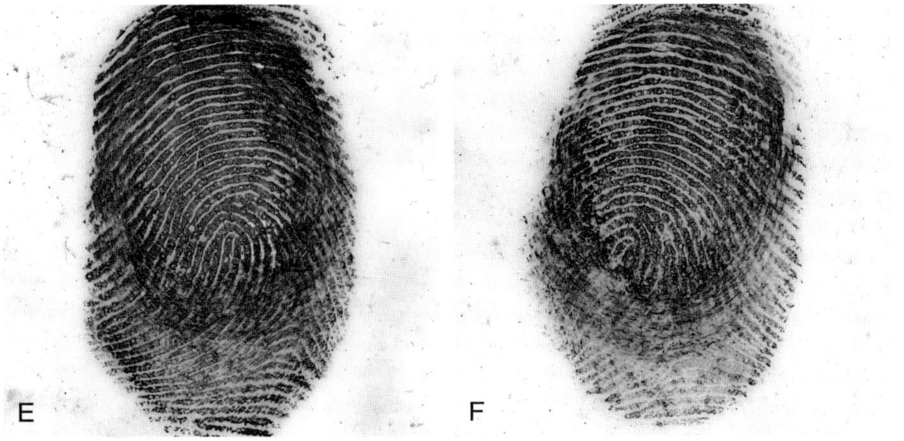

FIGURE 10-11—CONT'D
(e) Fingerprint applied with clockwise motion distortion. (f) Fingerprint applied with counterclockwise motion distortion.

The amount of pressure applied to the substrate affects the appearance of prints. Figures 10-12a–d depict very light to heavy pressure as a finger is applied to a white plastic substrate and the prints were developed with powder. Note the spacing between the ridges and furrows.

Figures 10-13a–c depict volar prints from adjacent fingers on one hand. Determining the simultaneity of deposition of digits or sections of a volar surface considers all the factors typical within any analyses, comparisons, and evaluations for consideration. The substrate, matrices, pressures, distortions, motions, sequences, and configurations of all details are all considered in the judgment of individual elements as individual prints and as an aggregate print. *Aggregate* is a better term than *simultaneous* because aggregate describes the examination process, whereas simultaneous describes the deposition process.

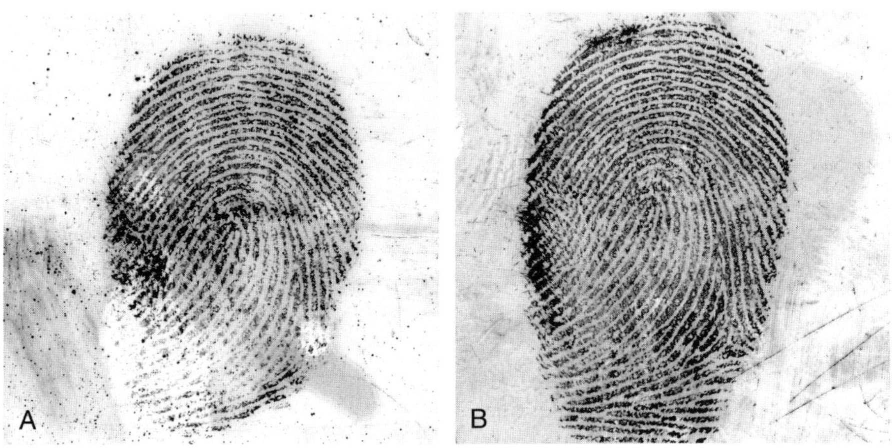

FIGURE 10-12
(a) Fingerprint applied with very light pressure. (b) Fingerprint applied with light pressure.

(Continued)

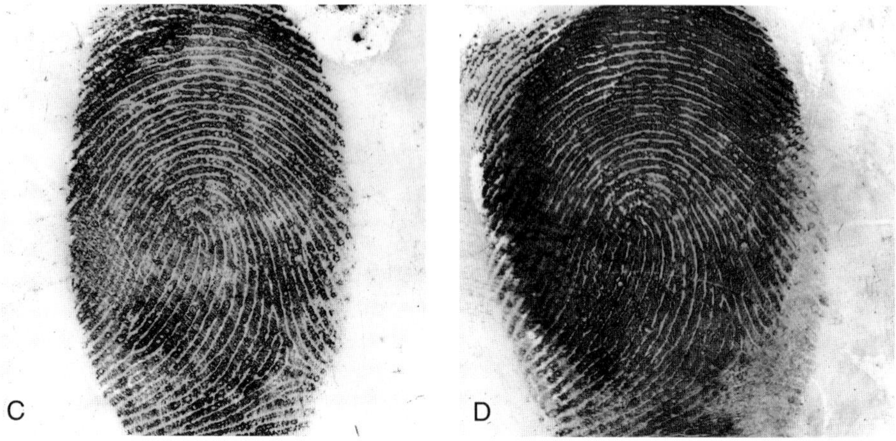

FIGURE 10-12—CONT'D
(c) Fingerprint applied with medium pressure. (d) Fingerprint applied with heavy pressure.

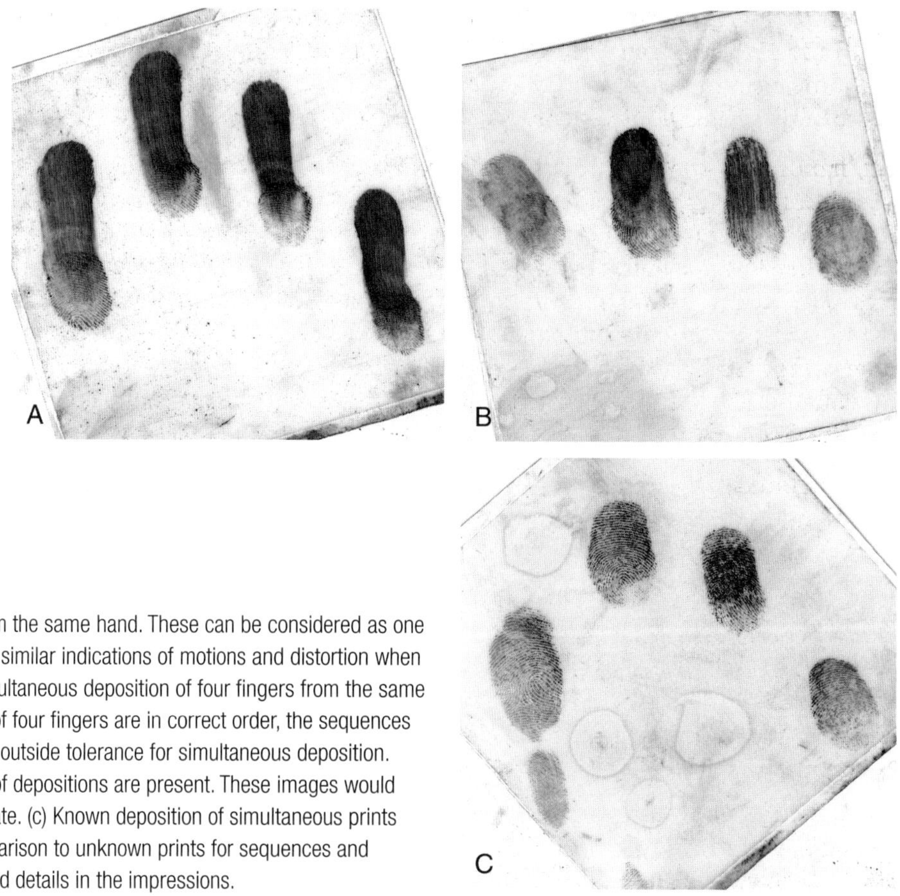

FIGURE 10-13
(a) Deposition of four fingers from the same hand. These can be considered as one image in an aggregate. Note the similar indications of motions and distortion when depositing the prints. (b) Nonsimultaneous deposition of four fingers from the same hand. Even though these prints of four fingers are in correct order, the sequences and configurations of details are outside tolerance for simultaneous deposition. Different indications of motions of depositions are present. These images would not be considered as an aggregate. (c) Known deposition of simultaneous prints that can be considered for comparison to unknown prints for sequences and configurations of fingers, tips, and details in the impressions.

The individual impressions on the substrates and the sequences and configurations of the details in the unknown and known prints are considered as individual prints and within an aggregate when considering whether they sufficiently agree or disagree and whether one aggregate volar surface is the source of the aggregate impression(s). Tolerance for positioning of the sections of the hand and fingers on the substrate must be considered. This is similar to tolerance for using many details on different elements of one sole in a distorted application of a shoe sole to a substrate or many land impressions on fired bullets to make a judgment in firearms examinations.

OTHER SKIN PRINTS AND IMAGES

Studying a wide variety of natural shapes and patterns leads us to accept unique patterns in any natural source and their images. The unique features of any natural source can be recorded as first-, second-, and third-level details. First-level is the general shape or outline of the source within an impression. Second-level is the specific path of the outline, and third-level is the texture along or within the path. The general appearances, paths, and textures within the outline of the overall print contribute to the aggregate of the image, no matter the source of these additional details.

Feet, hands, and ears have natural shapes of bones and tissues under the skin in addition to the patterns of the surface skin that contacts the substrates. Comparative measurements of patterns can occur for all features of the unique body. Where there is sufficient quality and quantity in the detail images of features of the body, comparative measurements can lead to examinations. Figures 10-14a–h depict variations in the recorded details of foot morphology and some comparative measurements. The tracings used in Figures 10-14 through 10-18 are limited demonstrations of a part of the comparative measuring.

Figures 10-15a and b show a foot impression with a variety of natural patterns. Many friction ridge examiners do not consciously consider the details of the other features of feet in impressions. It is better to consider all foot morphology, ridges, creases, and imperfections within the impressions.

Figures 10-16a–f show sets of prints from the same hand. The patterns of tissues under the skin of each hand will be unique. The expressions of fingers and hand can vary, as shown in the figures. During examinations, different expressions of the hand must be considered for tolerance of comparatively measuring recorded prints. All available details can be considered when conducting an examination.

Figures 10-17a–d show prints of palms both bare and when the hand is covered with a latex glove. Even if wearing gloves, the donor can deposit some details of the volar skin features, as the glove can fit the skin and hand contours while

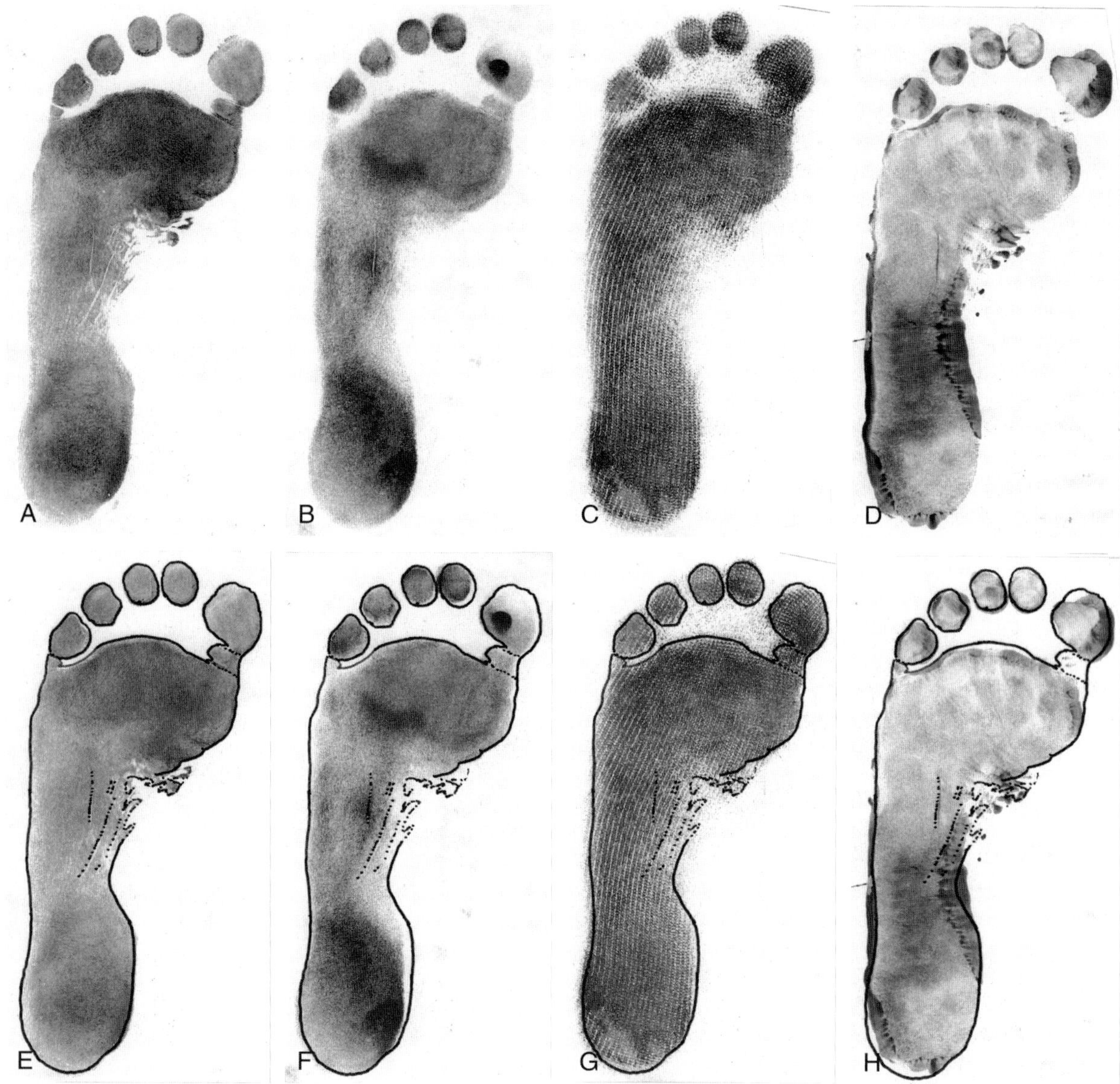

FIGURE 10-14

(a) A standard bare foot impression. (b) The same foot wearing hosiery. (c) The same foot wearing a sock. (d) The same foot, bare, recorded in dark, sticky residue. (e) Tracing on transparency film obtained from standard print (a). Dotted lines are placed on creases within the impression and along the jagged edge near the arch. (f) Tracing on transparency film of standard print (a) placed over (b). (g) Tracing on transparency film of standard print (a) placed over (c). (h) Tracing on transparency film of standard print (a) placed over (d).

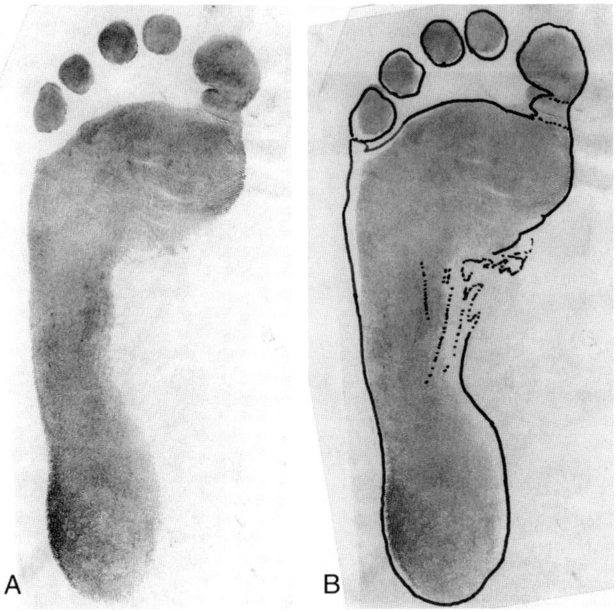

FIGURE 10-15

(a) Standard print from a foot of similar size as the foot that made Figure 10-14a. (b) The tracing on transparency film of standard print Figure 10-14a is placed over print Figure 10-15a. Consider any available details when conducting an examination to determine sufficiency. The size is similar, but the configurations of the widths at the arches and across the ball area are different. The areas by the little toes and big toe joints are different. There are no creases in the arch area of Figures 10-15a or b. The foot that made the impressions for (a) and (b) is actually the right foot of the person who made the impressions in Figures 10-14a–h. The images in Figures 10-15a and b were reversed to demonstrate that bilateral symmetry of patterns does not exist in foot morphology.

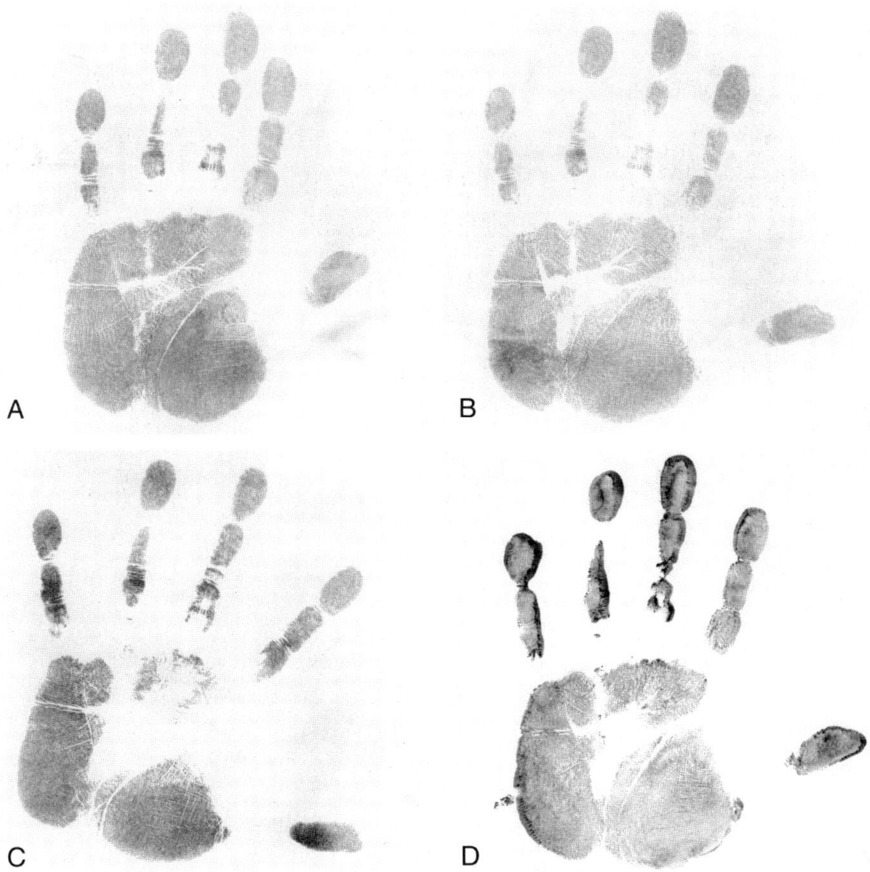

FIGURE 10-16

(a) Standard print from a hand. (b) Standard print from the same hand in (a) with a different expression. (c) Standard print from the same hand in (a) and (b) with yet another different expression. (d) Stain print from the same hand in (a), (b), and (c).

(Continued)

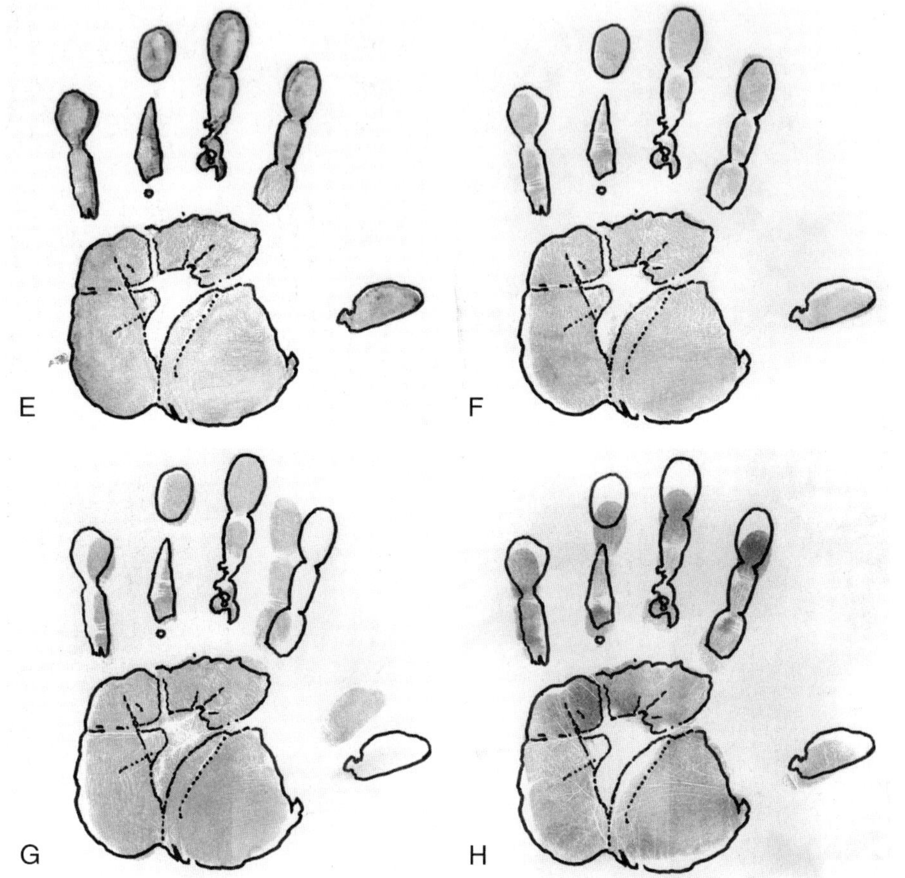

FIGURE 10-16—CONT'D
(e) Tracing on transparency film obtained from the stain print in (d). (f) Tracing on transparency film obtained from the stain print in (e) is laid over the print in (b). Some comparative measurements can still be obtained to determine tolerance for details during deposition of prints with differing expressions and different matrices. (g) Tracing on transparency film obtained from the stain print in (e) is laid over the print in (a). Some comparative measurements can still be obtained to determine tolerance for details during deposition of prints with differing expressions and different matrices. (h) Tracing on transparency film obtained from the stain print in (e) is laid over a print from a different hand.

contaminating surface residues are transferred between the substrate and the glove during contact. Note the sequences and configurations of the morphology or outlines of all the segments of the palm, some ridge and crease details of the skin within each segment, and the sequences and configurations of the morphological edges and details within the aggregate of each volar image.

Like foot and hand morphologies, ears also have unique structures of tissues underlying the skin with its unique patterns. Figures 10-18a–d show ear prints as compared to a variety of standard ear impressions.

Because ridged skin and pores are present in the muzzles of some animals, these prints are used like human inked finger prints for record-keeping purposes. Cows, sheep, and dogs are some of the animals that have ridge units and sweat pores on their muzzles. Figures 10-19a–d show prints from cows.

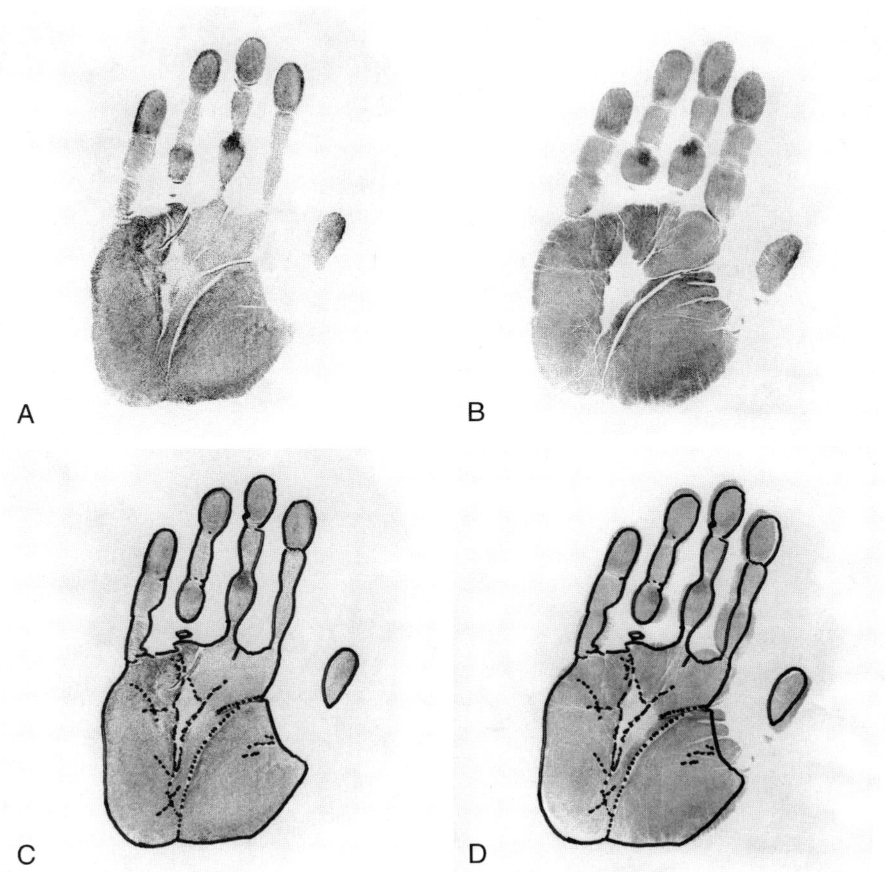

FIGURE 10-17
(a) Print deposited while wearing a latex glove with contaminating matrix and developed with powder. (b) Standard print of the same hand that made the print in (a). This hand made a print without a glove. (c) The tracing on transparency film obtained from the gloved hand print in (a). (d) The tracing on transparency film from (c) is placed over the standard print in (b). Different pressures affect the variations in appearances

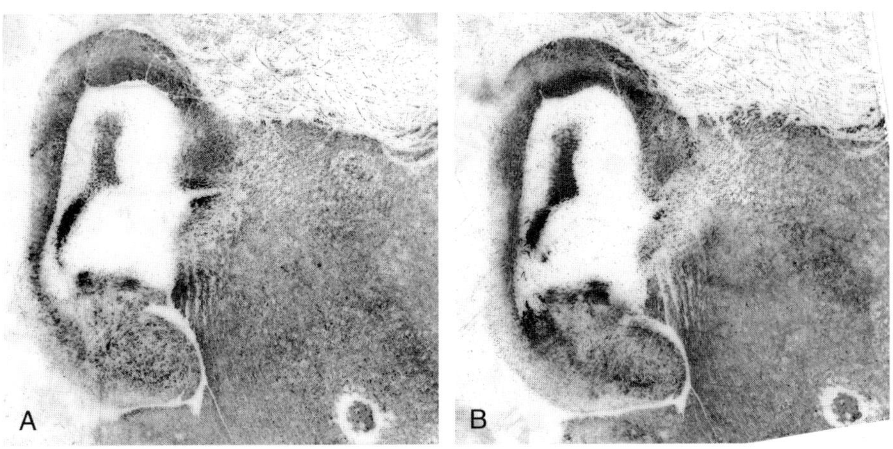

FIGURE 10-18
(a) An ear print developed with black powder. (b) A standard ear print developed with black powder.

(Continued)

FIGURE 10-18—CONT'D
(c) A tracing obtained from the ear print in (a). (d) The tracing from the ear print in (c) is placed over the print from (b). (e) A print from a different ear. (f) The tracing from the ear print in (c) is placed over the print in (e).

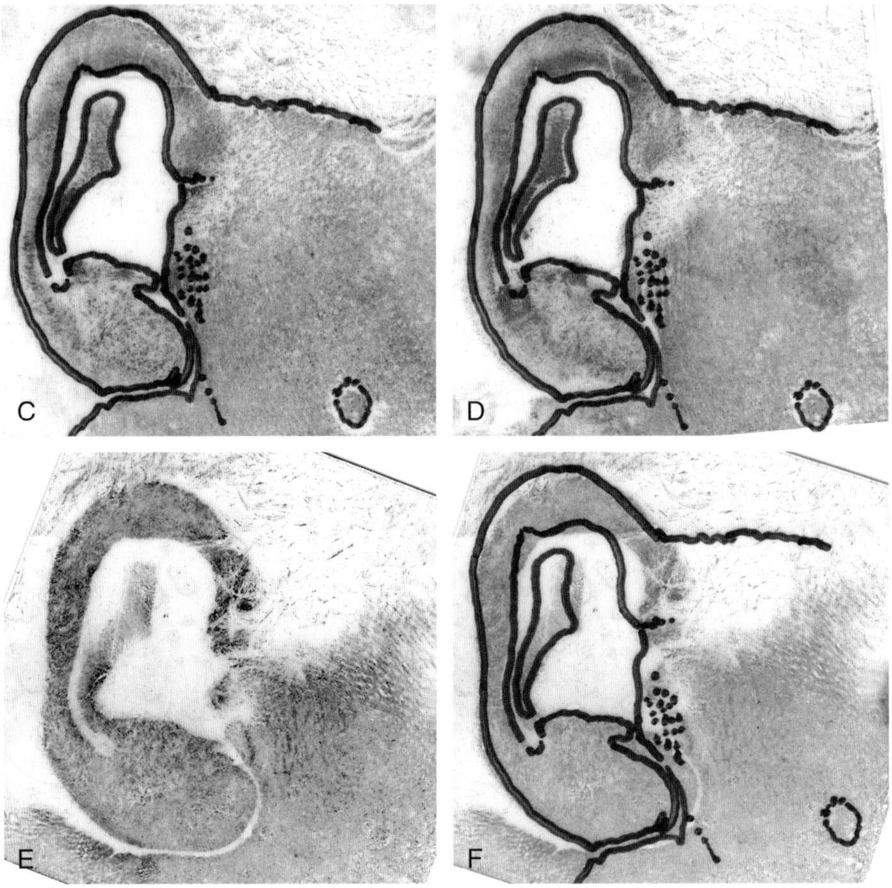

FIGURE 10-19
(a) Muzzle print from a cow. (b) Muzzle print from the same cow as (a).

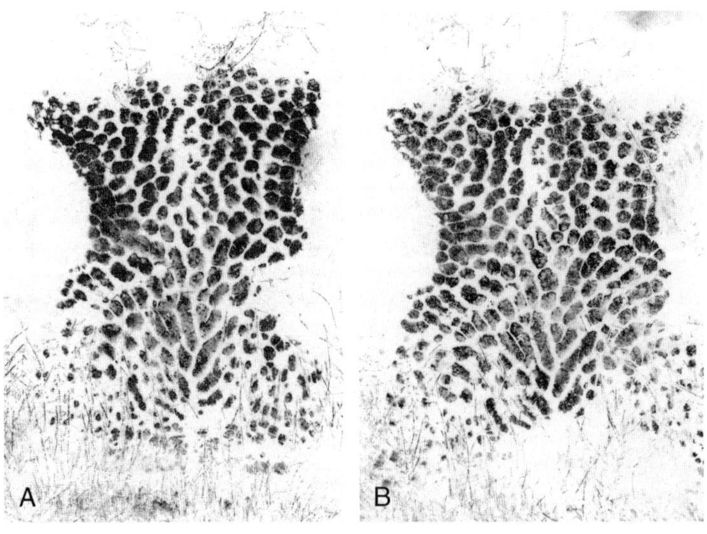

(Continued)

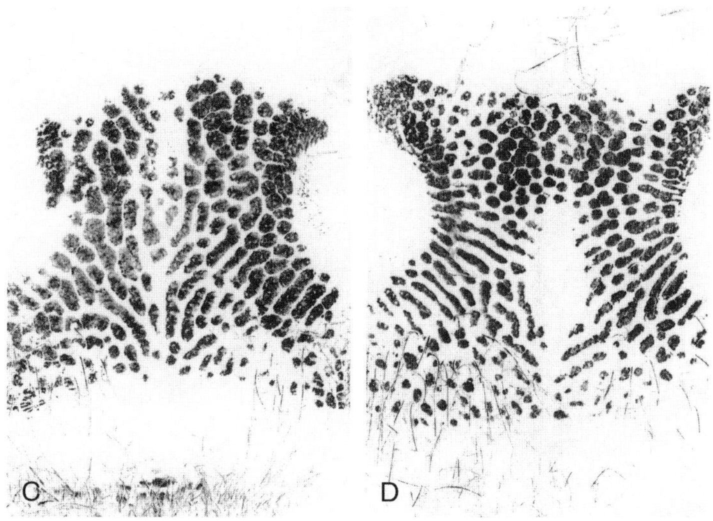

FIGURE 10-19—CONT'D
(c) Muzzle print from a different cow. (d) Muzzle print from yet another different cow.

Beyond people, animals can also have their natural features recorded as details in images for identification. Biometric technology is available for capturing images of other features of the body, human or animal. Even animals can have their features recorded for record-keeping and identification purposes, as evidenced by research and companies providing this service for livestock identification. Figures 10-20a–f show retinal scans from the eyes of cows, sheep, and goats. Retinas possess natural patterns of tissues and blood vessels. The retinal scans of animals seem to be replacing muzzle printing as a means of recording the identity of an animal. Retinal scans of features and patterns are easy to capture and record into a database.

Figures 10-21a–d show human irises. The eye's iris has a natural pattern of pigment and tissue and is now being used as a biometric record for identification.

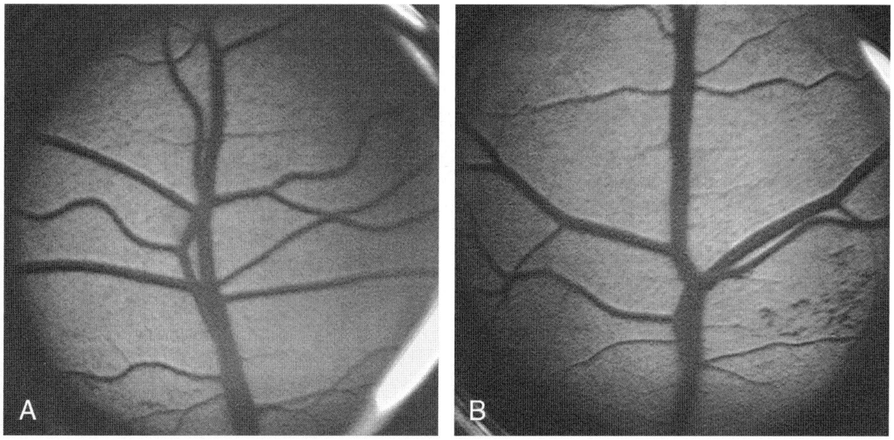

FIGURE 10-20
(a) Retinal scan from a cow's eye. (b) Retinal scan from a different cow's eye. (Retinal images in Figures 10-20a–h provided by Optibrand Ltd., LLC.)

(Continued)

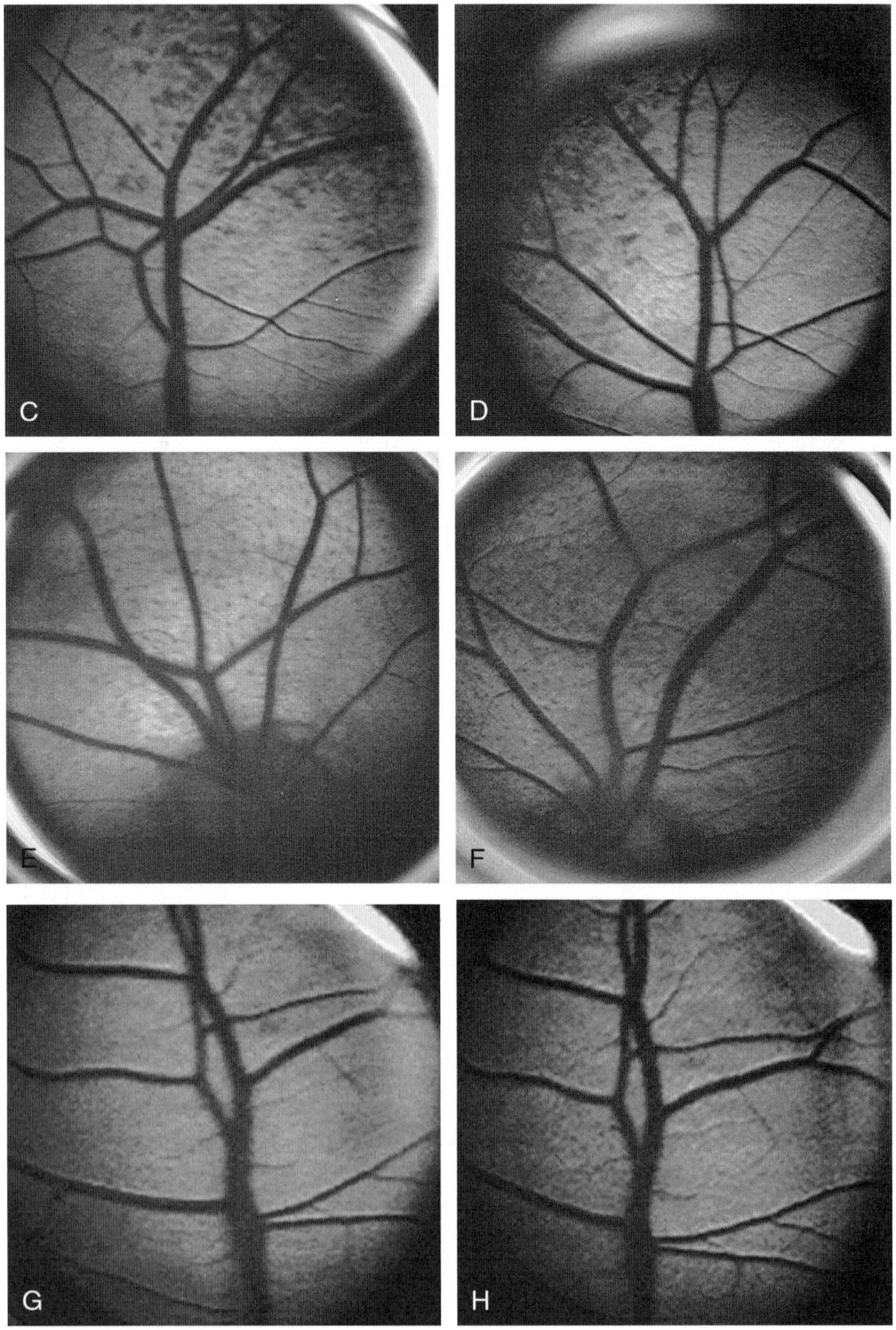

FIGURE 10-20—CONT'D
(c) Retinal scan from a sheep's eye. (d) Retinal scan from a different sheep's eye. (e) Retinal scan from a goat's eye. (f) Retinal scan from a different goat's eye. (g) Retinal scan from a cow's eye. (h) A different retinal scan from the same cow's eye in (g), demonstrating the variation of appearances of the two different captures of the retinal features.

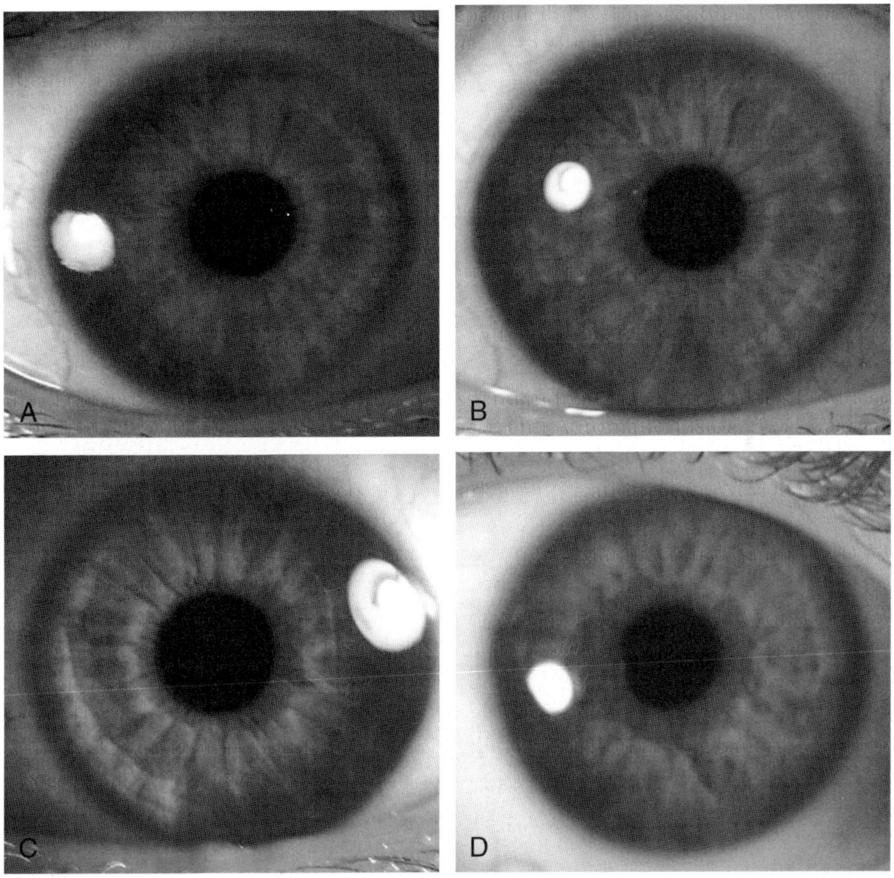

FIGURE 10-21
(a) Image of the iris from a human eye. (b) Another image from the same iris as (a). (c) Image from a different iris. (d) Image from yet another different iris.

CONCLUSIONS

The depictions in this chapter of various skins and tissues, including the influence of the morphology under the skin and their prints, emphasize the variations of appearances that occur when examining these prints or images. No two applications of the same skin to a similar substrate will result in identical prints. No two recordings of the same iris or retina will result in identical images. There will always be variation of appearances in the application of skin to a substrate. There will always be variation of appearances as an object is recorded. There is no such thing as a perfect match among impressions, prints, or images from the same source. It does not matter the type of skin or tissue, its underlying tissues, or the substrate. If it leaves a mark or impression in a receiving substrate, it can be examined.

For conclusions of examinations, refer to Chapter 6. The sufficiency and persistency of the repeatable and unique features must be considered when determining the judgment of conclusion. The natural patterns within and under skin have no repeatable specific pattern of features. The determinations of agreement and disagreement rest upon the quality and quantity of three levels of details of the persistent unique features of the source(s) as recorded in the substrates.

BIBLIOGRAPHY

Ashbaugh, David R. 'Ridgeology,' *Journal of Forensic Identification*, 1991, 41 (1), 16–64.

Ashbaugh, David R. 'Palmar Flexion Crease Identification,' *Journal of Forensic Identification*, 1991, 41 (4), 255–273.

Ashbaugh, David R. *Quantitative-Qualitative Friction Ridge Analysis: An Introduction to Basic and Advanced Ridgeology*, CRC Press, Boca Raton, 1999.

Babler, William J. 'Embryonic Development of Epidermal Ridges and Their Configurations,' *March of Dimes Birth Defects Foundation*, Birth Defects Original Article Series, 1991, 27 (2), 95–112.

Berry, John. 'A Lip Print Identification,' *Identification News,* June 1980, 12.

Black, John P. 'Pilot Study: The Application of ACE-V to Simultaneous (Cluster) Impressions,' *Journal of Forensic Identification*, 2006, 56 (6), 933–971.

Blake, James W. 'Identification of the New-Born by Flexure Creases,' *Identification News*, 1959, 9(9), 3–5.

Brandon, Mary, Kathy Egli, and Astrid Unander. 'Cloned Primates and the Possibility of Identical Fingerprints,' *Fingerprint Whorld,* 1998, 24 (91), 17–23.

Burns, Robert W. 'A "Kiss" for the Prosecution,' *Fingerprint Whorld,* October 1981, 28–33.

Champod, Christophe, Chris Lennard, Pierre Margot, and Milutin Stoilovic. *Fingerprints and Other Ridge Skin Impressions,* CRC Press, Boca Raton 2004.

Cowger, James F. *Friction Ridge Skin, Comparison and Identification of Fingerprints,* Elsevier Science, New York, 1983.

Cummins, Harold, and Charles Midlo. *Finger Prints, Palms and Soles—An Introduction to Dermatoglyphics,* Dover Publications, Inc., New York, 1961.

Dillon, D. J. 'The Identification of Impressions of Nonfriction-Ridge-Bearing Skin,' *Journal of Forensic Science,* 1963, 8 (4), 576–582.

Freinkel, Ruth K. and David T. Woodley. *The Biology of the Skin*, Parthenon Publishing New York, 2001.

Fuchs, Elaine. 'Scratching the surface of skin development,' *Nature*, Vol. 445, 22 February 2007, 834–842.

Hammer, Hans-Joachim. 'The Identification of Ear Prints Secured at the Scene of the Crime,' *Fingerprint Whorld,* October 1986, 49–51.

Hoag, Kenneth J. 'Lip Print Identification,' *Identification News*, 1978, 28 (11), 5–6.

Iannarelli, Alfred V. *The Iannarelli System of Ear Identification*. Foundation Press, Brooklyn, New York, 1964.

Jungbluth, William O. 'Knuckle Print Identification,' *Journal of Forensic Identification*, 1989, 39 (6), 375–380.

Kennedy, Robert B, Irwin S Pressman, Sanping Chen, Peter H Petersen, and Ari E. Pressman. 'Criminalistics - Statistical Analysis of Barefoot Impressions,' *Journal of Forensic Sciences*, 2003, 48 (1), 55–63.

Lightbourn, K. 'Identification from Pore Marks,' *Identification News*, 1978, 27 (7), 9.

Maceo, Alice V. 'The Basis for the Uniqueness and Persistence of Scars in the Friction Ridge Skin,' *Fingerprint Whorld*, 2005, 31 (121), 147–161.

Maceo, Alice V. 'Book Report—The Biology of Skin,' *Journal of Forensic Identification*, 2003, 53 (5), 585–595.

Massey, S. L. 'Persistence of Creases of the Foot and Their Value for Forensic Identification Purposes,' *Journal of Forensic Identification*, 2004, 54 (3), 296–315.

Meijerman, Lynn, Cor van der Lugt, and George J. R. Maat. 'Cross-Sectional Anthropometric Study of the External Ear,' *Journal of Forensic Sciences*, 2007, 52 (2), 286–293.

Montagna, William and P. Parakkal. *The Structure and Function of Skin* 3rd ed., Academic Press, New York, 1974.

Montagna, William, Albert M. Kligman and Kay S. Carlisle. *Atlas of Normal Human Skin* Springer-Verlag, New York, 1992.

Oatess, Richard T. 'Elbow Print Identification,' *Journal of Forensic Identification*, 2000, 50 (2), 132–137.

Osterburg, James W. *The Crime Laboratory–Case Studies of Scientific Criminal Investigation*, Clark Boardman Company, Ltd., New York 1982; 21–30, 34–37, 173–199, 217–231, 239.

Sherlock, William E. 'Ear Impression Case,' *AFTE Journal*, 1991, 23 (3), 850–853.

Taylor, Richard A. 'Flexure Creases–Alternative Method for Infant Footprint Identification,' *Identification News*, 1979, 29 (9), 12–14.

Vanderkolk, John R. 'Ridgeology—Animal Muzzle Prints and Human Fingerprints,' *Journal of Forensic Identification*, 1991, 41 (4), 274–284.

Vanderkolk, John R. 'Correction: Ridgeology - Animal Muzzle Prints and Human Fingerprints,' *Journal of Forensic Identification*, 1991, 41 (5), 317.

Wertheim, Kasey and Alice V. Maceo. 'The Critical Stage of Friction Ridge Pattern Formation,' *Journal of Forensic Identification*, 2002, 52 (1), 35–85.

Whittier, J. C., Jim Douber, Dave Henrickson, Justin Cobb, John Shadduck, and B. L. Golden. 'Biological Considerations Pertaining to Use of the Retinal Vascular Pattern for Permanent Identification of Livestock.' *Proceedings, Western Section, American Society of Animal Science*, Vol. 54, 2003.

Williams, Thurman Ray. 'Lip Prints—Another Means of Identification,' *Journal of Forensic Identification*, 1991, 41 (3), 190–194.

CHAPTER 11

It Just Does Not Matter

Science is about generalizations. The writings and examples in this book are my attempt to generalize the process of forensic comparative science examinations. Natural patterns are unique. There are no qualifications on the size or type of the natural pattern with that statement. Unnatural patterns are created by humans and are or can be repeatable by controlling the shapes when making those patterns through design specifications. Within the structures of unnatural patterns are natural patterns. Repeatable unnatural patterns have uniqueness within. If scrutinized closely, these unique patterns can be determined. Unnatural repeatable patterns can be damaged and acquire additional natural patterns.

As long as either type of pattern in the object is persistent between the times the unknown impression and the known impression are captured, an attempt to determine origin can be made by a trained and experienced examiner who understands patterns and their images. Specific sources can be determined in images possessing sufficient quality and quantity of the details of the unique features of those sources. The examiner, within the community of examiners, must have experiences, understandings, and judgments that follow the rules of nature and to be able to see, think, and judge comparative measurements. The experience generated from training, experience, competency testing, and peer review enables the examiner to render judgments that can be very accurate. As all humans must remember, errors can still be made within the very accurate domain of forensic comparative science.

There is no justification for requiring a predetermined minimum fixed quantity or quality of limited details of the features of the source. Quantity of details does not exist without quality of the same details. Requiring a fixed quantity of any aspect of the details without considering the qualities of those same details does not make sense. The fixed quantity and quality of details required from a unique and persistent source is not one unit of quantity or one unit of quality. One unit of quality quantity together is the least required relationship. When one unique unit agrees, the images came from the same source. Examiners are not perfect in determining sufficiency. Examiners must be above the minimum threshold of QQ = 1 and go beyond the irritation of doubt within self and within the community. That is subjectively above the objective threshold of 1.

There is no way to avoid judgment by the examiner. With variations in appearances, the examiner must judge whether the details agree or disagree sufficiently. Once those comparative judgments have been determined, an evaluation of the analyses and comparisons must occur. Without a determination of evaluation, there is no need to analyze and compare. The AACE+V model presented in this book is an intentional interlocked three phases of analyses, comparisons, and evaluations within all the influences of perception. There is no point in conducting partial perception.

Forensic scientists are often perplexed by the challenges of lawyers in pretrial hearings or during testimony. Forensic means a debate and formal argument. Hearings and trials are about debates and formal arguments. Many lawyers challenge evidence; that is their job. The scientist should expect challenges and arguments about every judgment in every case.

Criminal and civil laws do not cover every scenario of judgment that can occur in science. Many criminal and civil laws are specific, while many are general. The generality of laws, even the specific ones, is the reason there are appeals courts to determine whether a law was properly interpreted, followed, or judged during arrests, interviews, or trials. The generalities of nature must also be understood with the known natural laws that are determined. Sometimes, law pushes science and science pushes law. I know of no forensic science that is stagnant as scientists strive to learn more.

Many courts will conduct a *Frye, Daubert,* or rules of evidence hearing to determine whether an examiner follows an acceptable and valid science when rendering a judgment and expressing a conclusion of examination. These hearings might challenge the science, the scientist's understanding, or method used in the examination. Some hearings might result in a determination the expert cannot testify to a conclusion. Most hearings result in an allowance of letting the expert render the conclusion.

The determination by a judge in one case will affect the ability of an expert to testify in that case. The judge is a gatekeeper for allowing opinion evidence in the trial by the particular testimony of the witness in court. The examiner is a gatekeeper for the examination of evidence, judgment, and testimony within forensic comparative science. Each discipline within forensic comparative science should not have its own separate and distinct rules, regulations, procedures, and standards for conclusions. The more generalized, simple, and accurate the laws and rules are across all of forensic comparative science, the stronger the judgment and the testimony.

I believe in the generalities of comparative examinations. Whether natural or unnatural, the patterns within many varieties of objects need to be studied prior to examining images from a type of source. Each source must be understood for the persistence of the unique and repeatable features, and the variations of appearances caused by different depositions of those features onto a substrate. If two images are sufficiently recorded, they can be comparatively measured. The examiner who understands the source(s), the substrate(s), and the process of the examinations can determine a conclusion: The images share a common origin; the images have a different origin; a common origin was not determined, a different origin was not determined, or a common or different origin was not determined. The examiner's judgments are part of the process of applying the method of examination. Judgments are part of every comparative examination. The expert will make better judgments than the novice.

The examiners within the individual topics or disciplines of comparative science can all follow the same laws of nature when perceiving details of features with similar strategies for comparative measurements. Scientists strive to determine, challenge, and then follow those rules and laws. As long as sufficient persistency and uniqueness exist in the source, it does not matter what the source and substrate are. The source could be fingers, palms, soles, toes, lips, elbows, knees, wrists, guns, screwdrivers, hammers, tires, shoes, irises, retinas, animal muzzles, or patterned fur. The features within those sources could be ridges, creases, scars, cuts, nicks, gouges, stones, gum, mud, shades of colors, or any type of morphological contrast. Where there is contrast, there can be comparative measurement. The judgments of comparative measurements must take the examiner beyond the irritation of doubt.

Examiners must demonstrate training, competency, and proficiency with determining sources of images, no matter the source. Experts can recognize, know, and believe agreement or disagreement of patterns. While experts are not infallible, they can be extremely accurate in their judgments.

Only a few sources and features within nature's tapestries of patterns and human manufacturing are mentioned in this book. Many other objects can deposit images on all sorts of substrates. Ultimately, if a source has perceivable features that are persistent and unique and leaves two sufficient images, it does not matter what the object is. It does not matter what the substrate is as long as the substrate can maintain the pattern. It just does not matter.

Index

Note: Page numbers followed by *f* indicates figure.

E

N

O

P

U

V

W

Z